JAMES HILLMAN UNIFORM EDITION

9

Uniform Edition of the Writings of James Hillman
Volume 9

Published by Spring Publications, Inc.
Putnam, Conn.
www.springpublications.com

First edition 2008

Printed in Canada

Designed by white.room productions, New York

Cover illustration:
James Lee Byars, *Untitled,* ca. 1960. Black ink on Japanese paper.
Estate of James Lee Byars, courtesy Michael Werner Gallery, New York

Library of Congress Cataloging-in-Publication Data

Hillman, James.
  Animal presences / James Hillman. – 1st ed.
    p. cm. – (Uniform edition of the writings of James Hillman ; v. 9)
  Includes bibliographical references.
  ISBN-13: 978-0-88214-588-4 (hardcover : alk. paper)
  ISBN-10: 0-88214-588-6 (hardcover : alk. paper)
  1. Archetype (Psychology) 2. Animals–Psychological aspects. I. Title.
  BF175.5.A72H53 2008
  156–dc22
                                    2008019518

JAMES HILLMAN

ANIMAL
PRESENCES

SPRING PUBLICATIONS
PUTNAM, CONN.

The Uniform Edition of the Writings of James Hillman
is published in conjunction with

Dallas Institute Publications, Joanne H. Stroud, Director

The Dallas Institute of Humanities and Culture
Dallas, Texas

as an integral part of its publications program concerned with
the imaginative, mythic, and symbolic sources of culture

Additional support for this publication has been provided by

The Fertel Foundation, New Orleans, Louisiana

Pacifica Graduate Institute
and Opus Archives and Research Center,
Carpinteria and Santa Barbara, California

Contents

A Preface

The reader will find collected here essays and lectures devoted to specific animal forms as well as the major Eranos paper from 1984 addressing the theme of this volume as a whole: the presence of animals to the human psyche. I say "to" the human psyche rather than "in," since the latter preposition would suggest their enclosure within anthropocentrism. "To" leaves their location unassigned.

While reviewing the checklist of my writings to make the selection for this volume of the Uniform Edition I found that the theme of animal permeates works all along the way: Volume 5, animal images in alchemy; Volume 6.1, animal shapes of Greek gods; Volume 3, animal images in depression and the figure of the ape; and more philosophically in Volume 8, which includes lectures in Caracas ("Culture and the Animal Soul"), at Tenri University in Japan ("Cosmology for Soul"), and in Dallas, "Bachelard's Lautréamont." *The Dream and the Underworld* has a short chapter on animals, and the study of the goat-god of the ancient world, *Pan and the Nightmare,* opened the door to the animalistic animism in all the above-listed later writings already in 1972.

Yet these particular references do not reflect the full presence of animals infused in my work. My first piece of fiction, published in 1950, climaxes in a bullfight, and my first book on psychology, *Emotion,* published in 1960, aimed to lift repression from a force once called "animal spirits." I did not then make the connection between the vitality of the psyche and the psyche's animal images – that the "animal spirits" are indeed animal spirits! Now, at this late stage, I see that I have been consistently trying to preserve in psychology that which Cartesian rationality fears and condemns. Indeed, if there has been a steady line, an actual dominating narrative in my subversive service to psychology, it is what this present volume elucidates: the preservation of, even obeisance to, the animal spirits.

J.H.
March 2008

1

The Animal Kingdom
in the Human Dream

Polar Bear

During one of my itinerant teaching seminars on animal images in dreams, a woman handed me this dream:

> I was flying in an airplane piloted by my husband. As he was flying, I was looking at the scenery below. Then I told him, "Look, I see a polar bear under some water down there." My husband kept on flying. Then I looked at his radar screen and the polar bear had registered on it along with something else as two X's. Then my husband said, "I think I'll take a look," and he turned the plane around until we saw the polar bear again, still sitting under water.

When the dreamer is flying and piloted by her husband—what she is coupled with, to, by, in that syzygy—she looks down on the world as scenery. The scenery consists in the waters below, where there is a living animal. At first, the animal appears in the flying plane on the radar screen—an abstract kind of awareness of the bear in the flying, looking-down mind, which makes the husband say, "I think," and to respect, that is, look again, by turning the plane around, revising his forward direction. The polar bear registers as an X, an unknown quantity, in fact, as two X's, for the dream says, "The polar bear has registered on the radar screen along with something else as two X's." The bear is qualified by the number two; something else is with it, something more to it, a second bear, a ghost bear, resonance registering only abstractly. What is this double bear still sitting, sitting still under water? A Jewish legend says that each animal species has a corresponding one in the water. Is this bear in the water the bear that did not get into the ark? Why does this bear sit there in the waters below? Who is this bear? Why must they see it?

Another polar-bear dream from a woman in her thirties:

> A polar bear is after me. I am terrified and try to close a door to keep him out. A man goes after him, and then I see the bear come back, hurt. He has been hit by a car and his shoulder is all torn and bloody and he keeps looking at it confused. I feel sorry, anguished that this happened. I didn't want him hurt, I just didn't want him to hurt me.

The dream exhibits the familiar motif of pursuit by the animal. But does the bear pursue her because it comes "after her"—because she stays ahead of it, counterphobic to it, closing doors against the white animal that comes for her? An anonymous man goes after the bear, resulting in its being hit and bloodied and confused by a car—such is the strength of the "man" in this woman's dream and the vehicle of her drive. It can confuse the animal. But now there is reconciliation through pain: as the bear is wounded, she is anguished—a relationship conceived in terms of hurt. Perhaps hurt has opened the door between them.

A third dream comes from a woman of fifty-two:

> I see a large huge strong polar bear—gleaming white and standing on the very far edge of his earth—a point of ice and snow at the top of the pole, and facing blue, icy water. He stands on his hind legs, upright, and his head is thrown back, nose pointing to heaven, and he bellows, rends the air with anguish. Watching, I recognize that he is at the end of his rope from searching for his mate and child and calls out in terrible agony and helpless power.

Gleaming white, at the farthest edge of earth, at the end of his rope, at the top of the pole, upright and pointing to heaven, this bear—for all his power at that place—is in agony. Not because he is hunted or wounded but because in this extreme vertical northernmost pointedness he cannot find his mate and child; he is alone. Large, huge, and strong, yet helpless. What terrible anguish is rending the air of her dream? What must be heard? Witnessing this bear, to what is the woman bearing witness?

And now a fourth dream of a polar bear, this time from a man:

> I am hunting a white polar bear in very cold wilderness, making
> every effort to kill it. After several vain attempts, the white polar
> bear and I become friendly. It should be noted that although
> the atmosphere was a pure, clear cold, I was not wearing heavy
> clothing. Suddenly, I am drowning in the middle of a lake as my
> brother and the polar bear watch from the shore. Somehow, the
> white bear swims out and saves my life.

Not the brother "swims out and saves my life" but the white bear, paired
with "my brother" and, perhaps, more than a brother, at least in the
capacity of saving his life. The bear he has been trying to kill by making every effort (for so is how he tries to kill the bear: "by making every
effort") saves his life. The vanity of attempting to kill the bear, yet the
pursuit of it, has brought him into friendly affinity of hunter with the
hunted. And "it should be noted" that this dreamer is not wearing protective clothing. He has his own inner heat now that he and the bear
are friendly. Yet again: who, what is the bear that "saves my life"?

These four dreamers are modern Americans. They have no empirical
relations with polar bears: they are not hunters, explorers, zoologists,
Eskimos. I am rather certain they have not read the *Kalevala*, been to
the *Drachenloch* (Dragon's Lair), or studied shamanism. Nor do I believe
they know about the holy nature of the white animal in folklore.
I strongly doubt that the woman in whose dream the white bear howled
for its mate and child has read Thomas Bewick's illustrated eighteenth-
century *A General History of Quadrupeds* where it states that among polar
bears "fondness for offspring is so great that they embrace their cubs
to the last and bemoan them with the most piteous cries."[1]

Within this condensed context of a lecture I cannot pretend to
deal adequately with dreams, but were we anthropologists among the
peoples of the northern polar circle, we would recognize in this polar
bear what is called the "animal guardian,"[2] the master of animals who is
himself an animal and who is, more than being protector of the hunt or

---

1 T. Bewick, *A General History of Quadrupeds*, 3rd ed. (Newcastle Upon Tyne,
1792), 270.

2 I. Paulson, "The Animal Guardian: A Critical and Synthetic Review," *History
of Religions* 3 (1964), 202–19.

totemic ancestor (the great white bear as grandfather or grandmother), the supreme being in phenomenal form, as Ivar Paulson says, "among the oldest theophanies in the religious life of mankind."

These white bears could be theophanies, displays of divinities, presenting the dilemmas, the agonies, the potentialities in precise detail of what Jung called the "religious instinct." In each case we read how the dreamer deals with the white animal: behaves toward it, feels in regard to it, and where he or she encounters it. Yet a bear is more than, other than a religious instinct. An unknown quantity is left over from the reduction, the image of the polar bear itself, the other bear in the water, and we turn to animal dreams also for the animal's sake.

The dreams were given to me as an animal-dream collector to be used as I see fit, and I am grateful to all dreamers whose dreams I shall be recounting for their generosity. The dreams form part of a collection I began at the Jung Institute in Zurich in 1959 for a study group to inquire into animal motifs in dreams. The collection has grown over the years. I should hasten to add that though the material is honestly empirical, handed to me in written form by the dreamers and usually with no comment, or by analysts, the method of working these dreams is not empirical in the usual sense. No statistical frequencies, no correlations between dreams and the condition of the dreamers as in the fashion of the old dream books: when you see a polar bear in your dream, then you will catch a cold, or be lonely, find your life threatened, or saved, and so on. We soon gave up adducing the significance of this or that animal in direct relation with diagnosis and prognosis. Too simple. There is a strange gap between dream research and dream interpretation, between a scientific explanatory psychology and an understanding imaginative psychology. It is like the gap between the day world of nomothetic norms, inducing laws from many cases, and the night world of idiographic descriptions: how the dream animal appears in an image, and what it "means." Yet not "What does it mean to the dreamer?" because we did not have the dreamers. We thus were attempting to understand the dream animals as dream naturalists. What is the animal kingdom in the human dream? How does it behave? What does it want? What is the relation between dream animal and dream human?

Perhaps our first result was this struggle with method. The suspension (*epoché*) of dreamer, of therapy and of theory enabled us to regard the dream animal without benefit of therapeutic intentions or psychodynamic concepts more like a complex image, a depiction in words, an imaginative *poesis* of what Jung called the objective psyche. We did not then know it, but looking back many years later, we were on the road to another kind of dreamwork: an *essentialist approach to the dream* — toward what is essentially going on in the image. The animals led us to this approach, as if they were the essentials of the dreams, perhaps even essences. What I have been gathering from these animals has taken these many years to begin to find this first written formulation, which I dedicate to the spirit of Adolf Portmann.

Pig

As we turn now to further dreams, let me say that I know how difficult it is to listen at the same time to the dream and to discourse about it. I know that each new dream you hear adds to your hermeneutic frustration. I beg your patient receptivity and a willing suspension of the active quest for meaning.

A woman reports:

> I look down a deep, dark vertical tunnel. At the bottom, very deep, I gradually make out in the dim light, like firelight, flickering, the head of a pig. It has a human expression, of malice and triumph combined. I see its head pulled up and back at the very moment of its triumph. It looks at me with small black eyes, eyebrows raised; we look into each other's eyes.

The image places the woman and the pig in a direct connection that is vertical, and through darkness, and gradual. The pig is deep, and where the pig is, there is fire and an unsteady flickering light that comes from fire. At the sight of each other, malice and triumph combine in the pig — which is a *human* expression, as if not native to the pig. So it appears to the woman's looking-down perspective.

The woman, let us remember, is "above" the pig, and the dream says the depth is with the animal. Its head is the raised one, while hers looks down. The vision in the tunnel, a tunnel vision excluding all else, narrows the dream's focus into its essence: the intensity of direct gaze into the head of the pig, its black eye.

The motif of the animal's eye—being transfixed by its look, moved by its expression, its appeal, recalling on waking only its eyes—requires a moment's reflection about the eye as mirror of the soul and the eye as entry into the interiority of a creature. As the British naturalist E. L. Grant Watson pointed out, [3] we know the nature of an animal through its eyes: the hooded eye of the lizard; the slight bloodshot panic in the horse; the luminous cow's eye reflecting a dark inner softness as if glazed by its own metabolic ruminations rather than communicating outward; the obsidian bead-like eye of the mouse that hardly sees; the goat eye, cat eye, fish eye, spaniel eye, eagle eye—each distinct, and some even as metaphors for human traits.

Here the eye communicates triumph and malice, as if the soul of this pig is small and black.

The head of an animal as *pars pro toto* appears in animal cults and dreams. The head is the leading *eidos* of the animal, its idea or our reception of it as an idea, as if the head presents an animal's specific physiognomy, condensing and exhibiting the qualities of its consciousness. We may assume that the dreamer is beginning to exchange perspectives with the pig, taking in "pig" as an idea into her own head, and the fire stirred by this begins to enlighten her narrowed vision, a recognition that, while raising, uplifting the deep pig, she sees as a moment of malicious triumph for the animal.

What more is the woman seeing in that sow's head? The history of the pig in human culture suggests she is seeing into the depths of her flesh, which is so much like the pig's—its stomach, lungs, intestines so similar that anatomy from Galen through the Middle Ages used the pig's corpse as most apt analogy for the human. Also, the self-display of the pig: often pinkish, brownish, seemingly hairless, its jowls and dugs and belly, its rotund torso with folds at the neck, short legs and soiled behind, its copulatory habits, its omnivorous appetite like the human, enjoying everything. Even human flesh is said to taste most like pork.

---

3 E. L. Grant Watson, *Animals in Splendour* (London: John Baker, 1967).

This fleshly aspect of the pig makes the term an insult: a person called pig, swine, sow, or hog means greedy, dirty, sulky, coarse, obstinate, gluttonous, filthy, with bestial habits. Edward Topsell's mid-seventeenth-century *History of Four-Footed Beasts,*[4] following largely from Conrad Gesner's,[5] uses these epithets for the pig: dirt lover, beastly, milk-sucker, unclean, miry, fat, moist, greedy, loud. And there is depression in the pig; along with the dog and ass, the pig was a medieval emblem of *acedia:* laziness, sloth, inertia, the absence of spirit. Each species presents specific styles of pathologizings. Wallowing in an obese pig depression appears altogether different from doggedly chasing your own tail, gnawing buried bones, or lying in the dust with a hound-dog sorrow. The absence of spirit in the pig has its source in its association with the elements of earth and water. Its healing powers concerned mainly its bladder and fluids (milk, blood, lard, even urine), restoring life to old breasts and dried skin, curing the cough of horses and old men. Of course, the moist and muddy element is traditionally "feminine," and according to animal lore, the sow's brain shrinks more than that of all creatures with the waning of the moon. The pig's brain submits to the lunar tug and its rhythms in the flesh. Pigheadedness serves principles deeper than mere egocentric obstinacy. The sow will not receive the male, says pig lore, unless he first bend her ear, so keenly is this ear tuned to nature.

The abhorrence of swine, dogmatized by Leviticus 11:7, traveled with the faithful through all the monotheistic lands of Islam so that swine were militantly executed from the shores of the Atlantic all across to Indonesia. Even in Europe the devil was fond of appearing in pig shape; witches, too, rode them. Hogs destined for slaughter had first to be inspected by the local exorcist, following Mark 5:12 where Jesus drives devils into pigs.

Pig-loathing is even more ancient: Artemidorus (*Oneirocritica* 1.70) writes that pork is an auspicious dream symbol, because "while the pig is alive, it is of no use whatsoever... But once it is dead, it is more savory than the other animals who are, in turn, more useful while they are alive... "

---

4 E. Topsell, *The History of Four-Footed Beasts and Serpents and Insects* (London, 1658).

5 C. Gesner, *Historiae Animalium* (Zurich, 1551–58).

A bit of Islamic lore, from the *Nuzhat-al-Qulub* (Delight of Hearts),[6] a scientific encyclopedia composed around 1300) says that the sick pig is cured by a diet of crabs.

The curing of one animal by another – bears by a diet of ants; lions by a diet of apes – traditionally teaches psychological insights. Why would eating crab cure the pig? The cure must be homeopathic (like cures like) for the crab, too, is symbolically lunar, moist, and anti-heroic: Baldur dies when the sun enters Cancer; Hercules is impeded at Lerna by a crab seizing his foot, thus impelling the hero to redouble his leonine force. The astrological Crab arrives at the summer solstice when the sun "stands still" after its upward climb, a moment of watery depths and reflection before the hot dominion of Leo. Its astro-anatomical place are the breasts and the stomach, quite like the pig. Both are delicate, succulent, fatty foods. C. G. Jung's prolonged example of interpretation,[7] in which he demonstrates his psychology of dreams, rests upon the crab as its central figure. Jung takes the crab as the regressive libido, drawing the patient into the unconsciousness of a clutching old attachment, which in the case exposed was synonymous with cancer fears. "The crab," says Jung, "walks backwards."

Yet it cures the sick pig. Besides the general idea of renewal associated with the crab since Aristotle and stated by Artemidorus (*Oneirocritica* 2.14) that sea creatures "who slough off their old shells are a good sign for those who are sick," there is a more intimate particular relation between crab and pig. If the pig devours, the crab digests; if the pig uproots and lays bare, the crab tears apart, bit by bit, dainty, careful. What is obstinacy in the pig is clinging tenacity in the crab. (A crab's claw can grip thirty times its body weight, a human hand but two-thirds of its weight. The giant Japanese spider crab has an outstretched claw span extending to three meters.) The crab is a scavenger; it consumes carrion: digestion of the dead, the past, remembering. The pig goes forward, the carnal appetite for more. The boar charges; the crab moves off sideways, withdraws, backs out of the skeleton it inhabits. Walking backwards also expresses the bending backwards of reflection, the psychic activity *par excellence*,[8] and so the crab was familiarly paired

---

6 Hamd Allah Mustawfi, *Nuzhat al-Qulub* [1340] (Tehran, 1957).

7 See C. G. Jung, *Two Essays in Analytical Psychology*, Collected Works, trans. R. F. C. Hull, vol. 7 (Princeton Univ. Press, 1967), 123–65.

8 See C. G. Jung, *Structure & Dynamics of the Psyche*, Collected Works, trans.

with the butterfly in Renaissance emblems that juxtapose extreme differences of a secret similarity.[9] The regressive libido that Jung sees in the crab can also be imagined as the stomach libido, which goes beyond *fressen*, snout and orality, to *pepsis* in concealment. For, above all else, crabs know the art of hiddenness, while the pig is so fully, unavoidably there. (The constellation Cancer is almost indiscernibly faint, composed of only fourth-magnitude stars.[10]) Crabs hide: inside their own carapaces, no neck to stick out; in sand, by burrowing straight down; in borrowed shells, by closing trap doors; in the deep sea, by walking around with sponges hooked on their backs; in weeds; as a crab transferred from a green-weed aquarium to one with red weeds spends hours removing the green foliage from its shell and piling its back with red ones, re-dressing itself for its new environment. These silent, self-concealing, inward-turning behaviors – introverting, maybe paranoid – can cure the pig gone sick with an excess of its own piggish nature. Like cures like, and what cures the sickness of flesh is that creature that partakes of a similar nature but with an essential shade of difference.

I have been trying to evoke by means of amplification that flickering light in the tunnel, that *lumen naturalis*, that black-eyed pig consciousness that played such a role in the Demeter-Persephone cult of Eleusis. The milk-sucking fecundity, gluttony, and porcine revulsions, the rooting nose that legend says taught humans the art of agriculture, the flesh that taught the art of cooking, and the guts through which we learned about our own anatomy suppose a psychic value leading below their gross meanings to an underworld mystery of the flesh, like the whole joints of pork in Celtic graves for feasts beyond the grave. Each animal is a *psychopompos*, leading human consciousness to yield its theriophobic exclusivity, restoring participation in the animal kingdom. The pigs of Demeter-Persephone, those mystical pigs that die in the lesser mysteries as described by Karl Kerényi,[11] are the initiated themselves. (By perceiving the pig within the setting of a mystery,

R. F. C. Hull, vol. 8 (Princeton Univ. Press, 1970), 241–43.

9 See E. Wind, *Pagan Mysteries in the Renaissance* (London: Penguin, 1967).

10 See P. Lum, *The Stars in Our Heaven: Myths and Fables* (New York: Pantheon Books, 1948).

11 K. Kerényi, *Eleusis: Archetypal Image of Mother and Daughter*, trans. R. Manheim (Princeton Univ. Press, 1967), 55.

I can give up to it with devotion. My recognition of the divinity in my piggish needs allows it to yield its demands.)

The pig initiates consciousness into the subtleties of grossness: its exaggerated compulsive physicality is the very drive downward into the mystery of life's materiality, the Pluto-Hecate world of darkness under the earth of Demeter, requiring a dark eye that can see the psychic in the concrete, the subtle body in the gross obsession, that the *suksma* aspect is there in the midst of the *shtula*, that there is spirit, light, and fire in the fat.

A dream reported by an analyst from one of her cases shows this spirit in the pig:

> I saw a child of four or five, supposedly my youngest son, watching some little pigs with fascinated delight. They rose on their hind legs in play, and he, with his naked pink body, felt identified with them. He was particularly interested in their male organs, as they were also. He told them he felt his own as much bigger and stronger than usual, as big as a thick half sausage he pointed at me. I felt it was time for parental sex instruction, but he was not interested.

Again a pig arising, but now charm and candor, little boy Eros erecting, where "four" could as well be "five," that is, at this moment of Oedipal transition, the *quaternio* is indistinguishable from the sensate structure of Aphrodite-Ishtar. Instruction, initiation is constellated, but the usual roles are reversed: not she, the older ego, shall teach the pig-boy the usual normalizing rules, but the dreamer is being taught by the dream itself.

And that is the crucial point through all these dreams: the image is the teacher. We have to endure a laboriously slow method of dreamwork, frustrating our hermeneutic desire in order to hear the image. A dream brings with it a terrible urge for understanding. We want dreams decoded for their meanings. But the dream, like the animal in it, is a living phenomenon. It goes on displaying itself, pointing beyond itself to ever further interiority if we can hold back the hermeneutical desire so that the image can elaborate itself. If so, then does amplification help the image, and how?

Amplification

We have been following Jung's method of amplification because, as he says, "wherever it is a question of archetypal formations, personalistic attempts at explanation lead us astray,"[12] and "we resort to amplification in the interpretation of dreams, for a dream is too slender a hint to be understood until it is enriched by the stuff of association and analogy and thus amplified to the point of intelligibility."[13] By establishing the symbolic context through historical, philological, and iconological research we gain an objective core of meaning of the dream animal.

Critics of amplification contend that the method fails as an adequate scientific procedure on at least these three counts. *First*, the criterion of sufficiency cannot be met. By definition, amplifying means enlarging, adding details, enriching—so when does one achieve sufficient stuff? Where does one stop? Therefore, *second*, limits must be set arbitrarily in the selection of material by the analyst and patient according to their proclivities and the exigencies called heuristic. Therefore, *third*, amplification does not achieve an objective context in which "pig," say, inheres, nor can it impartially circumscribe the connotations of pig. Hence amplification cannot be called a method in the scientific sense but an anecdotal mode, imparting allegorical suggestions, wisdom, and moralisms. It cannot escape the charge of subjectivism.

A *fourth* criticism comes from another direction. This is the imagist critique. It charges amplification with failure to seize the actual dream image: that little pink boy with his sausage-like erection playing with piglets on their hind legs. We lose the image in the welter of amplificatory evidence. The dream is dissolved in a wider context and defended against by intellectualized knowledge. The import and complexity of the dream and its emotion is displaced from the dream onto the exciting and rich discoveries of amplification. We are led away from what is there to what is not there—the pig in contexts other than this actual dream.

---

12 C. G. Jung, *Civilization in Transition*, Collected Works, trans. R. F. C. Hull, vol. 10 (Princeton Univ. Press, 1970), 646.

13 C. G. Jung, *Psychology and Alchemy*, Collected Works, trans. R. F. C. Hull, vol. 12 (Princeton Univ. Press, 1968), 403.

For the imagist the dream has an inherent overdetermination. It is stuffed with its own grounds for archetypal significance. There can be no improvement on the dream or basis for the dream beyond the dream. The image has all it needs: pink, penis, body, nude, sausage, piglet, delight, felt, erect, upright, rose, play... What could more amplify the image than this coalescence, this layered density (*Dichte*) that makes each dream also a fiction (*Dichtung*)?

When archetypal psychology urges the maxim "stick to the image" (following Jung who writes, "To understand the dream's meaning I must stick as close as possible to the dream images"[14]), it is saying that associations and amplifications can do little more than the image has already done; associations and amplifications become substitutes for the dream itself. Whereas the dream, if stayed with, worked with, will release its archetypal implications of delight in the flesh, arousal as arising, erection as pointing, aiming, even instructing, and the sophistication of flesh into sausage—all of which suggesting an opus, an initiatory transformation of phallic consciousness.

Furthermore, says the imagist critique, with the solidification of this method by the Jungian school during the past seventy years, the pig in a dream no longer *points* as Jung said a symbol should, no longer *opens* into something unknown and of which it is the best possible expression. Instead, the pig now *represents*. It is a symbol "of." So, when the woman stares into the sow's head, a trained analyst knows the patient is staring into the black eye of the terrible mother, as John Layard[15] calls the pig. Pig-Isis is arising, and the woman is meeting her *materia prima*, a triumph of the "below" often graphically literalized as below the belt. She is confronting the "Archetypal Feminine" (Erich Neumann[16]), the shadow side of feminine nature and now will be coming to terms with the flesh as evil (malice), the devil in the swine, the witch—all represented by the pig.

I do believe the critiques can be answered, including the imagists. But to find the value of amplification we have to move the method

14 C. G. Jung, *Psychological Types*, Collected Works, trans. R. F. C. Hull, vol. 6 (Princeton Univ. Press, 1971), 320.

15 J. Layard, "Identification with the Sacrificial Animal," *Eranos Yearbook* 24 (1955), 390.

16 E. Neumann, *The Great Mother: An Analysis of the Archetype* (Princeton Univ. Press, 1963), 18ff.

from its base in what we might call the scientific fallacy, the idea that amplification of psychological material is comparable with methods used in historical scholarship or archeology. Jung, who in his youth wanted to become an archeologist, often couples the term amplification with the adjective "historical."[17] The method, however, is itself partly determined by its own historical context—the early years of this century and the parallel disciplines of anthropology, archeology, and philology: Frazer, Cook, Harrison, Lévy-Bruhl, Radcliff-Brown, Mauss. Amplification served the scientific claim of the universality of the archetypes and the collective unconscious.

By unearthing or assembling pig images, rituals, and etymologies, an objective meaning of "pig" would emerge—pig as symbol of the fecundating, telluric Mother Archetype, and this *reductio in primam figuram*, this singleness of meaning, served to account for all varieties of the figure. The demonic pig (its cloven hoof and dietary taboo) in severe monotheistic cultures, as well as the pig of ignorance (*avidya*), could be accounted for by rejection of the Earth Mother, while the tusked boar belonging to Ares or Vishnu could be accounted for by Neumann and Layard as expressions of the same negative mother, tusked as phallic, whom the Hero, like Odysseus, must meet as initiation and again overcome as a regressive enchantment toward primitive phallicism in the anima figure of Circe as the Hero proceeds away from the pig in the heroic course of developing consciousness.[18]

Singleness of meaning is, of course, just what amplification was intended by Jung to preclude. Yet the scientific fallacy is forced by its logic to ascribe a unified meaning to the figure. If a pig is winged, plays the flute, dances a jig, is carved into a church pew with a psalm-book, if it is a sun-god (Scandinavia), the highest and last zodiacal sign in the Far East, modeled with its torso dotted with stars, as found at Troy, or if it is naive, tender, fearful or jolly, and so attuned in hearing that Welsh Druids, who knew the language of birds for their divining,

---

17 See C. G. Jung, *Freud & Psychoanalysis*, Collected Works, trans. R. F. C. Hull, vol. 4 (Princeton Univ. Press, 1961), 329–30; *Civilization in Transition* (above, n. 12), 771, 733.

18 The victory of the lion over the pig (boar) was a Greek iconographical and literary convention. For example, in Homer, Patroclus was the lion while he was winning and became the boar as he died. See E. Vermeule, *Aspects of Death in Early Greek Art and Poetry* (Berkeley: Univ. of California Press, 1979), 88–92.

gained their foreknowledge of times from their pig companion, [19] or if animal psychologists today show the pig more intelligent than the horse, perhaps equal to the elephant, [20] and so perhaps one of the first animals to be domesticated [21] – these other spirited and sensitive implications fall out from the unified core of symbolic pig as earth mother, whether negative or positive. The arbitrariness of the method, however, belongs not to the *Handhabung* (handling), the heuristic way it is used, so much as to the scientific fallacy on which it is based.

If we retain the method and discard its scientific claim, then selection will not attempt an objective core of meaning, nor will the selection process derive from a set of tacit rules: cultural thematics before personal associations, imaginative texts before scientific texts, religious before secular, archaic before modern, folk culture before high culture, etymological before phonetic, Western before Eastern; all of which can be summed up in the principle: choose always wider and older materials.

Instead, we would follow Jung's idea of the heuristic: selecting from the data what works, what has *Wirkung* (effect). "Heuristic" is an idea taken from the healing arts; it is an artistic principle requiring an aesthetic economy to determine which few strokes evoke the essence most poignantly, going to the heart so as to amplify, extend, unfold an effect. The aim is to make the dream image display its full *plier* – implications, complications – not stuff it full or smother it with evidence: an imagistic sense of amplification rather than a data sense.

Because this essential economical stroke is a skill that requires cultural symbolic knowledge, fittingness is not fortuitous. We don't pull any-old-thing from the grab bag of symbols but select with a view to moving the soul by speaking symbolically with its images. Symbols are not things so much as rhetorical agents, ways of persuading images toward their

---

19 See A. Ross, *Pagan Celtic Britain* (London: Routledge, 1967).

20 See C. J. Warden, "Animal Intelligence," *Scientific American* (June 1951), 64–68.

21 Recent research dates the domestication of the pig no later than 6000 BCE; supposedly the dog and sheep go back at least as far as 7500 and 9000 BCE. Pig-keeping required settlements, and pigs were not suited to the life of food gatherers, nomads, and hunters. See A. H. Brodrick, ed., *Animals in Archeology* (London: Barrie and Jenkins, 1972), where it is also noted that "an aversion to pigs does seem to have existed from very early times in certain parts of western Asia" (32).

fuller scope and depth. They are like alchemical agents. They catalyze, dissolve, tincture the dream images, activating their *Wirkung*.

This offers an opportunity to make clear how I employ amplification and why I do so. First, amplification improves skill by providing *knowledge*, and, as I remember Karl Kerényi saying to me once after I was complaining about a boring, though learned, lecture, "aber das Wissen schadet nichts" (but knowledge does not harm). Knowledge is *the* technique of Jungian practice. For all the similarities in clinical training and therapeutic procedures, Jungians differ from other schools in one crucial aspect: knowledge of the archetypal imagination, the traditional deposit of symbol and ritual in art, culture, and religion. The grids from which Jungians work with the dream are patterns and materials like the dream, drawn from the thematics of the imagination. Jungians assume these patterns are the formal causes of psychic events and that the materials are the contents of psychic events, and that knowledge of them reveals the *telos*, the purposefulness, in the events. In Jungian psychology, knowledge of efficient causes – currently called "psychodynamic explanations" – takes a much lesser role.

Symbolical knowledge can of course lose its life, becoming routine formalisms, intellectualized materials, and prescribed goals. This frequently occurs with any knowledge; but merely because of the shadow of knowledge we should not forego knowledge itself.

Second, amplification presumes a *cosmology*. The pig or crab in a dream reaches across centuries and geographies because it is a visible presence of archaic and ubiquitous invisible processes. The symbolic pig is also an eternal, pleromatic pig full of all pigs everywhere, a cosmic pig there before I am here, dreaming before the dreamer. In that visible dream image are knitted together the pigs of Melanesia, the pig Aphrodite does not like because it killed Adonis, and my next *Wurstsalat*. So, a dream pig can no longer be a part of "me" only: as my laziness or dejection over my corpulence or as obscene compensation for a life-disdaining prissiness. The cosmic pig spills over the frames I put it in; its pleroma requires that every amplification seem too full. The cosmic pig can never fit into the fantasy of a personal private psychology. Its very appearance breaks such bounds and amplification is the adequate methodological response to this cosmic amplitude.

So, third, amplification is a *therapy*. By infusing the cosmic into the personal and releasing the personal into the cosmic, the method is a *re-ligio*, a re-linking, re-membering. I revive tradition as I recognize that I am – in relation with the pig – enacting what went on, for instance, in Leviticus, and what is stated in the Bible about pigs continues to be stated in the soul in my dreams. As these myths revive in me through the pig, the pig is restored to its role as a daimonic being, an inter-cessor, itself a *methodos* or path of *ta'wil* out of the egocentric secular worldview.

Fourth, amplification is itself a *ritual*, serving the image, much as if one would carve the pig in wood, paint piglets, or ceremonially slaughter, butcher, and roast it. Amplification brings out our hands and minds to the image: we offer time to it; we respond to its coming with gratitude. Our amplifications are a heaping up of offerings to it, *dulia* – not only that we may know it better but for its sake, that it be honored and attended.

Eagle

To show the power of amplification for giving the dream an imme-diately recognizable *topos*, let's begin with the amplification, then the dreams.

All birds, whatever their species, according to the bestiary books, are twice-born: once as an egg from the mother, and then born again from the egg. A bird brings the element of air, orientation from above. As Philo said, birds are messengers of God to strip us of material embroil-ments; they present the *intellectus agens*, the higher active mind that descends into the human sphere but is not born of it, which implies that the higher mind is an animal, that ideas and intuitions are winged bodies with quick-beating hearts that can strike us with claws and tear-ing beaks. The vernacular association of birds with sexual organs and behaviors recognizes that the *intellectus agens* comes also in those sing-ing, soaring excitements of sexual desire. The bird is like the physical force of the metaphysical.

Of the birds, the eagle is king and it appears as emblem of kings and kingdoms. At the cremation of a Roman Emperor, an eagle was released near the funeral pyre to conduct the imperial soul to the heavens. Only the eagle, it is said, can look directly into the sun, as Moses into the face of God, and only the eagle cannot be killed by lightning. The aged eagle renews itself by flying into the sun until its feathers become incandescent fire, and then, diving into water, it emerges young again. So Christ is this resurrected brightness, and the Logos that enlightens is an eagle like John the Evangelist who, in exile on Patmos, was taken up to heaven for his apocalyptic visions. Or, as the flight from Egypt, the Exodus, was accomplished on eagle's wings – the uplifting, inflating power of spirit over material entrapment.

The eagle "soon waxeth angry with spiritual arrogance" because its temperament is exceedingly hot and dry. There is militancy, even violence, [22] in its mission, for the eagle is always at war with lesser birds and creeping creatures: especially the dove – *d'aquila non nasce colomba*. [23] Mighty, battle-mad Ajax takes his name from the eagle (*aietos*). It seizes the frightened hare, the milky calf, the bleating lamb, the abandoned child; these weaklings fall prey to the seduction of a great grasp. Any beautiful boy like Ganymede can be carried away by the ascending impetus. Power. Knowledge. To wing among the lightning flashes untouched, forever, no more falls. Each day, an eagle tears at the liver of Prometheus, eating into the passionate organic soul of *ira* and *concupiscentia*, the Promethean drive consumed by its day-world ambitions.

As Emperor, spirit, logos, immortal, the shadow of the eagle is the senex, *aquilae senectus*, so there is much in eagle lore about renewal and aging. [24] It is said to die because of the increasing incurvature of its beak so that it either can no longer take food and starves or punctures its own throat.

We are able to expect that a dream showing movement in the eagle soul is of imperial, imperative force, bearing a large message, a collective mission. We can further anticipate upward-sweeping, inflating

---

22 Immediately after leaving the ark, the eagle committed the first murder by slaying a bird. God enabled it to escape punishment by the other birds by means of its high flight (L. Ginzberg, *The Legends of the Jews*, vol. 5: *From the Creation to Exodus* [Baltimore and London: The Johns Hopkins Univ. Press, 1998], 187 n51).

23 Italian proverb: "Eagles don't breed doves."

24 On the renewal of the eagle through "song, dance, and festival," see the story of old Eagle Mother told to Knud Rasmussen and retold by Nor Hall in *The Moon and the Virgin* (New York: Harper and Row, 1980), 105–108.

consequences and that something weak and exposed has been the bait. It might indicate the awakening of the *intellectus agens* as Logos in our culture and as a shamanistic initiation in archaic cultures. [25]

A woman dreams that she is going up the steps of the New York Public Library, when an eagle from towering height dives down on her, and she shields herself in terror. The dream stayed with her for years. This person, at the time of the dream, was a father's daughter and sheltered wife entrapped in the Egypt of her material security from which she slowly began an ambitious Exodus by means of further education and profession.

Another woman dreams:

> I am standing in our kitchen brushing my hair with my daughter's hairbrush before the mirror. With each brush a large amount of hair is pulled out. I realize my hair has holes, open spots, in it. I wonder if it will grow in again. I go on to a party and mention to several people about my hair having holes in it. I ask if they think it will grow in again. They say no. But each time I put my hand up to the holes, I feel small tight white feathers – like the cap on an eagle's head. It feels lovely and I enjoy having this secret.

In the kitchen, by the mirror, mother-daughter, loss of hair – a concatenation of familiar transformational motifs. In addition, here, the white eagle-feathered cap, appearing in the absence of her own natural hair, in the lacunae, the open spots of her head. Eagle-power emerges head-to-head and with it comes a paranoid potential: enjoying the loveliness of having this private secret in the midst of the "party," and despite what others say.

A younger man dreams:

> I am standing in the galley of the fishing boat on which I work. With me are the four other crew men and the captain around the table. I am becoming aware that there is a different animal associated with each of the five that they hold or have at their sides. What animals they are is obscure since the men and the animals are hidden in the shadows. In addition, I am spellbound at the appearance in the center of the air of a blindingly bright

---

25 On the eagle and shamanism, see the literature referred to by Mircea Eliade in *Shamanism: Archaic Techniques of Ecstasy*, trans. W. R. Trask (Princeton Univ. Press, 1972).

and luminous form, that of a snow-white eagle whose feathers are covered with midnight-blue stars and crescents. In awe I think the eagle wears the devices on the cloak of a wizard. The eagle alights upon me and spreads its wings. Gradually I become aware of nothing else but this royal creature, which continues to spark lightning from its form and grow ever brighter. I reflect this animal will bring good luck in fishing.

Because of our previous amplification of the eagle, we should not be surprised by the words in the dream: *blindingly bright, white, blue, luminous, center of the air, royal, lightning, awe,* or by the repetition of the Logos words *I think, form, reflect, become aware.* Notice the contrast between the gradual dominion of the eagle and the fading of the other men and their companion animals. Notice, too, how the motif of bright/obscure (hidden, shadow) is absorbed by the eagle who incorporates the midnight into its wizard-like form. As the royal blinding grows brighter, "I become aware of nothing else." This is the spellbinding effect of the eagle spreading its wings upon him. As Jung says, the archetype of the spirit is both wisdom and wizard, benefactor and sorcerer.[26] The effect is similar to the paranoid possibilities of the eagle-coverings on the woman's head. Both dreamers become privately centered.

The *raptus* effect of the eagle, by which I mean the identification with its vision, comes out in this dream of an elderly man:

> I am in a landscape bordered by mountains. Birds in the sky. Two eagles. Enormous, with a wingspan of some 30 to 50 meters. I can hear the swish of their formidable wings beating as they gyrate around in some kind of love play. The spectacle is awe-inspiring. Nearby is a fishpond. Dark fish in it. Suddenly I realize that on my left, as if hidden in a grotto just underneath the shore, is an enormous fish. It is black and facing the open water. A man connected with the place remarks that it is, or is not, dangerous. On waking, I was a bit scared The fish was dangerous. Maybe the eagles will catch the fish.

Here, as in the fishing-boat dream, light and darkness, sky and water, eagle and fish belong in the same image. In both dreams the dreamer expects the eagle to catch the fish, envisioning them as opposed.

---

26 C. G. Jung, *Archetypes and the Collective Unconscious,* Collected Works, trans. R. F. C. Hull, vol. 9.1 (Princeton Univ. Press, 1969), 413–18.

The black fish in the grotto is imagined in terms of danger (the eagle in terms of awe). His identification is with eagle power, as if he has already been carried to its place in the sky. Amplification can prepare us for these eventualities.

Giraffe

Concerning the giraffe, there is little of the usual lore to consult for amplification. Neither *physiologoi*, nor fairy tales, nor myths elaborate giraffes. It is not a familiar temple animal in Egypt, even if depicted, nor should it be confused with the fabulous *ki-lin* of China or the *zamar* of the Bible, though it is sometimes identified with both. Nor is there any representation of the giraffe in classical Greek art, for it is described only in later Hellenistic writings.

But there are giraffes in dreams. A young woman of high fashionable society, with anorexic traits, had two giraffe dreams. Another young woman dreams of coming down the Zürichberg in a small train with a giraffe beside her, but there is danger because its neck sticks up so high that it will collide with overhead wires and bridges. She wakes up anxious that the giraffe will get its head severed unless the train stops its descent. A third dream, reported indirectly, was from a mother, supposedly frigid, whose main concern was the sexual morality of her daughter: that she might get sullied.

Since we do not have the usual kinds of sources for amplification of the giraffe, we must open another avenue: cultural history. Giraffes belong in the cultural milieu of the courts; they were the delight of princes who presented them to one another as noble ostentatious gifts in Turkey, Egypt, Persia, Rome, and Renaissance Italy. Anne de Beaujeu, daughter of Louis XI, longed for a giraffe above all other animals and begged one from Lorenzo di Medici. The word *geraph, seraph,* from Arabic, supposedly means "the lovely one," and it was hunted and traded neither for its meat, nor for sport, but for its beauty, the coat, the long eyelashes and brush-like tail, its long dark tongue, the peculiar fluid lope, its silent, docile and elegant manner. It was eulogized by Renaissance poets; Poliziano saw in the giraffe the image of the cultured and intelligent man. Only in 1827 did the first giraffe arrive in Northern Europe, having been walked all the way up to Paris from Marseilles, causing extraordinary delight en route.

Depictions of the giraffe from African rocks through Persian manuscripts to eighteenth-century European drawings show a common anatomical misperception: the whole torso of the animal is drawn sloping upwards. The actual animal has a horizontal belly; nonetheless, the depicted image ascends, for this is the animal whose head is farthest from its body, its body farthest from the ground. To ground its head is ungainly. Its head is naturally in the trees, above it all, aloof, demeanor "exaggeratedly vertical" as the naturalist Wolfgang Schad says.[27] According to Heini Hediger,[28] its body has "remarkably few sebaceous [fatty] glands" (our anorexic dreamer?), and according to Adolf Portmann,[29] the giraffe has the highest development of its nervous center [cerebrum] of all cloven-hoofed animals. Also, it lacks any trace of that usual indication of aggression: upper canine teeth. Moreover, the mothering instinct, for which we turn to mammals as exemplars, in the giraffe is not so sure—at least as far as observed in captivity. Hediger's protocol of the first birth by a mother giraffe in the Basle Zoo reports that the mother feared the baby, ignored it, and trampled it so that the calf had to be reared by humans.[30]

An Arab dream book by Al-Damiri states that a giraffe may signify a worthy or beautiful woman, and it may sometimes indicate a wife unfaithful to her husband. It augurs financial calamity, or calamity to your property, and there is no guarantee for the safety of a person whom you may want to take to your homestead.

These warnings make sense in view of the distance of the giraffe from the common ground, its flighty defenselessness, and its beauty. In psychology, we might be speaking of the aesthetic anima—a docile, gentle, virginal quality of graceful awkwardness and heightened sensitivity, yet which has a killing kick if approached wrongly or too

---

27 W. Schad, *Man and Mammals: Toward a Biology of Form* (Garden City, N.Y.: Waldorf Press, 1977).

28 H. Hediger, *Psychology and Behaviour of Captive Animals in Zoos and Circuses* (London: Butterworth, 1955), 91–92.

29 A. Portmann, *Animals as Social Beings*, trans. O. Coburn (London: Hutchinson, 1963), 87–89.

30 I am not singling out the giraffe as sole example of awkward maternity, since infant mortality, infanticide, and neonate nurturing, both in captivity and in the wild, are complex subjects of research; I am simply noticing that the animal used by Hediger as witness for awkward maternity was the giraffe.

closely. A mother who is herself "frigid" fears that her daughter will become sullied, thereby losing their common giraffe totem. And the dream of the Zürichberg train tells the predicament of the giraffe: how to come down without having to cut off the head, which cannot negotiate the horizontal lines of communications and bridgings that run at cross purposes to that "exaggerated verticality."

First Conclusions

These amplifications have drawn upon three intertwined sources of "tellings" about the animals: classical symbolism (including lore, fable, etc.), ethnology or anthropology, and cultural history—in short, *mythos*. We have turned to the *Geisteswissenschaften* for the appearance of the animal in imaginative contexts. You will have noticed, however, that I have been slipping in a fourth source—natural history, extending amplification in a direction deriving from Adolf Portmann. The classical Jungian method uses textual sources: the symbolic pig rather than the pig of animal husbandry, laboratory psychology, zoology. The tradition of Jungian method has followed the traditional division of two kinds of comprehension: humanistic understanding and empirical observation.

Following Portmann, however, the pig reveals itself to the observing senses as a behavioral, aesthetic phenomenon—in short, nature, and not only as a philological, symbolical, textual one. *Selbstdarstellung* of the physical pig is another context of manifestation. Since each animal is a living form, as Portmann says, it expresses itself. All animals speak. They speak as metaphorically to the observational imagination as to the symbolic.

Consider the self-display of the pig, the crab, the giraffe. The giraffe's orange-and-white reticulated coat offers a gorgeous outward show. This coat, as zoologists have noted, does not conceal or camouflage—which is anyway a paranoid militaristic term originating in 1917 and misapplied to ecological conformity—but gives heightened visibility for communication at great distances. Giraffes must be seen; they do not call to each other. The pig's coat is its very torso, as if it were naked. Stuffed as sausage, compact as ham, it presents itself as flesh, meat. Loud, bulky, it goes after roots, while the giraffe extends into extremities and upwards with the trees into the air. (Taxonomy places giraffe and pig in the same large group of artiodactyla, or even-toed ungulates.)

Unlike either, the crab conceals its tender sweetness wholly within: who would guess the delicate articulated sectioning of its interior from the spiny, crusty, barnacle-covered, pugnacious external display. To know the crab, one must go into it, through its hidings and disguises in hard-shelled coverings, a body armor it sheds only during moments of mating. Compare their motions: the distancing of the giraffe by means of a singular galloping gait; the grounding of the pig with its short trotting; the scuttling of the crab, expressive of sidestepping. Compare their necks: the giraffe's, as if to hold head and torso apart, detached; the pig's, as if to keep them confluent; and the neckless crab whose head is in its body.

Or, return to the polar bear, hearing this report from Wolfgang Schad:

> Mating takes place towards the end of the polar night, at the end of March or beginning of April. The development of the embryo, however, is arrested until the end of October... Just at the onset of winter embryonic development resumes; in the midst of the most extreme cold, in January, deep within the snow caves over which arctic storms are raging, the tiny, naked, warmth-requiring young enter the world almost as embryos. Here causal arid teleological explanations break down. But the essential character of the bears is expressed all the more clearly... the complete independence of their strongly metabolic nature. In space as in time, these large carnivores withdraw from the surrounding world and time of year... surviving purely on the strength of their metabolism. [31]

That inner heat, independent of space and time, can withstand the dark night of the cold. The tapas of the shaman, "withdrawn from the surrounding world," the *opus contra naturam*, is given with their nature.

I am suggesting that we read the animal and not only about the animal. I am suggesting that the dream animal can be amplified as much by a visit to the zoo as by a symbol dictionary, and I am suggesting that we dream interpreters not reduce the dream to the symbol but reduce ourselves, our own vision, to that of the animal—a reduction

---

31 W. Schad, *Man and Mammals* (above, n. 28), 66–68.

that may be an extension, an amplification, of our vision so as to see the animal with an animal eye.

What does the animal recognize when it comes upon another animal? Without benefit of a bestiary, its text is the living form. The reading of living form, the self-expressive metaphors that animals present, is what is meant by the legends that saints and shamans understand the language of animals, not in the literal speech of words, as much as psychically, animal soul to animal image, speaking with animals as they come in dreams.

To read the animal, to hear it speak, requires an aesthetic and ecological perception for which psychology has yet to train its eye and find words that are not just allegorical moralisms, beyond metaphors of piggishness, mousiness, monkey tricks and bear hugs, beyond simplistic metaphor altogether, beyond grasping at the meaning of the animal; to that aesthetic apperception of what is presented, responding to the significance of its form, an appropriate, appreciative response, grateful that it is even there, that it has come to the dream, and that this visitation is a momentary restoration of Eden. For that short eternal while, and afterwards in varieties of recollection, there is in the dream of images, an original co-presence of human and animal, and when we are present to the animal, Adam is there and Eve, and we are in the Garden from which the animals were never rejected.

Dare we add one more Midrash to that Garden? It is not merely a nostalgia for unfallen paradise, immersion in innocence or lawless animality. The Garden is a mythical nature, the *topos* where things natural are also mythical and myth is presented as nature, where the animal and the name of the animal, natural pig and symbolic pig, cannot be fallen apart, ruptured, where each creature is sustained by the mythos of its nature, obedient to the lawful discipline of each according to its kind.

Animal Names

We need now to raise a question that should lead us more deeply into the nature of the animal in the dream. Why segregate dreams according to conventional species: pig dreams, eagle dreams, and so on? Why these rubrics? What is the fantasy in the method?

Clearly, the animal name as rubric places the dream within the bestiary tradition going back to Aristotle and Pliny and continuing to this day, where taxonomy follows the commonly recognizable forms of the animals – their appearances. The name bespeaks an image – a complexity of habits, presentation, style – by means of which each animal reveals its kind. Noah, too, entered the animals into the ark according to their kinds, and this is how they appeared to Adam, as species – each a morphological presentation.

Pig, Crab, Eagle assert that each animal kind is a recognizable essence, a concrete and visible universal, always the same. As such, these rubrics give essentiality to the dream, and as substantives, they give substance and power, like totemic authority to the dream as an entirety. Indeed, it is a pig dream, not a tunnel dream, because each animal name evokes the animal presence as the daimon in whose name the dream shall be told. Often, in practice, a dream is actually titled by the dreamer after the animal – which is unusual for a car dream, a flying dream, a sexual dream. These may be more common and more emotional, yet the credit of the title is given to the animal. And I do admit to taking the animal in the dream unvaryingly as its most significant element because it is the place where the psyche opens into beings of mystery and beauty who are creatures as we are and yet remain "other." The animal is that strange other I wish most to evoke during the analytical hour and from which, or whom, I hope further imagination will actively initiate.

To explore and to justify this sense of substance and power in the dream animal, to come to terms with this otherness, is our remaining task. First, however, we must recall in broad lines the modes of degradation of the animal kingdom that are still operative in the response of the interpreter to the dream and in the response of the dreamer in the dream.

Modes of Degradation

The many difficulties of the "dream-I" with the animal in dreams – perceiving the animal as dangerous, fearing its bite, pursuit by it, invasion by many of them – definitely correspond with the dreamer's devaluation of the animal in the dream – the desire to avoid, to control or to eradicate it, or in the dreamer's misperception (that familiar little phrase, "I thought...") of the animal and its intentions. The strained relation between human and animal in contemporary dreams recapitulates the Western tradition and its degradation of the animal.

The Western tradition regarding animals consists of four main strands: Hebrew, Greek, Roman (Stoic), and Christian—each of which composed of lesser threads reflecting different writers, economies, laws, and cults. The Bible places the animals in the original Garden and singles them out for salvation from the Flood. Dietary laws show a careful discrimination among animals, such as we find in Greek natural science, e.g., Aristotle's biological writings. Even if the animal is decidedly delivered into human hands (Genesis 1:28, 9:2), Proverbs 12:10 says, "A righteous man has regard for the life of his beast ..." And Ecclesiastes 13 says, "that which befalleth the sons of men befalleth beasts ... as one dieth, so dieth the other, yea, they all have one breath [*nepesh*, soul]; so that a man hath no preeminence over a beast." A long Greek tradition from Pythagoras through Plutarch and Porphyry also holds man and beast close together, and supposedly one of the three moral precepts of Eleusis was "do not be cruel to animals."

This Hebrew and Greek regard, however, seems not to have been the principal influence in later Western attitudes. In the main, Greek religious feeling expressed in the animal forms of the gods was followed by the Roman state cult of pomp, pageant, and cruelty. Despite Pliny's notion that animals are more dear to God than man, Lucretius's belief that animals are happier and higher than man, and the popularity of Virgil's third *Georgic*, Roman law gave the owners of animals *ius utendi* and *ius abutendi*, a position supported by the Stoic idea of reason of which animals were deprived.

As Greek gave way to Roman, and Hebrew to Christian, Ecclesiastes is nowhere mentioned in the New Testament. Where some Greek Fathers (Origen, Clement, Basil the Great) can be read to show profound sympathetic connection between man and the bestial soul, others (Gregory of Nyssa) attributed the Fall to one source: the animal mode of generation or bestial sexuality. The Serpent, after all, was an animal.

The main Christian line derives from the New Testament itself. Augustine writes,

Christ Himself shows that to refrain from the killing of animals and the destroying of plants is the height of superstition because, judging that there are no common rights between us and the beasts and the trees, he sent devils into a herd of swine and with a curse withered the tree on which he found no fruit. Surely, the swine had not sinned nor had the tree. [32]

By sending the devils into the swine, Christ, according to Augustine, made perfectly clear that animals were utterly beyond human concern. [33]

Aquinas's mode of degradation follows more the Stoic direction: animals have no reason; therefore, they have been completely delivered into our hands. When St. Paul says that "God hath no care for oxen," Thomas interprets this to mean that "he does not judge a man on how he has acted with regard to oxen or other animals." Thomas does note the Biblical injunctions to treat the animal well, but these, he argues, were necessary because the Jews were given to cruelty! Injunctions against cruelty to animals are because such cruelty makes the human perpetrator cruel or callous to other humans. The concern is not for the animal. [34]

---

32 J. Passmore, "Treatment of Animals," *Journal of the History of Ideas* 36.2 (1975), 197.

33 In *Confessions* V, 3.5 and VII, 9.15, Augustine recapitulates Paul's Letter to the Romans 1:23–25, explaining that the worship of animals, the sense of their divinity, is a falling from God, a worship of the organic and corruptible and the mortal rather than the immortal; the creature rather than the Creator. The paradigm of this sin of preferring the created over the Creator is the confrontation between Moses, who like an eagle could look into the face of the highest, and the red or golden calf. That scene has in its background the theriomorphic division between eagle and calf as represented, for instance, by the sign of the eagle on cattle enclosures in the ancient Middle East to ward off the rapacious bird of heights. Popular tradition holds that the eagle was anathema to the Jews, which shows – regardless of Babylonian and Syrian associations with the eagle – a psychological awareness of the dangers of the ascending spirit and its transcendent theology, i.e., John, the Eagle. The division between "calf" and "eagle" can lead to the division between nature and spirit, created and creator, as emphasized in the theologies of Paul and Augustine.

34 St. Francis of Assisi, raised from parochial obscurity by a fin-de-siècle biography (Paul Sabatier's *Life of St. Francis of Assisi* [1893], trans. L. S. Houghton [New York: Charles Scribner's Sons, 1928]), is often held up by Christian apologists as exemplar of the love for animals inherent in Christian doctrine. Not only, however, does Francis have little theological influence, but this story is told in the anonymous *Fioretti di San Francesco* (Little Flowers of St. Francis): when Brother

Kant continues the rationalist mode of degradation. Animals "are not self-conscious and are there merely as a means to an end."[35] Like Aquinas, he points out that kindness toward animals will develop humane feelings toward mankind. Again, the concern is not for the animal.

My point ought now become horribly clear from this passage from a sermon by Cardinal Newman:

> We, in our turn, have no duties toward the brute creation; there is no relation of justice between them and us... They can claim nothing at our hands; into our hands they are absolutely delivered. We may use them, we may destroy them at our pleasure, not our wanton pleasure, but still for our own ends, for our own benefit or satisfaction, provided we can give a rational account of what we do.[36]

The moral philosophy of Aquinas, Kant, and Newman did recognize that the animal suffered. It is a sentient being if not a rational one. Animal nature is brute in regard only to the absence of reason; reason, of course, being the distinguishing mark of the human, sign of the divine Logos. For Descartes and Malebranche, however, even the sensitive soul is gone. Cruelty to animals is therefore logically impossible because they are incapable of feeling. "They eat without pleasure, they cry without sorrow, they desire nothing, they fear nothing, they know nothing," says Malebranche. They are machines. The Cartesian Jacques Rouhault argued that an organ makes more noise when it is played than an animal when it cries out, yet we do not ascribe feelings to an organ.[37]

Even our diet is Cartesian, or Christian, according to one Japanese cultural analyst: only in Western societies can meat play such a prominent dietary role because only here does the ontic distinction

---

Jonathan, Francis's disciple, being ill, had a great longing for pig trotters, Jonathan cut the foot off a living pig. "Saint Francis rebuked him, but with no reference whatsoever to his callousness. He urged him, only, to apologize to the owner of the pig for having damaged his property." (Passmore, "Treatment of Animals" [above, n.32], 200.)

35 "Duties Towards Animals and Other Spirits," in I. Kant, Lectures on Ethics, trans. L. Infield (New York: Harper and Row, 1963), 239–41.

36 J.H. Cardinal Newman, Sermons Preached on Various Occasions (London: Longmans, Green, and Co., 1908), 79–80.

37 See Passmore, "Treatment of Animals" (above, n.32), 204.

between man and beast allow it to be delivered into man's hand, an ontic distinction that is ritually commemorated three times a day.[38] Like one of the faithful facing East, our faith in human superiority is confirmed with bacon at breakfast, at the hamburger stand at lunch, and over chicken dinner in the evening with Grace—thank thee Lord and bless this food. The animal as meat belongs to our religious beliefs. Compare, for instance, what an Igloolik Eskimo said to Rasmussen: "The greatest peril of life lies in the fact that human food consists entirely of souls."[39]

The historical degradation continues to appear in dreams. A young woman from an inner-Swiss Catholic canton dreams:

> I pass a glass case of small stuffed animals of different kinds, and birds too, on display. As I come nearer and look more closely, I am surprised to see that they are all alive and moving.

We can enjoy this little dream as the psyche's response to Descartes. The animals that, at first, seem stuffed with conceptual labels, available only for objective study, insensitive, dead, are actually suspended in the glass vessel of the psyche, in one's actual "case"; and, if we step closer to this animal display, we, and they too, will be surprised to see that they are alive, and moving.

The inevitable counter-impulse to callousness is sentimentality, which in regard to animals, especially its British moralists from the eighteenth century onward, reaches culmination—and another mode of degradation—in this twentieth-century prayer written for British Girl Guides:

> Hear our humble prayer, O God, for our friends the animals... we bless thee that thou carest for the dumb creatures of the earth... especially for animals who are suffering; for all that are overworked and underfed... for all wistful creatures in captivity, which beat against the bars, for any that are hunted or lost or deserted or frightened or hungry... [40]

---

38 S. Toyoyuki, "The Meat-Eating Philosophy," in M. Hyoe and E. Seidensticker, eds., *Guides to Japanese Culture* (Tokyo: Japan Culture Institute, 1977).

39 S. Giedion, *The Eternal Present: A Contribution on Constancy and Change* (New York: Pantheon Books, 1962), 290.

40 See C. W. Hume, *The Status of Animals in the Christian Religion* (London: Universities Federation for Animal Welfare, 1957).

The degradation of pity still places the animal's fate in human hands. Roles are now reversed: man may now be seen as bestial, the animal as lovable, but the animal remains pathetically dependent and lower.

The most familiar mode of degradation is evolution theory. *Homo sapiens* is well at the top of the tree. Yet Darwin's theory was received initially and by many still today as a degradation of mankind. Simply by returning humans to the animal kingdom, Darwin had put us too close to the ape, that species which has carried through the centuries one or another aspect of the culturally repressed, whether it be knowledge, drunkenness, brutality, *figura diaboli*, or polymorphous pleasure. A psychological reason for why evolution theory met such resistance is that the ape is in its shadow.

Notions of evolution influence dream interpretations. The lower the evolutional place of the animal, the more the creature is supposed to develop, as for instance in the well-known case reported by Medard Boss, where progress in therapy showed an analogy with development of the animal images according to the evolutionary scale, beginning with insect dreams, until the animals disappeared from the dreams altogether. Jung, too, saw the lower animal, serpents for instance, to be indicative of cold-blooded reflex actions, far from human. [41]

The implied teleology in evolution theory, however, is not that all kinds of animals strive toward the human estate, but that each species achieves its own perfection, like oysters and sharks that have not changed in millions of years. A frog is not "better" in a dream than a fish, a dog than a wolf. There are no wrong or negative animals, in dreams or otherwise. An alchemical caution says, "You cannot make a milk-cow out of a mouse." Each animal has its own perfection: it does not improve into another species. A mouse brings its own virtue into a dream, and evaluative comparisons across the species are odious because they desert the image and insult both the mouse and the milk-cow.

A reversal of evolution theory is the devolutional view of animals, sometimes called animalitarianism. [42] The beasts are fallen from the

---

41 C. G. Jung, *Aion: Researches into the Phenomenology of the Self*, Collected Works, trans. R. F. C. Hull, vol. 9.2 (Princeton Univ. Press, 1969), 369.

42 Animalitarianism, or the innate superiority of animals, is discussed with historical documentation by Arthur O. Lovejoy and George Boas in their *Primitivism and Related Ideas in Antiquity* (New York: Octagon Books, 1965).

human condition, and fallen for their sins. Monkeys especially were once humans, but because of their sinful habits, which anyone can see, they became monkeys, grew hair, lost speech, and foul their own habitations. Jung, at one point, puts the devolutional view more subtly in this question: "Are the psychic functions of animals remnants of consciousness?"[43] Implied is the fantasy that intelligence precedes instinct, instinctual reactions being remnants of more individualized and malleable adaptations that have devolved into segmented inborn release mechanisms.

Jean Servier gives the devolutional view a beautiful twist. He tells a tale that animals in North African cultures he has studied are said to be richer than we. Why? Because the rich give and the poor receive; since humans have speech and fire, and animals haven't, we have been given speech and fire by the animals. Their richness is hidden; they carry an invisible fire, an inaudible word.

The Animal Kingdom Within

The animal as hidden benefactor opens into a series of views in which the animal is interiorized into the human soul in one fashion or another—as phylogenetic traces, as totemic ancestry, as inborn release mechanisms and from this animal we are descended or instinctually empowered. It is this animal face of the psyche that we see in dreams.

"Understand that you have within yourself herds of cattle," says Origen in the third century (in Patricia Cox's translation), "flocks of sheep and... goats... and that the birds of the air are also within you... You see that you have all those things which the world has."[44] Not merely are we each an ark, a microcosm containing the animals, but they serve a functional purpose inside us.

We need the animals, says Laurens van der Post, because animals are reflections of ourselves. We can't know ourselves unless we see ourselves reflected in them. They make possible our reflective consciousness; indeed, we owe them fire and speech. Remember the pig in the tunnel, the flickering firelight... Does that dream image not imply

---

43 C. G. Jung, *Archetypes and the Collective Unconscious* (above, n.26), 502.

44 P. Cox, "Origen on the Bestial Soul: A Poetics of Nature," *Vigiliae Christianae* 36 (1982), 115–40.

that the animal is immersed in a *lumen naturalis,* which we gain from it? Examining the animals on the cave walls of France and Spain, Clayton Eshleman claims that these first moments of reflective consciousness in humans occurred by means of "naming the animals" and placing them "out there," for they were drawn on those walls wholly by interior vision in the claustrophobic dark.[45] Microcosm before macrocosm. As if the origin of the species, animal, is within the soul.

Grant Watson, the British naturalist whom I have mentioned already, says, yes indeed, we have thrown the animals off and out. Not evolution, not we as developments on top of the animal chain, going back to amoeba. Rather, we have thrown off from our Adamic natures these animal parts. Out there roam the hyenas, gorillas, and little white lambs that we have cast from ourselves. Of course, Adam knew the names of the animals, and the cave man could so truly paint them; they were parts of himself. Each animal has its specialized calling, bespeaking specific human characteristics, and even contemporary laboratory psychology and zoology recognizes that one particular species is ideally constructed to give answers to each particular human problem.

A complete elaboration of the specific function of each species is the plan of the Polish/French physician-philosopher Hélan Jaworski. His formula is succinct: "Zoology interiorized becomes physiology—physiology exteriorized becomes zoology."[46] The animals out there are our human organs; our organs are interiorized animal species.

Batrachia (frogs and toads) present the skin: human sweat, sebaceous and sudorific cells have their analogy in the cutaneous exudations of frogs and toads. Crustaceans are limbs—even their eyes are on stalks, and a separated claw can be grown again. Snakes have lost their limbs for the sake of digestion, interiorizing their locomotion to locomotor peristalsis. They digest for days, defenseless and soporific, aided even by their spinal column and their jaws that can dislocate to accommodate meals larger than themselves. Fish, the skeletal structure; molluscs and octopus, the female genitals; insects, the external equivalent of the

---

45 C. Eshleman, "Preface" to *Hades in Manganese* (Santa Barbara: Black Sparrow Press, 1981).

46 H. Jaworski, "Batrachia, Reptiles, Birds—Their Significance," *British Homeopathic Journal* 48.3 (1959). See also J. M. G. Twentyman, *The Organic Vision of Hélan Jaworksi* (Richmond Hill, Surrey: New Atlantic Foundation, 1972).

human vegetative nervous system, hence their symbiosis with the plant kingdom. Higher mammals are exteriorizations (or "excrescent souls" in older language) of the human psyche and its emotions. Monkeys, for instance, are all hands, even their tails are hands. Swinging, picking, grooming, teasing: they are the presentation of manipulative abilities. The lion is courage; the fox, cunning; and the leopard, cruelty. Further, "if all living forms happened to disappear, man, dissociated into each of his different parts and organs, could recreate them again."

This homeopathic vision offers deep organic kinship, all the while maintaining human superiority. We can recreate the animals one by one from our organic functions, but only all of them together, each contributing its specifically circumscribed function, could recreate man. Animals remain partial functions. Into our hands they are still delivered.

The idea of the animal as an interior function of the human continues in depth psychology. Freud writes,

> Wild beasts are as a rule employed by the dream-work to represent passionate impulses of which the dreamer is afraid ... (It then needs only a slight displacement for the wild beasts to come to represent the people who are possessed by these passions ... a dreaded father is represented by a beast of prey or a dog or wild horse.
>
> Many of the beasts which are used as genital symbols in mythology and folklore play the same part in dreams e.g., fishes, snails, cats, mice (on account of the pubic hair), and above all those most important symbols of the male organ—snakes. Small animals and vermin represent ... undesired brothers and sisters.[47]

Wilhelm Stekel carries this further. The toad is a womb; wet, slippery animals (snails, frogs, etc.) are to be taken as feminine; dog, snake, and bird are penis equivalents. The flea is a phallus because it is fresh, lively and aggressive. Ernest Jones explains why animal images represent the sexual libido:

> Doubtless the feature of animals that most attracts ... is the freedom they display in openly satisfying needs, particularly those of a sexual and excremental order ... Children often owe their

---

47 S. Freud, *The Interpretation of Dreams*, trans. J. Strachey (London: George Allen and Unwin Ltd., 1954), 357–416.

first experience of sexual activities to the sight of animal copula-
tion... Animals therefore lend themselves to the individual representation of crude and unbridled wishes. [48]

Now hear Jung regarding the animal:

People don't understand when I tell them they should become
acquainted with their animals or assimilate their animals. They
think the animal is always jumping over walls and raising hell all
over town. Yet in nature the animal is a well-behaved citizen. It
is pious, it follows the path with great regularity, it does nothing
extravagant. Only man is extravagant. So if you assimilate the
nature of the animal you become a peculiarly law-abiding citizen,
you can go very slowly, and you become very reasonable in your
ways... We have an entirely wrong idea of the animal; we must
not judge from the outside. From the outside you see, perhaps, a
pig wallowing in mud, but that is partially because man has made
the pig what it is; judged from the outside that pig is dirty... But
it is not for the pig. You must put yourself inside the pig. [49]

That was Jung, fifty years ago. Contemporary analytical psychology
has transformed that basic empathy for the animal into an idealization of a theoretical abstraction: instinct. Today, mostly, the animal
in a dream functions to represent a phylogenetically older level of the
psyche, often referred to as "instinctive," "chthonic," "primitive," or
simply as "the body" from which the modern ego is judged to be too
far removed. The dream animal compensates an overrationalized and
denaturalized human condition.

An article by Mario Jacoby well presents the contemporary Jungian
view: "Animal dreams are first and foremost compensating for the
constantly inherent danger of the loss of instincts in humans." [50] The
instinctual basis of human nature is like an inner *menagerie* in which
all species must be cared for, else they become ravenous or die out.
Any animal that becomes too devouring represents that partial drive

---

48 E. Jones, *On the Nightmare* (New York: Liveright Publishing Corp., 1951),
69–70.

49 C. Douglas, ed., *Visions: Notes of the Seminar Given in 1930–1934 by C. G. Jung*,
2 vols. (Princeton Univ. Press, 1997), 1:168.

50 M. Jacoby, "Das Tier im Traum," *Studium Generale* 20, no. 3 (1967): "Tier-
träume haben... in erster Linie die Bedeutung, die im Menschlichen ständig in-
härente Gefahr des Instinktverlustes zu kompensieren."

to which the human has become victim. For instance, falling prey to the herd instinct shows in sheep and goat dreams, the power instinct shows in lion and eagle dreams. A mouse that gnaws in the dark represents the sexual stirrings that one regards as insignificant and yet are feared as disturbing: "The dream animal is thus an image of a specific instinctual behavior."[51]

The animal "represents." It has a single function: the rodent gnaws, the sheep gather in herds. This mode of understanding follows an old allegorical *topos*. Gregory of Nyssa, for instance, contended that humans become toads through lust, vultures through cruelty, and tigers through anger. The rubric of each animal kind becomes confused with each animal having but one so-called instinctual function. The method is like a medieval bestiary where each animal serves to moralize in terms of Christ. Here, each animal serves to moralize in terms of an ego that sees a stereotypical aspect of itself in the behavior of the animal.

Besides the unexamined theoretical assumptions that divide human nature into an instinctual unconscious and a rationalized cultural consciousness between which operates a system of compensations, where animal symbols function as servo-mechanisms, this compensatory view does not, as Jung says, put yourself inside the pig. And, it neglects the humor of each animal style. Fables, cartoons, toys, and children's tales worldwide show that each animal is funny, fun to watch, and also a mode of play.

The Household Mouse

Consider the household mouse: it has not merely a single function and its image in a dream is not merely a symbolic representation of that function. That flattens the mouse, making its incursion into the dream too understandable. "Inside the mouse" means to do justice to the rich, complete being that each animal is, with its intricate adaptive manners of eating, breeding, nurturing, moving, its coloring and eyes, its geography. Each animal presents not only a way of surviving and self-preservation; it shows also patterns of defense and pathologizing, and, as well,

---

51 "Das Tier im Traum ist also ein Bild eines spezifischen Instinkverhaltens." (Ibid.)

ways of relishing the world through specialized senses and intelligence. Mice don't just gnaw; they listen. And they are beautiful.

If you put yourself inside the mouse, you can sit there quiet as a mouse and hear the world, its little tonalities, its whispers, and to do this you must remain very nearby and yet very hidden—every muscle alive and still (and "muscle" and "mouse" are etymological cousins)—so as not to interfere with what's going on, the sounds, the smells, by calling attention to yourself. Intent, intense, you follow well-regulated, almost puritan paths because you can succumb to paralyzing hysterical fugues if found by a cat or a snake. On your little grey back you carry the suddenness of the *invenio*, the unexpected—breaking into the familiar—like the return of dead souls, especially little ones (children), like the lecherous passions and thirst for drunkenness of humans trapped in households. You must be both surreptitious, humble, mousey, and yet brazen, cheeky, hurry-scurry, because thieving is in your nature, breaking and entering, through cartons, grain bags, walls; whatever is laid up and stored away is subject to the inventive genius of the mouse, inspiring the inventive response to build a better mousetrap, for you are like little mercurius, tricky-micky, who does not allow paranoid partitions by making holes and opening the ways that humans fear as "contamination," the profligate spreading-out through quick-breeding or through fleas and disease. [52] And the cat, who would control the household for its egocentric comfort, needs you to hunt, so you are satisfied with leftovers, crumbs, whatever falls to your greedy modesty.

Beware of trapping the mouse of the dream in theories of sexual repression and functional compensation. Instead, by putting yourself inside the theriomorphic imagination, you may save the phenomenon from the theories. This was, after all, God's concern, saving the phenomenon "animal"—or is it a noumenon?—for which he commanded an ark be built. The world could go under, its cities, forests, and plains,

---

52 Hediger (*Psychology and Behaviour* [above, n. 29]) writes, "Man must declare war on mice, not only in zoos, but everywhere; we have no choice, it is either mice or men ... Owing to their smaller size mice are able to get into places ... [and] hide there and this is important bearing in mind that they carry disease ... As well as plague they can also carry typhus, severe enteritis, leptospirosms and tularemia; they frequently carry salmonellosis and virus infections, also bad fungal diseases ... The above list is by no means comprehensive ..."

and all its people excepting one nuclear family. But what must survive of all that He made are the seeds of creation—the animals.

Body

I want to carry my critique of depth psychology's view of animal images further than its assumptions about instinct versus culture, and further than its use of each animal as an allegorical disguise for these so-called human instincts. We also need to question the identification of animal with body.

"Body" is a curious word in English, tending to mean a limbless, headless, central mass, a torso or trunk, unarticulated and coagulated, clumped, and even inert. Often it is a collective noun: a body of water, a body of soldiers, a body of writings. Its derivation is obscure: the anglo-saxon *bodig*, going back to the Old High German *botah/potah*, is probably related with the German *bottich*—brewing tub, cask, vat. This relation is doubtful and there are no others. The word is an orphan, without cousins. Pokorny's giant etymological encyclopedia does not elaborate it. Onians's masterwork on the ideas of body organs and functions does not discuss the very word in the book's title.[53] Thass-Thienemann's two-volume Freudian study of language claims that "in language the human body is the primary reality and the references to the body and body processes are prior to any object references."[54] Yet Thass-Thienemann forgoes examination of the prime word, body, to which he claims all others refer.

"Body," the primary referent of phenomenology and the transcendent metaphor of school after school of therapy, remains a curiously unreflected word in the English language. Perhaps this unreflectedness is precisely what body signifies, a kind of dumb, brute event, direct, naive, and unarticulated. It seems to be the root metaphor of the naturalistic fallacy in psychology. Therapeutic attempts to differentiate body, awakening it and reaching psyche through it, e.g., the body therapies, may thus be attempts to work through—not "body" as such—but consciousness trapped in the naturalistic perspective.

53 R. B. Onians, *The Origins of European Thought about the Body, the Mind, the Soul, the World, Time, and Fate* (Cambridge Univ. Press, 1954).

54 T. Thass-Thienemann, *The Interpretation of Language* (New York: Aronson, 1968, 1973).

Animal images can differentiate this naturalism. Instead of locating the animals in the body, we can break up "body" into animal imagery. A variety of animal pairs pull the many chariots of sexual love (as depicted in murals in Ferrara),[55] thereby differentiating the sexual body into a swan-like style, a pig-like style, or a manner of mating like two turtle doves. Physical life (instinct) is always imaged.[56] Body is always carried by the soul in a specific fashion. And this carriage derives from the soul's images. The animal images are thus carriers or vehicles of bodily existence. Or, better said, there is no such thing as "body" as such, as there was no word for it in Biblical Hebrew, but there are many varieties of animal images more relevant to actual behavior and more precisely efficient for capturing its patterns than the general concept "body."[57]

When animals are equated with body, one of two things tends to happen. Either the animals must represent the stupidity of the body,

---

55 Here, the ancient Christian moralistic idea of the "animal skins" or "coats" (see J. Daniélou, "La Colombe et la ténèbre dans la mystique Byzantine Ancienne," *Eranos Yearbook* 23 [1954]), which encase the spiritual essence of human being in bestial clothing, ourselves enclosed in biological existence, is revalued by the Renaissance imagination. The animal images become fantasies, vehicles for transporting our biological drivenness into differentiated patterns of enactment and reflection.

56 For a psychologizing of the term "instinct," see my *Re-Visioning Psychology* (New York: Harper and Row, 1975), 244–45, and my "Essay on Pan," in *Pan and the Nightmare* (Putnam, Conn.: Spring Publications, 2007), xxiii–xxvi.

57 The differentiation of "body" by means of animal images is adumbrated in this passage from Jung's Zarathustra seminar (3 June 1936): "The body is the original animal condition, we are all animals in the body, and so we should have an animal psychology in order to be able to live in it... Since we have a body it is indispensable that we exist also as an animal." (J. L. Jarrett, ed., *Nietzsche's Zarathustra: Notes of the Seminar Given in 1934–1939 by C. G. Jung*, 2 vols. (Princeton Univ. Press, 1988), 2:967. This "animal psychology" would be to return the "body" to its "original animal condition," that is, to imagine and experience "body" events as animals—although not in the fashion of Jaworski, Jacoby, etc. Rather than a singleness of function (sheep equal herd instinct, etc.), we would experience any zone and organ, any physical sensation and behavior with theriomorphic imagination; e.g., sometimes when I argue I am as tightly armored as a crab, nipping and pinching; sometimes I am a lion imperious; at other times I act like a monkey, chattering and escaping every which way. Muhammed Ali, when speaking of his boxing style, used theriomorphic imagination for his "bodily" movements: "Float like a butterfly, sting like a bee."

that it is low, driven, and desirous, a headless and burdensome beast, as W. B. Yeats says in his *Last Poems* ("The Man and the Echo"):

> Waking he thanks the Lord that he
> Has body and its stupidity.

Or the animals are praised for their marvellous instinctual sureness, the wisdom of the body as the natural superiority of the million-year-old inner animal. To become healthy and normal, one must only let the animal lead by following the body.

Another poet, Gerald Burns, questions psychology's idealization of the body:

> Analysis of mind is incomplete
> when "body" means something normal
> and how one twists in vain or rage
> escapes the attention;

By assigning animals to the body, we normalize their specific peculiarities. They disappear in a collective noun, that tub as melting pot. They lose their names. We neglect that an ape body differs from a horse body, and that again differs according to the horse in the image. Does it kick at the stall slats, pull a beer wagon, take sugar with its lips? What color is it and where is it and whom is it with? A dream animal is in the image and not in the body.

Besides, the animal in a dream presents not my body, whatever the word connotes, but its body, the essential otherness of its shape and motion, the self-display of *its* physical presence.

Beyond Interiorization

There was a time when psychoanalysis had to interiorize the animals, degrade them into an "inner psychic menagerie," that microcosm of Origen, that standard Latin *topos* of the animal soul as a jungle or zoo within the human being.[58] Interiorization into instinct, into body,

---

58 "Le Roman voit donc l'*animus* inférieur comme une espèce de jungle, ou comme ces parcs d'Orient remplis de fauves pour chasses royales. C'est l'esprit, soutenu par la volonté, qui est alors le chasseur et le dompteur qui doit tuer ou apprivoiser ces monstres de l'âme, éliminer ou soumettre ces énergies qui lui sont étrangères" (The Roman thus sees the lower animus like a species of the jungle

were ways to reclaim what had been thrown out and away and to bring the animals into an inner feeling of kinship. After the extreme ontic otherness of the Stoics, Romans, Christians, and Cartesians, where the animal was merely amusement, property, meat and machine, interiorization at least gave the animal kingdom a habitation in the soul.

The soul, however, has undergone a long process of subjectivism. It is no longer the psyche in the Platonic sense (I inside it). Soul has taken on the interior personalism of Augustine (it inside me), culminating in the introspective identification of all soul events as "mine," my emotions, my body and its needs. Thus the mouse in the dream is my trepidation; and the pig, my greed. Immanence has lost its otherness, which Jung tried to restore with his notion of the *objective* psyche, where images exist in their own right. Like the fox in the forest, which is not mine just because I see it, so the fox in the dream is not mine just because I dream it.

For the animals to exist in their own otherness, they have to be kept safe from the law of compensation that declares "the dream is strictly causal," always in compensatory relation with "the conscious mind."[59] So long as I can affect the animals in my dreams by the stance I take in day-world consciousness, the transcendent otherness of the kingdom within cannot be distinguished from my unconscious psychological life, the sins and wishes of emotions that the animals have been forced to represent.[60] They reside not inside human nature but inside our view of human nature; our subjectivist personality theory constructs

or like these parks of the Orient filled with deer for royal hunts. It is the spirit, supported by the will, which is then the hunter and the animal trainer who must kill or tame these monsters of the soul, eliminate or subdue these energies that are foreign to it). (Y. A. Dauge, *Le Barbare* [Brussels: Collection Latomus, 1981], 606.)

59 C. G. Jung, *Practice of Psychotherapy,* Collected Works, trans. R. F. C. Hull, vol. 16 (Princeton Univ. Press, 1966), 334.

60 The reduction of each animal to the single meaning of a stereotypical trait also results from what Emile Mâle calls the "mania for symbolism" (*The Gothic Image: Religious Art in France of the Thirteenth Century,* trans. D. Nussey [New York: Harper Torchbooks, 1958], 48). The symbolic view of thirteenth-century cathedral sculpture—reading each beast and composite creature to be symbolic of religious psychology—makes use of the animal for subjectivist functions. But Mâle says the craftsmen were not carving animal *symbols:* they "delighted in nature for its own sake." It was the animal itself that inspired artistic invention. Thus the animals are so vivid and profound. They are not symbols but *true images,* animals as they are, even if not lifelike copies from actual nature.

the cages of the inner zoo. The law of compensation has delivered dream animals wholly into human hands, the hands of our humanistic interpretations.

What I have been criticizing as functionalism, symbolism, or subjectivism can be subsumed under interiorization. Animal image as representation of organ, drive, or *Daseinsweise* is still a degradation, even if this mode is the most subtle and psychological. Lost is the animal as other, its ownership of itself as a self-possessed creature with its own nature not assimilable to mine. Can we leave the animal out there in its otherness and yet retain its psychological import and our kinship with it? Can we remain psychological without interiorizing?

Henri Frankfort[61] wrestles with a similar question regarding the animal-god relation in Egyptian religion. First of all, Frankfort says, the term "animal gods" is wrong. They were not totemic figures; there was no sacred bonding with the animal, and the animal did not function as a symbolic representation of a god "in the way that an eagle elucidates the character of Zeus": "There was nothing metaphorical in the connection between god and animal in Egypt." No functionalism. No interiorization. Rather, "animals as such possessed religious significance for the Egyptians. Their attitude might well have arisen from a religious interpretation of the animal's otherness. A recognition of otherness is implied in all specifically religious feeling." Here Frankfort refers to Rudolf Otto.

"We assume, then," says Frankfort, "that the Egyptian interpreted the nonhuman as superhuman, in particular when he saw it in animals—in their inarticulate wisdom, their certainty, their unhesitating achievement, and above all in their static reality. With animals the continual succession of generations brought no change...They would appear to share...the fundamental nature of creation:" its repetitious, rhythmic stability. Each animal confirms that living forms continue; they are eternal forms walking around. An animal is eternity alive and displayed. Each giraffe and polar bear is both an individual here and now and the species itself, unchanging, always self-creating according to kind. Each polar bear presents the eternal return of the polar-bear spirit as a guardian, a *spiritus rector*, from which, according to Ivar Paulson speaking of the

---

61 H. Frankfort, *Ancient Egyptian Religion* (New York: Harper Torchbook, 1961), 8–14 ("Sacred Animals and Otherness").

circumpolar arctic peoples, the very idea of a God arises. Gods "originated within the animal world itself, that is, with the actual animal."[62]

This offers an answer to the question about the nature of the animal rubrics, the general bestiary names, e.g., Pig, Eagle, Crab. Species names go back to Adam in the garden of myth. Each species is a primordial substance or living archetype as visible image to which the question of origin, being temporal, cannot apply. The origin of the species is outside historical, empirical knowledge. The species can be apprehended themselves as origins, as revelations of eternal forms, and so theories repeatedly turn to them for the secret of origins.

In the animal image is the eternal return in Eliade's sense, the *ricorso*, not as a death instinct, repetitious into entropy, but issuing forth ever the same from creation, as the thundering herds of buffalo to the Plains Indians were always the same buffalo charging up from the earth each spring, not subject to history, each species breaking through history. Repetition as renewal, a blessing, a witness to continuing creation. So, when the last giraffe, the last white bear falls dead, it is also the first giraffe whom Adam named and who was on the ark. Its fall is the extinction of an eternal seed, a divinity killed – deicide.

"Their certainty, their unhesitating achievement, their static reality" (Frankfort) confirms in humans an animal faith. We rely on the term "animal" to express our unquestioning confidence in the reality of being. What we abstractly call "instinct" is a behavior of certainty, exhibiting faith in repetitious, static realities, "following the path," as Jung said, "with great regularity." The Western cult of change through human will, its belief in historical progress, of course declares these witnesses of primordial faith in the reality of continuity to belong to a lesser kingdom or declares them already by definition extinct, that is, soulless, irrational, or mechanical. But the recovery of these forms in our dreams can restore that animal faith in the repetition of continuing realities, that animal certainty, as Frankfort calls it, or preservation of the species, as biology calls it. The animal is the unhesitating answer to nihilism: it must go on, each according to its kind. In each animal the ark is recapitulated, and the Garden. *In illo tempore*, this morning in your dream.

---

62 Paulson, "The Animal Guardian," (above, n. 2), 218.

The otherness of each animal form is what I believe Adolf Portmann's scrutiny of concrete nature brought us to see and feel for thirty
years at Eranos. (Curiously, his lectures were for many years the last
ones, each year closing with this disguised tribute to the animal kingdom, as more recently it has been closing with the theme of Egypt
where, too, the animal could not be more honored. Closing lectures
that, by ritually invoking the animals, bespeak our faith in the continuity of Eranos.)

Portmann insisted that "appearance, like experience, is a basic
characteristic of being alive."[63] All living things are urged to present
themselves, display themselves, to show *ostentatio*, which was a common Latin translation of the Greek *phantasia*, fantasy. Each animal's
ostentation is its fantasy of itself, its self-image as an aesthetic event
without ulterior function. Portmann brought many kinds of evidence
for these "unaddressed appearances." For example, the small transpar-
ent oceanic creatures that live in the interiors of other larger creatures
or below the depths where light can reach, having no visual organs
themselves, and whose brilliantly vivid and symmetrically patterned
forms serve no functions, neither as messages to their own species, as
attractions or warnings, nor as disguises. Sheer appearance for its own
sake; unaddressed. "Here, self-display is realized in its purest form.
Appearance is the result of a very specific structure of the plasma; it is
its own purpose."[64]

Appearance is its own purpose—does this not say that the animal is an aesthetic creation, that the animal eye is an aesthetic eye, and that the animal is compelled by an aesthetic necessity to present itself as image?

Portmann's radical insight into the biological necessity of the aesthetic explodes the sheerly functional notion of animals, struggling
to feed and breed, ever in fear and trembling, their *demeure* as mere
territory or possessive property, and whose reason for being on earth
is sheer preservation without spirit, without sport, without play. And
we see, too, how human psychology, by using this narrow view of

63 A. Portmann, *Entläßt die Natur den Menschen? Gesammelte Aufsätze zur Biologie und
Anthropologie* (Munich: Piper Verlag, 1971): "Das Erscheinen ist wie das Erleben
ein Grundmerkmal des Lebendigen." (84)

64 "Hier ist Selbstdarstellung in der reinsten Weise verwirklicht. Die Erschei-
nung ist das Werk einer ganz spezifischen Plasmastruktur, sie ist ihr eigener
Zweck." (Ibid., 86)

animal life, cannot take their images in dreams otherwise, implying that the way back to the animal kingdom for humans must be only through brutalism and bestiality—sex, body, territory, fight or flight, release mechanisms, imprinting; nature still red in fang and claw. Then a behavioral, biology-based psychology must view the aesthetic as a secondary accompaniment of more species-preserving functions or as incidental decoration. Psychology has refused to see that the animal kingdom is first of all an aesthetic ostentation, a fantasy on show, of colors and songs, of gaits and flights, and that this aesthetic display is a primordial "instinctual" force laid down in the organic structure.

Our attempt to deliteralize interiorization has taken a second step. First, we had to see that the interiority of animal images is not inside us. Now, we are led to see that this interiority is also not inside them. Their *Innerlichkeit* is in their appearance. The interior selfness of the animal appears in its displayed image. Interiority need not follow anthropomorphic and subjective notions of memory, experience, and intentionality. Not self-consciousness but self-presentation.

I am continuing here with a theme I began to formulate last year as a "depth psychology of extraversion"—the turn to the world as a psychological arena where any event displayed to the senses is also an imaginative form. From this depth perspective of the world, all things are displays, and imagination and perception, invisible and visible, intuition and sensation do not fall apart when discerned with an animal eye.

How to gain this animal eye? How to put yourself inside the pig? We have touched upon several ways: making phylogenetic correspondences with human embryology; interiorizing the animals as human physiology; seeing stereotypical behaviors as allegories (the greedy pig); discovering the symbolic essence by means of amplification (the devouring earth-mother pig). Now let us move beyond correspondences, symbolization, interiorizing, and living forms as metaphors. Let us attempt another entry into the animal kingdom. Can we climb aboard the ark?

A man dreams:

> I am walking with my wife outdoors somewhere. We notice a lot
> of ants; we get interested in them, even getting down and looking
> at them from eye level. Maybe even picking them up like being
> one of them. Seeing things as they do.

In the next dream, the wife kneels down to a dog in order to show some children, who cannot learn the dog's trick, how to do it. And the dog then easily performs its trick.

By bringing our superior postures to the level of the creature, kneeling to it, condescension, we begin to see as they do; a transposed eye. Gods retain this animal eye. Their animal heads and animal masks display their animal consciousness. The head of the animal on the human torso maintains that lower, immanent vision of creatureliness—creator and creature, God and animal, in the same figure.

To see with the creaturely eye is an act of imagining the world so that it appears in continuing animation, in a continuing play of creation with which human consciousness participates by means of imagining acts. Not the creative imagination as some wondrous gift that creates images, art, and ideas. Rather, the transposed eye itself releases what is into its own createdness, each event as a presentation of creativity. The human imagination is not the creator, does not create; it sees the creative, creatively in the world's ongoing *Schau*—its *Spiel*.

Spiel, "play" in English, is rooted in the meanings to dance for joy, to rejoice, be glad—as the Hebrew legends of the animals who chant and sing praise. The word "play" is packed with animal motions. It means to strut, dance, or otherwise display oneself as a cock bird before hens; to move about swiftly with a lively capricious (goatlike) motion; to fly, to dart to and fro, to frisk, flit, flutter, oscillate freely; the play of light on shining, glinting, bright surfaces (like feathers, shells, scales)...With animals in mind an idea of play stands forth as the revelation of fantasy in action, its free motion, its animated joy in the presentation of an image. With animals in mind, play is the visible display of the invisible, free of purpose, of function, other than its own display.

The phonetic link between play and display—and I have learned from Paul Kugler[65] that such links may indicate profound connections—suggests that the animal's urge to self-revelation is reason enough for its creation. That is precisely the help it offers Adam: the animal continually reminds that the play of creation is revelation. To be is to be seen; beauty is given with existence. As Portmann shows, to be seen is as genetic as to see: the organic structures of patterning,

---

65 P. Kugler, "The Phonetic Imagination," *Spring 1979: An Annual of Archetypal Psychology and Jungian Thought,* 126–28.

coloring, and symmetrical display are as genetic as the ocular organs that allow seeing the display. In fact, the coat is genetically prior to the eye that sees the coat. It is this beauty of the phenomenal and its everlasting return of the same that the animals reveal, as if they revel in their own fantasy—not information, not communication, not metaphor, beyond understanding and meaning, the beauty of these amazingly complicated and "other" living beings. It is as if they say, look at us with respect—re-spect, which means, "look again"—as if Adam's eyes were made to see their images, or to see them as archetypal images.

Inside the ark it was dark, of course, for the ark was covered with pitch, inside and out (Genesis 6:14). By what light, then, did the creatures see? What is the vision of these seeds[66] in the ark, the essential vision? Jewish legend says that God sent the archangel Raphael to Noah with a book of wisdom in which were written all the secrets and mysteries. By means of this book, Noah knew how to fulfill his task and gather the animals. With him into the ark he took this book and it was made of sapphires, and by means of its light all the creatures in the ark could see.

The incorruptible substance of the *caelum* is the light by which the corruptible animals see. The natural animals have an imaginal vision; the physical world perceives by a metaphysical light. To restore to our human eye that sapphire light we must be pressed in among the animals against the pitch wall. The way to the imaginal lies in the animal.

Implications of this blue sophic light are to be sought in the writings of Gershom Scholem, Henry Corbin, C. G. Jung, and in the fifty yearbooks of Eranos. We come to these conferences for the sake of that light. For my part, let me suggest only that the eye that sees by a sapphire vision is brought by the animal in the dream. The blue vision is inside the pig and we get inside the pig for the sake of its sapphire light. Interiorization is not them in us but we with them inside the ark.

Why do they come to us, the animals? If not a part of us, if not subjective partial drives, symbolic representations of stereotypical styles, but presences, *daimones*—what do they want inhabiting our dreams?

---

66 "Noah needed the ark—to unite with it, to sustain the seed of all, as is written: *to keep seed alive.*" *The Zohar* 1:59b (Pritzker Edition, vol. 1, trans. D.C. Matt [Stanford Univ. Press, 2004], 341).

Why does the polar bear come through the door, the eagle descend to sit among men?

A woman dreams:

> There are a lot of tiny animal creatures who have fragments of an original knowledge, guidance, which they preserve jealously with great tenacity to keep it, and them, alive. I watch them guarding these fragments, and scurrying around, building, or rebuilding, their living place, and I feel reassured and hopeful. I know (without being able to say why it is so) that these holy fragments will last forever, go on forever, yet will help only if these creatures give them their utmost care and attention.

Are these creatures the animal guardians that the creation may perpetuate, and do they claim a similar careful attention from us? Can we know the answer without attending to them, speaking with them? We may guess why they come, but let us yield the degrading beliefs that they come for our subjective purposes, to compensate our omissions. Perhaps, they fear the loss of human kinship, that they have already been excluded from the next ark, or that the Gods have deserted them so that they are like a displaced people merely an ecological problem for administrative solutions and charitable pity. Imagine—pity for an eagle! We cannot know what they come for until we first start to wonder, until we turn the plane around and look into the water where the bear waits, until we feed deep, deep upon that pig's black and peerless eye, until we condescend to the ant. These theophanies, are they calling the dream soul into their kingdom?

We know the record of extermination. The animal kingdom, from the caveman through Darwin on the Galapagos and Melville on the whaler, is no more. Insecticides lie on the leaves. In the green hills of Africa, the bull elephants are brought to their knees for their tusks. We long for an ecological restoration of the kingdom that is impossible. Yet it is a noble longing, for it houses a utopian impulse, an impulse that can be satisfied in the nowhere world of the dream. There, their souls and ours meet as images. The dream is an ark in which all living forms according to their kinds can abide during the eternal cataclysm that is coterminous with the ark. Do they come to remind of the cataclysm that occurs whenever humans fail to see by a blue light,[67] fail to see that the invisible is in the perceptible, an invisible that shadows appearances with their "otherness," unaddressed to our needs and meanings. Do they come so that we may still see beauty, even to save beauty?

The restoration of the animal kingdom is thus a restoration of ourselves to that kingdom via the dream where motifs that we encountered in dream after dream of the research extend beyond the heroic stereotypes of mythic amplification[68]—the animal as fearful and dangerous, its conquest and our superiority—to motifs of learning from the animal, amazed by its beauty, touched by its pain, reconciliation with it, being borne, helped, saved by the animal. These dream motifs restore the reason given in Genesis 2 for the creation of the animals as succor (ezer). The terrible wildness of animals disappears in messianic times say both Jewish legend and the Sybilline oracles. These moments of restoration appear in dreams: saved by the swimming bear, piglets arisen and delighting, the animals restored to life in the glass case.

It has been said many times at Eranos that the soul is in exile—from its Platonic possibility, the terre pure, the Temple. But that restoration may require another more prior: recovery of the ark and Eden, a recovery expressed today as an ecological nostalgia for a topos, a perimeter where human and animal share the same kingdom. But the dream itself encloses us protectively in the saving ark, in the originating garden, and there in the dream, we may recover the habits of the crab and the

---

67 J. Hillman, "Alchemical Blue and the Unio Mentalis," *Sulfur* 1 (California Institute of Technology, 1981), 33–50. See also "The Azure Vault: *Caelum* as Experience," in *Alchemical Psychology*, Uniform Edition of the Writings of James Hillman, vol. 5 (Putnam, Conn.: Spring Publications, forthcoming).

68 Heroic stereotypes of mythical amplification (Hercules as paradigm) are precisely those which set animal and human against each other. Giedion (*The Eternal Present* [above, n. 39], 273) writes: "The age of the supremacy of the animal—of the natural order—reaches back immeasurably ... Man then severed himself... The first step in this severance was the dethronement of the animal. Another approach to the world was evidenced in Greek myths. The animal is here dethroned: dethroned forever... A new figure arose: the hero ... The animals which appeared on the walls of the caverns—bulls, lions, snakes, boars, birds—are transformed in the Greek myths [of Hercules] to fabulous man-hating monsters. A tragic situation arises: a demi-god, himself in slavery, has to accomplish their destruction. There is no memory of that bond which once held man and animal in one embrace. The emergence of the hero symbolized the end of the zoomorphic epoch."

mouse, the knowledge of the pig, the animal coat, the animal tail, the animal eye.

Is it possible that it is we who are delivered into their hands to guard us from our own extinction? Yet we cannot summon them. They are other. It is for them to come to us. Will an eagle dive? Will a crab take hold tonight? Sleep, and hope for a pig.

2

Imagination is Bull

What you may expect from the next fifty minutes is an account of what you have been enduring and enjoying here for the past many weeks – the curious confusion of imagination and bull that is our peculiar Dallas activity. In fact, my fifty minutes hold even bolder promise than the activity of the Institute of Humanities and Culture. You shall hear great tales of myths and origins; how bull came into the world; the nature of inflation; of money and the bull market; why the bull of imagination disrupts convention; why Blake said, "Jesus the Imagination"; why Johnny can't read; and finally, and necessary to every American public address, what's wrong with this country, how we got this way, and how we may still be saved. These fifty minutes must promise all this because the theme of this talk and my talk itself is bull from beginning to end.

Greet the Bull

Now let us be introduced to the great bulls of myth so that we do not talk bull behind their backs. Let us invite them into the arena, one by one.

Here is a most famous one, the bull of Poseidon whose priests (if we may call them that) were known as *Tauros*. This bull rises from the sea (as do many others in many cultures) toward the end of Euripides' play *Hippolytos*. Remember the moment when the young man, cursed by Aphrodite (because he neglects her) and by his stepmother and his father, drives his four-horse team along the coast and the great bull appears:

> We saw a wave appear
> a miracle wave ... To the shore it came,
> swelling, boiling, crashing ...

> But at the very moment when it broke,
> the wave threw up a monstrous savage bull.
> Its bellowing filled the land... And sudden panic
> fell on the horses...The horses bolted:
> their teeth were clenched upon the fire-forged bit...
> the bull appeared in front to head them off,
> maddening the team with terror.
>   (*Hippolytus* 1205–25)

And in that chaos the chariot overturns, killing the virginal, noble youth.

Another tale of Poseidon's bull. This, too, shows the power of Aphrodite over the fate of those who refuse her. The wife of the king of Crete, Pasiphae, would not propitiate Aphrodite. The goddess took her revenge by infusing Pasiphae with a monstrous lust for a bull. This white bull with soft dewlaps and sinuously curved horns was Poseidon's bull, out grazing with her father's herds. Pasiphae's desire for him knew no bounds, so she charged Daedalus, the old master-craftsman, to construct a hollow sculpture of a cow on wheels. He covered it with hides and into it she placed herself so that she could deceive the bull. From this union the dreadful minotaur was born—that bull-headed creature imprisoned in the labyrinth who fed on the best young men and women. You may see the minotaur whose lust (a selfish gene from its mother?) consumes young men and women, even the best of them, in many of Picasso's etchings and paintings. He shows the minotaur with the body of a man whose mind is encased in the head of a bull, consuming youth with imaginary passions and unable to puzzle its way out of the maze of desires, unable to meander slowly through the labyrinth of life.

Europa is another female figure attracted to the bull, this time Zeus on the seashore.[1] Europa wreathes garlands on his head, holding out flowers "to his snow-white lips," as Ovid writes. Zeus, the bull, kisses her hands. Europa then mounts his back "little knowing on whom she rests." Soon she is in deep water, and carried off toward Asia, tho' the bull lands them on Crete.

Is this a founding tale of Europe's ever-fertile imagination because it rests on the back of an imaginary bull? Underneath, an entire continent

---

1 Ovid, *Metamorphoses* 2.833–75.

is an animal spirit of desire to be carried away and a recurrent swimming towards Asia: Alexander, the Legions, Crusades, Marco Polo, Prince Henry the Navigator, Columbus, Lord Clive... on to Gallipoli and Iraq.

Now, one of the biggest and oldest bull stories we have: the *Epic of Gilgamesh* from Babylonia. Ishtar, the goddess of love, has had her advances refused by Gilgamesh and Enkidu, the heroic pair of mighty friends. They rudely mock her, enumerating all her love crimes and seductions and, after ridding the world of her bull, they parade through the streets of Uruk chanting, "Who is the most glorious of heroes, who is the most eminent among men?"

Hercules, too, is a bully and a bull-slinger. He overcomes the bull of Crete, and the river bull from whom he wrests a horn. He pits his strength against the bull, limiting his imagination of it to only its physical power and the danger of its horns. If Hercules and Gilgamesh are bully-boys, Dionysus *is* the bull. The Chorus in Euripides' *Bacchae* sings,

> Come Dionysus
> come and appear to us
> come like a bull;

and the women of Elis cry for Lord Dionysus, the "Noble Bull," he who roared like a bull, "raging with a bull's hoof."[2]

Early, too, are the founding bull stories of Egypt. For instance, one that makes clear that from its very birth, bull brings confusion. The Egyptian text says,

> I am the male of masculinity
> I slid forth from the outflow between her thighs...
> I broke forth from the egg...
> I escaped in her blood. I am the master of redness.
> I am the Bull of Confusion, my mother Isis generated me...
> I took shape, I grew, I crawled about, I crept around, I grew big,
> I became tall...
> The flood it was that raised me up...
> I am the babe in the Primeval Waters...[3]

---

2 W.F. Otto, *Dionysus: Myth and Cult*, trans. R.B. Palmer (Bloomington: Indiana Univ. Press, 1965), 166.

3 R.T. Rundle Clark, *Myth and Symbol in Ancient Egypt* (New York: Thames & Hudson, 1959), 87.

With the arrival of bull unreason rules, confusion reigns: erotic, heroic, civic, destructive—and maybe also creative. For example, the Persian creation myth says that Ahuru Mazda creates a bull named Gosh before he creates the hero Gayomart, and from them come all things of the world—earth, waters, tree, stars, moon, sun, and ox. This bull is the only beast mentioned at the beginning and he is representative of all the beasts. At Lascaux, on the cave wall, there is a giant bull with all sorts of other animals traced on its great body.

If Lascaux represents where painting begins, the bull is given the rank of *prima inter pares*. Similarly, in India, Nandi who carries Siva on his back is the lord of all four-footed creatures. Not the lion is king; it is bull who keeps the beasts alive. Imagine that! If the bull sustains the mythic spirit animals, then bull keeps our animal spirits alive and well. Bull has a guardian function within the ark of our physical souls.

Animal spirits was the term used in psychological explanations throughout Western history until modern times. It referred to what "goes on inside." Today we might translate animal spirits into the soul's vitality, emotions, hormonal or autonomic or lymphatic systems, or the unconscious psyche, or deep brain functions. Imagine that! Bull is good for your health.

To keep the animal spirits living and well is precisely the intent of a paper by the Harvard history professor William G. Perry in favor of bull: "In a university setting good bull is therefore of more value than 'facts.'"[4]

We could now continue with more bull stories from other cultures' myths; certainly more from India, other parts of Asia, the Nilotic peoples, or the Celts who are famous for their extraordinary gifts of bull. But let us rather move on.

Bull about Bull

Huge, direct, terrifying is the oncoming bull. We are cowed in its presence. That face, forming masks cultures over, that huge scrotal bag, the horns and tongue and cloven hooves—must fertility be so forceful? It charges, rushes, throws, tramples. We cannot hold our horses.

---

4 W. G. Perry, Jr., "Examsmanship and the Liberal Arts: A Study in Educational Epistemology," in M. Rainbolt and J. Fleetwood, eds., *On the Contrary: Essays by Men and Women* (Albany: State Univ. of New York Press, 1983), 161.

The word for the animal relates with bellow and bell. The roar of the bull is the sound of the sky god himself. The Greek prefix *bou-* (our bovine) means huge, monstrous power. Bullies are ruffians; tough cops are bulls. The root of the word: *tauros* is thick, stout, like a four-by-four hunk of wood.

Besides the enormous horned force – and horns, symbolists say, signify spiritual energy – there is a second root to "bull" that is closer to our usage when we say, "that's all bull, full of bull, cut the bull." *Bulla* (Latin) means bubble, bauble, trifle, vanity, inflated, expanding quickly and quickly passing; whence comes the Papal Bull or edict named for the hot bubble of lead with which the Pope's pronouncement was sealed.

Hence bull in the dictionary of English means to fool, mock, deceive, trick, and cheat. A bully is a gallant, a darling, a sweetheart. *Bullatus*: ebullient, inflated, bombastic, full of air. A bull market, therefore, can be strong and come on with a Merrill-Lynch rush or deceive like a South-Seas bubble, full of irrational exuberance, a sweet cheat. Incidentally, the etymological root of this second bull (*bulla*) – both in its connotations of trick and full of air, and as Papal Bull of authority – is *ubal, phal,* same as *phallus.*

While we are engaged with origins of bull, let us note an explanation from antiquity for our vulgar use of "bull" for worthless untruth, i.e., objectionable, revolting bullshit. Pliny described a *bonasus,* a species of bull whose horns were bent in on each other in such a way that it could not fight. "It has therefore," Pliny writes, "to depend on flight, and which in flight sends forth its excrements, sometimes to the distance of three *iugera* (104 Roman feet), the contact with which excrements burns those who follow, like a kind of fire."[5]

When confronted with a great animal power, whether in the shape of an actual animal or an animated image, we in our culture rarely bow down to it, sing to it, or dance in its honor, nor do we even run for cover. Rather, our usual move is to interpret. We wave the hermeneutic wand to make the force go away by transforming it into a meaning. Our modern propitiatory rite is to look up "bull" in the symbol dictionary. Bull dissolves into "moon," "father," "fertility," "thunder" ... and

---

5 *Naturalis Historia* 8.16.

takes on names from Gaelic to Hebrew to Latin to Urdu accruing ever more mythic tales as we research. Civilized men and women in institutes of humanities and culture have met the bull with their own sort of bull: what they say about the bull. Myth, after all, is what is said about what is said: the bull about the bull.

What does this bull about the bull tell us? First of all, we see that the bull releases extraordinary imaginative power. The power of its image is like the power of imagination itself. The range seems unlimited: bull is both Father and Moon Mother, soft rain and thunder, seminal and fecund, meat and mystery, natural and spiritual, raging and Venusian, earthbound and cosmogonic, a mass of blood, muscle, and horn, and the celestial constellation governing light-footed springtime. Perhaps, then, "bull" is another way of saying "imagination." Perhaps, then, imagination is simply "bull" as rationalists have long complained.

Consequently, I am adding another body to the list of substances we have already reviewed, another *pars pro toto* such as bull as blood, as horns, as testicles, as eye, as face, as hide. Let us propose that the most recurring, enduring, and sacred essence is its "b. s.," its myth-making power. What bull breeds best are fantasies.

Then the stories we have seen and the interpretations take on another sense. Gilgamesh and Enkidu are punished for destroying the cosmogonic imagination, and so, Gilgamesh, in that tale, had to seek personal immortaility since the eternal cosmos was no longer open to his imagination. When the Egyptians worshipped the bull, then it was not simply a fertility divinity of life but the fecundity of imagination that kept all their gods alive. When Pasiphae, Europa, and the women of Elis fell so desperately, hungrily, for Poseidon, Zeus, and Dionysus, it was not for simple sexual lust but for the "trip," the release, the ecstatic move out and the unforeseeable progeny that comes from union with imaginative power. And regarding the heroes—Mithra and Hercules—overcoming the bull by taking its horns or slitting its throat does not found anything more cultural than cults and militant action. Deeds without image, as Rilke said.

Aleph

I have been proposing an equation: bull = imagination. But not all imagination is bull. I would locate our bull in a specific place, the non-place of origins, those beginnings called "creation myths," the founding imaginations that "make up" the ground of culture and its inseminating starting point. For example, the first letter of the alphabet, where all words start, is *aleph* (Hebrew, Semitic, Arabic) and *alpha* (Greek). This letter comes straight from the bull, for *aleph* derives from a glyph that represents the face of an ox or bull. The bovine *aleph* is a breath letter, a vowel. It holds the "ah" of wonder and the "ah" of pain, and the great, affirmative, open throat of assent. "Say Ah," says the Doctor, "Open wide." He does not say, "Aum."

This bull faced *aleph* still appears in our words "elephant" and "alphabet"—again that curious proximity of beast and spirit. How hard for us to draw the necessary lesson: that the aspiration of our civilization to be literate, that everyone be able to read and write words of letters, in short, that humanism begins with the ABCs, close to the face of the great beast, and that in the word itself is the bull. We cannot help but speak bull. "A" is not for apple and the Fall but for *aleph* and the bull.

"A" is not merely for referential speech: that apple there to which I am pointing. Language does not have to be chained to the fall of reductive explanation downward to some evidential fact. "A" is for *aleph*, the bull face, the bull force, the hot air of speech that overblows, giving us things to say and to say to things. Not only referential but reverential; speech said to the apple in praise, not merely about the apple in description. We may learn words for applied information, but we must learn them so we can bellow back the mind's confusions that long for speech.

The ABCs are for the soul's sake so it can find words for its bull. The bull is the first poem, and all poems have bull in them; each is a made-up conceit carrying huge weight on its shoulders. Poems come trotting out, snorting, and civilization drinks from them the lifeblood of imagination on which its culture depends. They are both edicts of authority lasting centuries and yet tricks, cheats, deceptions—mere sounds in letters.

I think Vico had this bull in mind when he invented his theory of language by imagining the earliest humans stumbling their way into speech, which, he said, was utterly poetic, wholly imaginative: "Living in bestial solitude, men… expressed their passions by shouting, grunting and murmuring, which they did only under the impulse of the most violent passions."[6]

The bull in the imagination of origins look to Crete. Crete has been imagined as the cradle of Western civilization; and the excavations of Arthur Evans uncovered bulls of every sort, and leaping, dancing youths and maidens somersaulting over the backs of charging bulls. On Crete, Evans's own imagination runs rampant; he reconstructs the whole palace, the whole culture, paints it red, endowing our Western history with another origin myth. There, too, Jane Harrison suddenly imagines her ritual theory of myth; Karl Kerényi, the origins of the Dionysus cult; Martin Nilsson, the Minoan origins of Greece culture; Arthur Pickard-Cambridge traces drama and tragedy to Cretan bull sacrifice. All bull — myths of origins. Crete, place of bull, and when we go there to land our creative theories and reconstructions of origins, we are close to the bull.

More bull stories of origins. Coinage: Bernard Laum lays his bet on the ceremonial dismemberment of the bull as the origin of bits of money. The spit on which the animal was roasted (*obelos*) became the coin (*obolos*) as the piece of bull meat stuck to the spit. Bull sacrifices, so these writers say, were the first form of taxes and the treasuries of temples originate in the closed places where sacrificial bulls were kept. The ancient Roman currency, the *as*, means "piece of roast." The ancient Spartan iron coin originates in the sickle-shaped knife used to kill the sacrificial bull. Still more: Athenian financial officials were called *kolakretai*, which means "receivers of limbs." The limbs were pieces of the sacrificial animal that were also money. Delve deep enough into money and you find it based on bull. No wonder we succumb to and yet distrust economic prophets. Even when their pronouncements are dressed in statistics, we sense they are full of bull. No wonder, too, that money brings panic, confusion, ecstasies, joys and madness, especially when we try to hold its flow with rational accounting. Balance sheets,

6 G. Vico, *The First New Science*, ed. L. Pompa (Cambridge Univ. Press, 2002), 152.

transparency, cavernous vaults with massive steel doors try to keep the life in the money under control, as do other measures in which we pen the bull: bonds, securities, safes, obligations, fixed assets. Nonetheless, money is a wild ride because it is truly blood money, perhaps never severed from the bull, Dionysus, in one of his many carnal shapes.

I have been persuading you to accept the idea that myths of origins and the origin theories of myth are bull stories. These myths of the beginnings of letters and words, of money, of civilization are founding myths—not tellings of how things were once or then but how they are now. The same old bull is continuing as we make up myths that account for our foundations, whether in etymology, history, or religion. Ontologies are filled with bull. They are great sustaining forces that carry worlds on their backs. When we say, deprecatingly, "it's all bull," in response to a theory or an idea, we are standing in the tracks of the ancient mythical heroes, the bull slayers. Today's rationalist doesn't leap or dance or sling or tease with the bull; he re-enacts Mithra, Hercules, Theseus—the heroic enemies who kill the bull.

When we turn to imagination, we let in the bull. Yes, it breaks up the bourgeois china shop. Yes, it disrupts the plebian conviviality of the TV-ad beer party and causes wild rides in the rodeo arena as in the stock market. Yes, it can burn you with its excrements if you chase it, as Pliny said.

Yet, at the same time, the beginnings are with bull: the first letter, the first treasure, the first creature, the guardian of all other creatures, and so perhaps of all other letters, of literacy itself. Imagine: the bull at the head of the word, its chief and king, which means nothing less than literacy begins in bull: power stories, sex stories, hero stories, marvel and miracle—and creation stories about how it all began, told with stubbornly bull-headed insistence of their real truth, even pawing up the earth in search of physical proof. To win the day with one's tales one must rather bull one's way through. It is the far-flung that prevails, and the body of the beast must come with its breath into the line, into the phrase. Make way for the alphabet; it walks like an elephant.

To state it again and another way round: no bull, no imagination. No imagination, no foundations. And—no imagination without its concomitant excremental excess. Baubles of hot air, rhetorical hyperbole amplified with a bullhorn, far-flung fantasy, crap. All this follows the bull and follows the mythical imagination as it plows forward. Imagining indulges itself in excesses. What a load! Yet, just where we protest, "That's a load of crap," the beast is breathing an uprising of a founding image. Imagination is wasteful because it is fecund like nature. Superfluous fantasy is the first flaring of imagination, the *materia prima* of creation.

What then holds the two—hot air and true imagination—in felicitous consort? How keep the fertile bull and cut the crap?

El Torero

The tales themselves answer: the bull is met with discipline. Just like the rite of learning by rote your ABCs. Where we find the bull, we also find the tight disciplined spirit of the *miles*, or soldiers of Mithra; stock market chartists; picador and toreador formalisms; rules of slaughtering and quartering; dancers and acrobats and rodeo riders; and the slow painstaking disciplines of scholarship and archaeology. Pasiphae's lust calls for Daedalus's craft that constructs the mechanical cow and the intricate labyrinth to hold the Minotaur. Bull sacrifice (*bouphonia*) means not merely a literal slaying, overcoming the beast of sex and money, blood and nature.

Rather, sacrifice of the bull means dedication of your raging, bloody-minded, dumb-headed extravagances to their own originating powers. Making method of the madness by discovering the generative imagination charging through your fury. Bull sacrifice takes one's bull to the altar of the image, making myth of mere bull, fecundity of mere force, outrage of rage, art of nature.

Two tales of philosophers show them to be disciples of bull and practitioners of bull sacrifice. Pythagoras walked over to a bull grazing in a field and spoke into its ear, persuading it to no longer eat nefarious bean plants, after which the animal ate only "human food." Empedocles "had an ox made from myrrh, frankincense and the most precious spices and divided this [invention] to the gathered assembly in ritual manner."[7]

---

7 M. Detienne, *The Gardens of Adonis: Spices in Greek Mythology*, trans. J. Lloyd (Hassocks: Harvester Press, 1977), 57.

Simply said, bull sacrifice is an act of recognizing the sacred in bull. Recognizing its spirit, sniffing the air of its potentialities. Sir William Osler, one of the greatest physicians of his time, was given this information in a dream:

> A huge plain in a valley beautifully situated... Scattered on the grass in thousands were big bulls, of all breeds, all lying down and at the head of each one a patient breathing the exhaled air from its nostrils. This had been found to be a panacea – consumption, cancer, everything. It had to be bulls' breath, because it was so much stronger. Sometimes there were two patients at one bull's head... the patients were only using one nostril, at the other a valvular machine was attached for collecting the air in reservoirs so that none of it was lost. This was sold in cylinders. An hour three times a day was the duration. I strolled about among the patients many of whom I knew. All were doing well. It was a great cure![8]

These tales from Detienne and Osler could be read as examples of psychoanalytic sublimation: raising beast to spirit as the cure for what's wrong with bull – too confused by passions. The inflation sublimates to spices and breath, ritually. Lower to higher: that would be the cure.

I think not. Rather, these tales suggest another founding role for bull: the discipline of aesthetics. Go back, now, to the Egyptian story of the baby bull sliding forth from its mother and declaring itself to be the Bull of Confusion. Well, confusion is the very mark of aesthetic imagination according to the eighteenth-century philosopher Alexander Gottlieb Baumgarten who invented the field of aesthetics as a philosophic discipline in its own right. Logical reasoning misses the nature of the arts altogether, for they can be grasped only in their confusion: "Confusion is a condition of finding truth," as Croce writes, explaining Baumgarten.[9]

The confused profusion of springtime, that Merry Month of May, during which Venus blossoms and the sun shines in the house of Taurus in the Zodiacal calendar, places that beautiful valley in Osler's dream and those fragrant spices of Empedocles' ox in an aesthetic world of

---

8 C.G. Roland, "Sir William Osler's Dreams and Nightmares," *Bulletin of the History of Medicine* 54 (1980), 438.

9 B. Croce, *Aesthetic as Science of Expression and General Linguistic*, trans. D. Ainslee (London: Macmillan, 1909), 195.

the senses, where the very word aesthetic (sensuous perception) derives from the Greek syllable meaning "to breath in."

Cure bull with the discipline of the arts.

In all this it is crucial to remember the Nativity *crèche*, which makes a substantial distinction between the ox and the ass—a distinction again going back as far as Egypt, where Seth, the ass, was enemy of Osiris, the bull. Osiris, the creative mystery force of the undying soul; while Seth was shown as an ass-headed man, an image of sexual lewdness, a potency of another kind.

The potency of bull includes another moister, softer element. It must, else it could not be fertile, could not affect the soul. Astrological knowledge, which is another system for imagining origins, places the Moon and Venus each differently, but both comfortably, within the zone of Taurus; and the word *tauros*, according to the ninth-century Byzantine scholar Photius, was used for the *pudenda muliebria*, the vulva (Liddell & Scott, *tauros*). This lexicological fact makes great sense if we remember what extraordinary fantasies arise in the mind of men when they imagine the *tauros* of women, even fantasies of cosmogonic proportions that account for origins of all things of the world, and all its evils too.

Rather than the straight sexual force, it is the curved horns from which the potency of bull comes. These horns are hollow, containers of air. Gilgamesh, for example, uses the huge horns of his bull sacrifice to hold anointing oil.

We err when we read the bull's horns with the mind of Aristotle, as if they posed a two-horned dilemma. To the bull they are not opposites, nor to the poet who works more closely with bull than anyone. Poems and myths need no opposites, no Lévi-Straussian constructs into abstract pairs. Bull's horns work together, both at once: no either/ors in imagination. The toreador is caught by the tip of a horn only when he takes a stand too far to one side, wavering from the central focus—the bull's eye.

The onrushing force forces upon us the discipline of stepping back. Kerényi refers to Thomas Mann who refers to Sigmund Freud concerning the moment of stepping back "like the toreador poising himself for the death stroke."[10] More than stepping back to reflect or to conceive an interpretation, the move is a leaning onto the mythic imagination for backing so as to be enabled to meet the animal surge.

We have to realize here that the very idea of two-horned opposites begins with the bull of Dionysus. It is he who comes on with horns so often, and it is for him that his celebrants wear horns on their heads. The opposites, too, are bull, an awesome image become an epistemic logic. Better to take them in a Dionysian fashion with Dionysian logic, as theater—either comically on the head of the cuckold or tragically as antagonistic struggles on stage, or off—masks, figures, contentions of persons and places, rent by their agonies, leading us to compassion. The horns of the bull present not a problem but a drama.

Rituals under the Arch

We are close to a close. I promised at the start that I would give an account of the origins of all things in fifty minutes—about the stock market and money, about imagination and founding myths, about this Institute, about how bull came into the world, and about what's wrong with America.

Now to deliver on that last: America.

Thomas Wolfe (the elder, not the one in the white suit) wrote that we are lost in America as if nostalgia were forever our mood: "A stone, a leaf, an unfound door... O waste of loss, in the hot mazes, lost, among bright stars... we seek the great forgotten language, the lost lane-end into heaven..."[11]

What did we do wrong, why have we been driven out? Was it crossing the oceans, leaving our ancestors behind? It is that we have built our entire citadel on the illusions of hope? The City on the Hill, a hill of sand? So many answers: here is ours for this evening.

Might it be that we have slain the mythical imagination of our own soil, the great founding beast—not the red Indian to whom our nos-

---

10 C. G. Jung and K. Kerényi, *Essays on a Science of Mythology: The Myth of the Divine Child and the Mysteries of Eleusis,* trans. R. F. C. Hull (New York: Pantheon Books, 1949), 5.

11 T. Wolfe, *A Stone, A Leaf, A Door: Poems* (New York: Charles Scribners Sons, 1945), 27.

talgia often turns, but the native bison, the horned bull of this land? The hunters on horseback and later from train windows could shoot down thousands in one day, neither for meat nor for purse, leaving their carcasses to rot on the plains. The slaughter of the soil's totem is a blood-crime, a pollution of the American soul. Murder of the ancestral animal, a mythical genocide that made mythic perception no longer possible, a genocide backed by Hercules, Mithra, Gilgamesh, and the ancient struggle at the foot of Sinai—the Bible's word against the pagan bull. Could it be that the slaughter of our native bull, in which some Indians themselves had their part, has been replicated in our heart, so that we Americans have extinguished and left to rot our native myth-making imaginal power that could found us? And so, in quiet desperation, to reconstitute this animistic imagination, we have conceived other originating myths for our people and our land with a substitute paganism—Walden Pond, Leaves of Grass, White Whale...?

Then, in the bull's place, its fat ghost, the steer, dulled as an ox, no longing roaring its stories, penned, cornfed, testicles gone, the bull becomes chopped meat, feasted upon obsessively, ritualistically, communally, no other remembrance of mythical power than the mechanical bull and the swagger and brag of the urban cowboy. Under the golden arches, our contemporary altars to Mithra, a *taurobolium* in ketchup, the dead gods are celebrated in strange misshapen recurrences of antique rites. The burgher's burger, a thick secular wafer in a debased myth that is liturgically living because we do not know it is a myth. A uniform daily observance of the native animal god, with his and her *epitheta deorum*: Burger King, Big Boy, Big Mac, Dairy Queen, Hamburg Heaven.

At the Foot of Sinai

I would like to recall one more bull, a Biblical bull at the foot of Sinai. No more dangerous bull exists in the whole good book; it is, this bull, the very archetypal base of the historic distrust of imagination, and the consequent bull slaughters by bull slingers of the American West.

Turn please to Exodus 32, and place a marker also in Psalm 22:12.

As Exodus reports, while Moses went up Mt. Sinai and received the Law from Jahveh, the people grew impatient; and they had his brother, Aaron, fashion their smelted gold jewelry into the statue of a "bull-calf" (*New English Bible*), which the people called God; and they made offerings to it, feasted and drank and made merry. Well, this was too much for the Biblical God, who had taken them out of the land of Egypt with its many gods and many images and its worship of Apis/Osiris the bull, and Hathor the cow; and the Lord's wrath waxed hot, and then Moses' anger waxed hot; and he, when he saw the people dancing before the Golden Bull-Calf smashed the very tablets of the Law he had received on the mountain; and he put his own people to the sword—three thousand of them. This image had remembrances in it not only of Apis and Egypt and Ishtar and Babylonia but of all the many gods and statues and images of all the other Mediterranean and Asian and African bulls and oxen and cows and steers and calves of all the surrounding heathen, pagan, polytheistic, animistic, iconophilic peoples: all that bull that the Bible stoutly denies.

At the foot of Mt. Sinai, an enmity was absolutely established, and confirmed by ruthless extermination, between the monotheistic people of the Bible and all those surrounding; an enmity that appears again in Psalm 22 when the singer as the voice of the Bible's chosen people complains of being surrounded: "Many bulls have encompassed me/Strong bulls have beset me round... Save me from the horns of the wild-oxen."

The great Biblical sin of the Hebrews was bull worship. "There is no sorrow that falls to Israel's lot that is not in part a punishment for their worship of the Golden Calf."[12] And this sin occurs at the very moment of, in the very shadow of, the reception of the Torah. Above and below. And it is made of trifles, baubles, trinkets of women! Just bull. When the solitary goes up the mountain to encounter the highest spirit, the rest of the tribe returns to bull—to dance and feasting.

The bull returns significantly one more time in the Torah. Numbers 19 describes ritual purification by burning a red heifer, supposedly the most mysterious rite in the entire scripture. Here, the bull story says that the ashes remaining from burning the heifer's "skin and her flesh, and her blood, with her dung" shall be gathered for purification. But—whosoever touches the heifer in the rite, even the ashes, shall be

12 L. Ginzberg, *The Legends of the Jews*, vol. 3: *Moses in the Wilderness* (Baltimore and London: The Johns Hopkins Univ. Press, 1998), 120.

unclean. The essence of the heifer both defiles and cleanses, cleanses and defiles. You cannot touch bull without becoming perplexed – and therefore without stimulating imagination.

Psalm 22 was transferred into the New Testament at the crucial moment of Jesus's dying on the cross. His last words recite the opening of that Psalm. Christian commentators have easily read the scene of soldiers mocking Jesus in terms of the bulls in the Psalm. Bull is present, if concealed, in the phonetics of the language; *tauros* (bull) means thick, stout, and *stauros* (Greek) means a stake, the cross of wood itself.

All in all, bull is not a major image in the New Testament: *tauros* appears only four times and *bous* (oxen, cattle) only eight times. (The ox in the manger is not in the Gospels. It bulls its way in through the fantasy of folklore and via Isaiah 1:3.) The scarcity of bull in the Christian Bible could be grounds for not noticing its bull and also for taking it so literally.

The extrapolation of Psalm 22 into the New Testament makes bull the enemy of Christ, present at, perhaps participant in, the crucifixion. Bulls seem always to be called on when a sacrifice is to happen. Always a sacrificial victim somewhere. When Jerome established the convention that identifies St. Luke with the bull, it was because Luke's Gospel stressed sacrifice.

The most vividly bloody sacrifice during the early years of our era was not the image of Jesus on the cross but of the *taurobolium* enacting Mithra's slitting the bull's throat and the Mithraic devotees bathing in animal blood. Julian, the emperor, who tried to restore the earlier cults, partook twice in this bloody exercise.

Yet the Mithraic and Christian bull stories of sacrifice differ decisively. These two religions contested for dominance in the early years of our eon. The Serapian one, too, which was the most popular religion in first-century Augustinian Rome. All three turn on the question: Whose bull wins out? Serapis *was* the bull; Mithra slits its throat; Christ is sacrificed by it – or instead of it? Or substitutes for it; it becomes the victim; it becomes the bull. This shift from the active heroic Mithra to the subtle passivity and imaginative fertility of the Christ figure who assumes the place of the sacrificial animal gives a founding mythic power, the fertility of bull, to the Christian imagination.

> Following the overthrow of Mithraism and the simultaneous tri-
> umph of Christianity, the bull faded away into the realms of sur-
> reptitious superstition and the secret pagan practices of peasant-
> ries ... bull had no place in the Christian Church nor in Christian
> art ... Both in West and East the religions of Christianity and of
> Islam have pushed all pictorial representations of the bull either
> into the bullring or on to the farm. [13]

Did it vanish – or merely vanish as a depicted animal; instead continuing all the more powerfully in the bull that suffuses through Christianity itself, its dogma, rhetoric, and theological imagination.

I am suggesting that the bull does not need to play an overt role in
the New Testament since it is implied already in the mystery of the
blood, with its echoes through the Mediterranean world of the sacrificed bull. And, that blood continues to empower our religious imagination with fecund confusion – is it actually blood? Is it merely and
only wine? And if wine, then is it the blood of the Dionysian wine god
who, too, is slain?

The stories of passionate debate, the warfare and martyrdom oc-
casioned by that healing fiction founds an entire culture and a civilization perpetuating through centuries. Of course, dogma attempts
to end the bloody confusion by nailing meaning down with one literalism after another. Papal bullying attempts to end all bull, thereby
committing the profound psychological, even archetypal, error of
forgetting that it is bull that allows Blake to say, "Jesus, the Imagination," which can never be fully yoked nor led around with a ring
through its nose.

We may go on making mincemeat of it; we may break its horn and
slice its sac and burn into its hide our trademark, becoming the bull-
slaying antagonist with his technological knife of efficiency, cutting
out imagination as a confusing variable. But bull keeps coming – inflating even its killers. Horsepower cannot carry us away from it. We
cannot outride the ghost; ever-fresh fantasy rises in the seas of the
mind. Nor can we become St. Luke's fortress of repression as Moses,
Gilgamesh, Pentheus.

---

13 A. Fraser, *The Bull* (Reading: Osprey, 1972), 79.

Suppose the archaic bull spirit could be summoned here, in these Western lands that, like the Mediterranean, are territory of the bull. Would bull not come forth first in the old ways we have reviewed: power, beef cult, *macho phallos*, baubles and crap, excessive wealthy fecundity, spilled blood, confusions that stand for freedom, and the curse of inflation that goes with any cosmogonic vision. American, Texan, bull-slinging — is it a ghost rising? If it is, then we have learned something from our excessively grand tour this evening. Power-maddened bull can tear us apart and also make us ridiculous with its fraudulence and flatulence. The answer is discipline. We become disciples of bull, crafting and shaping imagination, riding its back by hanging on, propitiating with our words, our very talk, our "b.s." as *pars pro toto*, that resurrects the totem animal, welcoming in, as we do at these conferences, what we have lost so that we no longer be lost.

3

A Snake is not a Symbol

*O*ften I begin a workshop on animal images with the snake. The snake works like a charm, freeing people of their insidious notions of snake symbolism and, therefore, of animal symbolism in general. The questions I ask sound like this: "How do you understand a snake image?" "What does a snake mean?" "What's your interpretation?" I have assembled and condensed the replies:

1. The snake is renewal and rebirth, because it sheds its skin.
2. A snake represents the negative mother, because it wraps around, smothers, won't let you go, and swallows whole.
3. It is *the* animal embodiment of evil. It is sly, shifty, sinister, fork-tongued, and it is cursed by God to slide on its belly because of what it did to Eve and Adam. The Book of Revelations says that the serpent is the Devil himself.
4. It's a feminine symbol, having a sympathetic relation with Eve and goddesses in Crete, India, Africa, and elsewhere.
5. The snake is a phallus, because it stiffens, erects its head, and ejects fluid from its tip. Besides, it penetrates crevices.
6. It represents the material earth world and as such is a universal enemy of the spirit. Birds fight it in nature and heroes fight it in culture.
7. The snake is a healer; it is a medicine, and we see it still on the signs of pharmacies. It was kept in the healing temples of Asclepius in Greece, and a snake dream was the god himself coming to cure.
8. It is a guardian of holy men and wise men – even the New Testament says that serpents are wise.
9. The snake brings fertility, for it is found by wells and springs and represents the cool, moist element.

10. A snake is Death, because of its poison and the instant anxiety it arouses.

11. It is the inmost truth of the body, like the sympathetic and parasympathetic nervous systems or the serpent power of Kunda-lini yoga. That's why the sophisticated folk medicine among native Americans, South Asians, Chinese, and Africans, for instance, relies on parts of snakes for remedies.

12. The snake is the symbol for the unconscious psyche—particularly the introverting libido, the inward-turning energy that goes back and down and in. Its seduction draws us into darkness and deeps. It is always a "both": creative-destructive, male-female, poisonous-healing, dry-moist, spiritual-material, and many other irreconcilable opposites, like the figure of Mercurius.

This twelfth interpretation of the snake takes all the other eleven and turns them into steps in a program in which the snake is finally explained by the final step: the unconscious psyche.

What has really been said by this last term that is not better said by the image itself, its fascinating flickering tongue, its rattle or hiss and quick strike, its reticulated glistening skin, its coil and sidewinding, the panic rising on sudden sight of it? Why must we exchange the living image for an interpretative concept? Are interpretations really psychological defenses against the presence of a god? Remember: most of the Greek gods, goddesses, and heroes had a snake form—Zeus, Dionysus, Demeter, Athene, Hercules, Hermes, Hades, even Apollo. Is our terror of the snake the *appropriate* response of a mortal to an immortal?

For instance, a black snake comes in a dream, a great big black snake, and you can spend a whole hour of therapy with this black snake, talking about the devouring mother, talking about anxiety, about repressed sexuality, and all the other interpretative moves that we therapists make. But what remains after all the symbolic understanding is *what that snake is doing*, this crawling huge black snake that's sliding into your life. The moment you've caught the snake in an interpretation, you've lost the snake. You've stopped its living movement. Then the person leaves the therapeutic hour with a concept about "my repressed sexuality" or "my cold black passions" or "my mother"—and is no longer with the snake.

The interpretation settles the emotional quivering and mental un-
certainty that came with the snake. In fact, the snake is no longer
necessary; it has been successfully banished by interpretation. You, the
dreamer, don't need the snake anymore and you then form the habit of
not needing dreams anymore either once they have been interpreted.
Meaning replaces image; animal disappears into the human mind.

There are various ways of keeping the snake around. It can be imagined as a felt presence and talked with; it may need to be fed and
housed, painted and modeled. It can be honored by attentions, like
recalling it several times during the day: by "doing something for it" – a
physical gesture, lighting a candle, buying an amulet, discovering its
name. It can be brought closer by visualizing it, sensing its skin, its
strength. Now imagination replaces meaning, and the human mind
gives itself over to the animal presence.

This is the psychological and imaginative work of *animating the image*,
giving a life-soul back to the snake that may have been removed from
it by your desire to understand it. The snake may have no objection
to being understood. It may be pleased with your turning to herpetol-
ogy books about snakes, by your visit to a zoo to watch them, by your
reading of ancient serpent mysteries. But whatever you do, consult with
the snake first so that you do not insult it by following your own plan
without recognizing its arrival in your life. Its arrival is a summons to
divert your intentions from yourself at least partially toward it.

Animating the image – that is the task today. No longer is it a question of symbolic contents of dreams. Over a hundred years ago Freud
brought us back to the old traditions of symbolism and the old traditions of dream meanings; then Jung explored these symbolisms and
meanings even more widely and deeply.

But then both Freud and Jung made a move that we no longer want
to repeat. They both translated the images of animals into crystal-
lized symbolic meanings. They didn't let what appeared express itself enough, but moved toward satisfying the rationalizing – and often
frightened – day-world mind. "This *means* that." Even Jung's method of
active imagination, which does animate the image, is less for the sake
of the animal's soul than for yours, the dreamer's. "Pinned and wriggling
on the wall," said T. S. Eliot about the modern mind's mode of opera-
tion. Eliot's image suggests the psyche's butterfly unable to wing its
way beyond diagnostic labels and interpretative meanings.

Once you've translated the great snake into your omnipotence fantasy or penis envy, or you've translated it as a mother symbol, the Great Mother, you no longer need the image, and you let the image only say one thing, in two words: "Great Mother." Then it disappears. You don't want that black snake really anymore. You want to work on your mother complex, your personality, and so on. This still leaves the soul unanimated. That is, unalive. The images are not walking around on their own legs. They've been turned into meanings, as Aniela Jaffé wrote about Jung whose main myth was the myth of meaning.[1] Now, let's try to leave meaning, and the search for meaning, and the meaning of life, so as to stick with the animal image.

In our eagerness for conceptual meanings, we ignore the actual beast. We are no longer astounded by its facts, or wonder over its presence—that, for instance, a snake dislocates its jaw to swallow an animal larger than itself, that its digestive system works without chewing, without teeth or gizzard or cud, like a rhythmic peristalsis that squeezes its meal against the snake's backbones, crushing its prey into a digestible pulp. Or, for instance, the fact that its discarded skin after shedding appears to go on shedding.

Lives without meaning hunger for meanings, and psychologists feed the hungry with the living presences of animals. Patients as carnivores, devouring the flesh of their dream animals to satisfy their gluttony for knowledge. Or, have we psychologists become taxidermists, disemboweling the snake, stuffing it with concepts, and preserving it as a carefully fixed meaning?

---

1 A. Jaffé, *The Myth of Meaning in the Work of C. G. Jung*, trans. R. F. C. Hull (Zurich: Daimon, 1983).

4

Horses and Heroes

The delicacy, the gentility—that's what we often miss, seized as we are with the thundering hooves, the muscled flanks, the headstrong force of a galloping Arab, ears laid back, neck stretched into the wind. But remember the delicacy of a horse's lips, its lashes, its throat, its leg bones, the sweetness of its stable smell, the nuzzling. "...Her long ear/That is delicate as the skin over a girl's wrist," writes James Wright about horses in his poem "A Blessing."[1] And, impressed as we are with the plow horse, the dray horse, the packhorse, we forget how much they belong to the airy element as if all horses had wings, flying through the wind, tail streaming, nostrils flared wide, the air rushing through their innards—wheezing, whinnying, panting, rumbling, snorting, farting.

The young heroes of Greek myths rode their horses into the air: Bellerophon on Pegasus, Phaethon driving his father's chariot of the sun, Hippolytus racing off the roadside to his death. They couldn't hold their horses, and they crashed.

Usual symbolism attaches the horse to the earth and the sea, to Poseidon, the sea-god: the waves, the horse's mane; its stallion thrust, the god's unstoppable power; its hoof, the magic of fertility. When this ferocious strength is perceived in a woman, the horse is demonized into the witches' steed, the nightmare, the panicky madness of a runaway.

Although horses may be work horses and farm horses pulling their loads of civilization, dream horses still carry heroes on their backs, both in the images of dreams and in the invisible myths that accompany these images.

---

1 J. White, *The Branch Will Not Break: Poems* (Middletown, Conn.: Wesleyan Univ. Press, 1963), 57.

Crusaders and Conquistadors; Mongols and Huns; Mohammed's faithful, riding to convert the vast expanses of the Arabian world; Apaches in Arizona; gauchos in Patagonia; the cavalry advancing into native lands, followed by the Iron Horse on railroad tracks—all the extraverted push into distance accomplished on horseback. Heroes and saviors: Paul Revere; the Pony Express; Teddy Roosevelt's Rough Riders; the dashing escapes of kings and queens. Washington, Lee, Sheridan—statues in the parks of bronze men sitting on bronze horses. Napoleon's horses dragging an army's material across Poland to Moscow, their carcasses stiff in the snow; and Hitler's horses, tens of thousands, bearing the *Wehrmacht* on their backs. Clint Eastwood, John Wayne, Tom Mix, Roy Rogers, the Lone Ranger...

And still they carry us, as Broncos and Pintos, Mustangs, Pacers, and Colts, and as the power hidden under the hood. Even driving across the lawn and the golf course, we're still riding horses.

That horse power still brings sudden death on the night roads and highways to so many boys at the verge of bursting into full life—boys like Hippolytus and Phaethon, and Diomedes, that son of Mars and mythic king of Thrace whose horses ate his human flesh. The steed that can so strongly carry life leads that same life to its funeral in the solemn procession of the riderless horse.

But all this about horses is the easy part. This is symbolism and the history of the horse. What of its mystery, the horse that asks to be relieved of carrying the hero on its back? What of the horse of the soul against whose neck a young boy can cry his loneliness and speak his secret wishes, the horse a young girl curries and combs and loves with more devoted passion than anybody anywhere?

Have you cared for a horse? Had its saliva on your hands, watched its colic, felt its patience when being shod, carried water on a January morning and heard its mouth suck it back? Have you ever had to put one down? Or dreamt of a hurt horse?

Within the headstrong extraversion and noble courage that gallop across continents and centuries, marking the migrations of civilizations and their conquests and retreats, within that heroic impulse lies the delicacy, something internal and so invisible that only dreams seem able to recall.

Rituals, called "the horse sacrifice," aim to release that invisibility within the heroism of the horse, marking a separation of horse from hero. These rituals are the hard part, and they amaze with their pathos. For instance, when the Buddha took up the ascetic path, he dismissed his charioteer and had no further use for his horse, Kanthaka. This separation from his master broke the horse's heart and it died of grief. Thus did the Buddha do away with his no longer needed horsepower. Kanthaka is remembered in Buddhist statuary as a little horse figure of faithfulness near the great seated Buddha, the horse reduced to a minor potency in Buddhism's constellation of images.

The great Hindu horse sacrifice (asvamedha) reaches back to the fourth millennium BCE. A conquering king would let a prize horse wander freely to graze accompanied by a band of young warriors. The territory covered by the horse became, as it were, the king's grazing grounds – the horse representing the limitless libidinal energy of expansion. "When this stately animal... had wandered over the earth for the full cycle of a year, extending its adventurous stroll of conquest as far as it pleased and wherever it chose, it was then escorted home again to be slaughtered with the most elaborate and solemn rites."[2]

Once the king was established, the expansionism that took him to the throne was no longer needed. The way of conquest is not the way of rule. One god or animal vehicle supports ambition, while another god or animal vehicle maintains what has been achieved. Thus, kings as kings are often presented as lions, elephants, bulls, eagles, that is, as supreme lords of consistency rather than as conquering heroes. By their steeds you can recognize their characters.

This brings us to Mars, the god of battle rage. You will have noticed that the horse in the Hindu story is accompanied by an honor guard of warriors. The Roman sacrifice of the October Horse makes this relation between horse and conquest even more explicit. Each year on October 15 on the field of Mars outside the city walls, a horse was killed by a javelin thrust to honor Mars. The scholar of early Italic religion, Georges Dumèzil, has collected the texts and explains the rites and their reasons. It was always a winning horse, for instance, the right-hand trace-horse of a winning chariot. Why a "winning" horse?

2 H. Zimmer, Philosophies of India, ed. J. Campbell (Princeton Univ. Press, 1951), 134.

"Because Mars is the specific divinity of victory and prowess." And, explains Plutarch (*Roman Questions* 97), "they sacrifice to the gods creatures that are particularly pleasing and appropriate for them." Mars likes horses because horses are like unto Mars. Of course, the Buddha had to let Kanthaka go: giving up the horse meant also giving up the martial way. [3]

In dreams, too, horses are carefully slaughtered, sometimes flayed, put to death with a bullet, bled from the neck, buried in a pit. The dreamer is shocked, afraid for his or her own life, as if the death of the horse signaled the death of his own vitality, the forward-carrying energy that is ready to get up and go into the day. Do these images of agony, which the horse endures in dreams belong truly to the horse, or is it being sacrificed for its heroic master, the dreamer who cannot give up expansionist ambitions?

Alchemical psychology teaches the "horse sacrifice" much less literally. It makes use of the horse's belly, *venter equi*, as an image of inward heat. Alchemy employs metaphors of fire for the intense concentration needed for soul-making. (In fact the alchemists were called "workers in fire.") The heat of the horse's belly referred to the digestion of events, brooding and incubating, instead of flaming up with martial temper. It is an inward heat, a contained fire.

Rather than slaying the horse or letting it go in order to be free of its force, alchemy suggests getting inside the horse, like Jonah in the whale. We interiorize and contemplate the urge to press forward, to run wild, to panic, to win. Instead of free-ranging conquest, you on top of the horse with reins of control in hand, you climb down and stay inside your animal drive, enveloped and cooked by its heat.

Alchemical psychology also uses an image of horse manure for this introverting heat. The closed glass vessel that holds the psychological stuff being "processed" may be kept warm at a steady temperature by burying it in horse dung. The steady heat refers to a slow and long focus on one's soul life. (*Focus*, by the way, is Latin for hearth.) The glass vessel invites looking into and seeing through actions for their images. Stashing your soul stuff in a pile of manure means paying

---

3 G. Dumèzil, *Archaic Roman Religion*, trans. P. Krapp, 2 vols. (Chicago Univ. Press, 1970), 1.215–27.

attention to the residues of your horse-driven urges and actions. You become conscious of the horseshit component of your drivenness, the consequences of the life you have sped through and ridden over. As you stew in this fermentation, another kind of awareness begins to form.

From this perspective of the horse sacrifice and of getting inside the horse, rather than riding it heroically, we can look at the story of the Trojan horse told in the *Odyssey.* The Greeks were foiled again and again in their attempts to take Troy—until they built a great wooden horse that the Trojans, after much debate, took inside their impenetrable walls as a gift to honor the gods. As we all know, the wooden horse was hollow and packed inside with the strongest of Greek heroes who then rushed out of the horse's interior, sacked the city, and carried the day.

We all know the horse was hollow, but why didn't the Trojans suspect? Their imaginations were limited; they were still warriors; their horse had not been "sacrificed." The Greeks had taken the war to another level, from battle to the imagination of epic, from heroes to homecoming. After ten years of fighting, they got inside their own martial rage, their own need to conquer. They took Troy from the inside (not merely inside the walls literally but metaphorically, imaginatively). They could imagine an end to the war—the hollow horse as artful image of that imaginative act. They entered its belly, as in alchemy.

So Troy fell, but it fell to Homer. He conquered Troy with the Greek language, transforming battle into story, inventing in poetry what may or may not have happened in literal history. But for this to happen and for culture to rise from the ruins of conquest, the horse had first to be hollowed, its martial drive become epic image.

5

The Rat

"**Y**ou rat!" Deceiver, betrayer, cheat. In fact, "You *dirty* rat!" Slinky, slimy, nasty, and mean, denizen of the tenement hall, sewer sludge, the garbage heap. Rats came into Europe from Asia, following the invading tribes, bringing the plague with them in the fleas and lice on their fur. Wherever humankind goes, rats go too. Nothing keeps them out. They are hard to trap, hard to kill. They live where we live, in big cities with crowded slums, like pariahs living off what we cast out. At night they take over the streets, scurry through the gutters, eating and breeding—and escaping. No palace is immune, no brownstone safe from the incursion of rats. This intimate knowledge of civilization's underside is precisely the boon the rat offers.

The rat is persistent and intense. Like the rat terrier, its catcher, it doesn't let go, so we speak of the obsessive aficionados of a discipline as rats: water rats, ballet rats, *rats de bibliothèque*. No nut is too hard for them to crack; they never stop gnawing as their incisor teeth never stop growing. Thus Ganesha, the pot-bellied good-natured elephant god of India is carried on the back of a rat who gets through anything and opens the way forward.

It knows the city; it has street smarts. A cheerful, pleasantly domesticated woman dreams: "I am riding the London tube (the underground) and I'm followed by a rat-faced man; I am frightened and try to find the escalator back up." What might this rat-man show her, were she not to retreat upward but to stay in his company below? Perhaps something of the labyrinthine ways of the deeper levels of human civilization.

Another dream of rat-disturbed domestic tranquility, from a male psychologist around forty years old: "I'm coming home. The light over the carport is out—I pull in anyway. Suddenly, rats come at me from behind some stuff. I can't see where they are coming from. One jumps on my shoulder and I wake up with a jump. A full 'startle reaction.' I am wide awake and panicked."

Home is no longer a secure port. The guiding light over the entryway is out. The stuff (stored away, piled up, unused, kept to be sorted?) releases its ghosts. Rats. Was he himself a pack rat, storing stuff, both outer and inner? The dream says clearly that the rats are coming from behind the stuff, but he says just as clearly that he can't see where they are coming from. His light must be out too, or he wants to deny the source of the rats.

The rat on his shoulder clearly wants to get to him. It wakes him up with its jump. It gives him a jump-start. Does this tell us something useful about panic attacks? It might be both a paralysis – and a radical awakening.

The animal on the shoulder, sometimes a monkey, sometimes a parrot, here a rat, puts the creature right where your own head sits, parallel, equal. You may now be of two minds about something, see things with another perspective, with a doubled metaphorical understanding. Is this the awakening that this psychologist needs? Is that why the rats come at him, to him, for him? Even if he cannot see, he now at least may listen, because the animal on his shoulder has his ear.

A man of great goodwill and kindness tried to make a new career in real estate. He couldn't make the pitch, couldn't con, couldn't close. Out of a dream came a figure whom he called "Rat." The first words Rat said to him in an imaginary conversation were: "You have no nose." Rat began accompanying him on sales calls. They talked in the car before he walked into a house. Our man began to find quick answers, which sprang to his lips to his great surprise, instead of vague sales talk that he had learned on tape. He began to avoid traps laid for him and showed some teeth when cornered. And he spent the late nights studying, under Rat's tutelage, wising up about zonings and regulations, about the maze of laws and small print in bank loans. (Remember, rats are used by high-tech science for their learning capacity.) He also began to look out for number one, himself, thereby gaining confidence and being less paranoid that he was always being taken, being deceived by everyone. Until he knew Rat, he only knew the rat's unconscious effects, those shadowy suspicions of others and gnawing doubts about himself.

The rat may certainly not be placed among the heroic animals, nor does it appear among the major sacrificial animals in religions. Nonetheless, it plays a leading part in Eastern astrology, where the Rat is the first of the twelve zodiacal animals, equivalent to our first sign, Aries the Ram. That the year, or any cycle, begins with the ram seems evident to us who have inherited the Western traditions. The ram's headstrong forwardness, its huge spermatic balls and long thin sprouting penis, its slit eyes almost covered over by its thick skull that takes on as challenge and bashes into whatever it encounters – all this belongs to the restless thrust of spring and the fresh start.

But to begin with the rat? The Korean shamans say it is "the totem of the force that sets the year on its course." Evidently, if it begins with the rat, the "new year" must slip in slyly, from underground, out of the dark alley where least expected. At the beginning, you are not quite sure what can be trusted; in fact, you are not quite sure what is really a beginning and what is decay. The rat keeps decay and life together, just as the laboratory rats hold in their infected grotesquely distorted bodies the hope for better health and longer life.

When the rats desert a sinking ship, as the saying goes, while the captain bravely goes down, is the rat a traitor and the captain a hero? Or is the rat moving toward a new beginning while the captain goes to the bottom stubbornly unable to change. The rat desertion is also the beginning of a new cycle. It is on the side of life, off for a new start. For survival, the rat is the fittest.

6

Lions and Tigers,
or why there are two Great Cats

In the great order of things, it seems there had to be both lions and tigers. One kind of big cat couldn't cover the territory. The difference between them is like day and night. Yet, anatomically, they are just about the same. Stripped of skins, their carcasses—except for a slight variation in facial bones—would appear identical to the ordinary eye. Not so the coats, the habits, the habitats, and the manner in which they walk through our dreams and into our societal imagination—as different as day and night.

Lions belong to the veldt, to open ground with light cover, to the plains of Africa; tigers belong to hillside thickets, the jungles, and the river beds of Asia. Lions live in groups, accurately called prides. They hunt in teams. Tigers are solitary. Lions like to keep dry and out of trees; tigers swim, often seize their prey in deep water, and use trees. Lions are mono-colored, a tawny yellow that symbolism ties to the sun, to gold, and to all the heroic virtues of undeceiving single-mindedness. Tigers are striped with contraries: orange and black, white and black. As different as day and night.

Tigers live (or once lived) in the lands of shamans – India, Indonesia, Siberia, Korea—and so the tiger is not a pelt that dresses solar heroes like Hercules or Samson. Tiger skin (like those of its mythic kin, the panther, the leopard, and the jaguar) provides the classic seat for the yogin or holy man, as the tiger (or panther) draws the chariot of Dionysus, the lord of mysteries, and as the tiger appears in Asian paintings, lurking behind bamboo lit by the moon.

The young warrior, like David in the Bible or a Masai in Kenya, slays a lion for his test, while Zen stories tell of another kind of test. The master does not fight the tiger; rather, he enters the tiger's cave and both go to sleep.

Both warrior and sage must come to terms with the great carnivorous rage to live, which also means meeting death head on. These big cats are like the intensity of physical passion. They desire flesh because they are the flesh's desire. And so we imagine lions and tigers as "man-eaters" and love to present them on TV stalking and killing and then plunging their heads in the bloody innards of their prey. The warrior by spearing the lion dominates what could dominate him, thereby incorporating on another level the lion's ferocity. By wearing the pelt, meditating upon it as does the sage (like Shiva on the tiger-skin), or laying it out on the game-room floor, human and animal find a new symbiosis. The sage finds that union with the great carnivore by letting it pass from him. He sleeps. The tiger sleeps. Daniel, too, passed the night in the lion's den (Daniel 6:18–23) unscathed, and Jerome wrote the Latin Bible in his monk's cell with a sleeping lion at his feet.

In Rudyard Kipling's *Jungle Book*, little Mowgli walks side by side with his panther protector—a child's heroic fantasy. But in addition to Kipling's colonial Raj messages, the book implies a mystic's initiation into the secret languages of nature. Mircea Eliade's shamanism study[1] says that the tiger carries the neophyte on its back into the jungle—that metaphorical region of the unknown, the dark beyond, the other side. The tiger, he says, was the master of initiation in Central Asia and Indonesia.

A young woman dreams of escaping downhill from hostile pursuers. Others in her company jump on horses while she gets on a tiger. Her way down and theirs differ. (Not only does she choose the tiger over the horse; the tiger favors her, else it would not allow her to ride its back.) With this impulsive choice of animal vehicle she is also announcing something of her fate, something about which animal divinity will carry her into lower terrains and which one she will use for escapes. She is also distinguishing herself from "the others" in her psyche who take the more conventional ride.

Whereas the lion can stand in for the king of Judah, for the crusading Christian king, for Christ's disciple Mark and other saints, even for Christ, the tiger seems contrary to that entire noble tradition. As

---

1 M. Eliade, *Shamanism: Archaic Techniques of Ecstasy,* trans. W. R. Trask (Princeton Univ. Press, 1972).

William Blake wrote so famously in his poem "The Tyger": "In what furnace was thy brain?...Did he who made the Lamb make thee?" Blake put that tiger "in the forests of the night," implying that it brings darkness with it. The tiger carries our cultural shadow—sinister, double-colored, perhaps the duplicitous representative of the "other side."

Curious, too, that Chinese astrology places the tiger in the zodiac where Western astrology has the double-bodied sign of the mercurial Twins. As different as day and night, lion and tiger; or, as Chinese philosophy says, as different and necessary as *both* yang and yin.

Because yin brings the "death" of yang, to those who follow only the monocentricity of the lion, the tiger is imagined as a killer, particularly cruel, even evil. And—feminine! So our European-based languages have expressions for women as tigresses of passion, jealousy, and revenge.

Oddly, gender distinctions attach themselves to the two big cats, as if lions were male, though, as most people know, the females do the hunting and fostering that allows survival; and as if tigers were female, yin, west wind, night, lunar, and, like the Central American jaguar, enemy of the solar-power eagle. The use of gender to divide the world into opposites obfuscates the fact that both cats are both genders, as Noah insisted, and that the casual psychological labels "masculine" and "feminine" become cover-ups for weak thinking, falsifying the complex implications that the big cats bring with them.

Nonetheless, the psyche does divide lions from tigers, and it divides other animals, too, by means of gender. I once saw a child's drawing of her parents as a lion and a tiger. The mother was the lion. This drawing was similar to two others brought to case discussions over the years. In one, the patient painted himself between two elephants, mother and father. The mother had the tusks. In the other, a girl painted a dream in which her mother was a wolf, her father a fox. In one man's dream, he is in his family's living room with his parents. He "notices a lion and a panther there too, but his parents then are gone." Were the lion and the panther the "animal souls" of his parents, and was the lordly lion the mother spirit, the surreptitious panther the spirit of the father?

The child's perception, like the dream, often picks up what the conscious mind does not notice. The dreams and the drawings show what's underneath, what psychoanalysis calls "the unconscious." (Jungian psychology would say the dreams and drawings show the anima of the father and the animus of the mother.) In these instances, the mother is perceived to belong to the tribes of lions, the wolves, and male elephants; the father, to the more devious, cunning, and less confrontational world of tigers, foxes, panthers, and tuskless elephants.

Whether the fox considers itself "devious," whether its habit of preferring a sinuous path, its agility in slipping through narrow openings and hiding in holes, and its versatility in outwitting the hounds and the hunters, are adequately described by such adjectives as "devious," "clever," "stealthy," "wily," "foxy" is really a *moral* issue. For us, these terms signify deceit, as if all creatures should look us straight in the eye and walk the narrow path of predictability. Perhaps the value the fox places on "devious," like the tiger on "duplicitous," includes virtues such as boldness and pride, prudence and perspicacity. Although our descriptive terms may be accurate in taking true account of an animal's nature, their acuity is corrupted by our deeply buried moralistic suppositions.

When the main character, Dr. Abbey, falls apart in Michael Ventura's novel *The Zoo Where You're Fed to God*,[2] it is to the tiger's enclosure that he goes, the tiger who calls him, the tiger's eyes he looks into, the tiger who watches over his madness, his sanity, and the strange mysteries of passion and tenderness. It could not have been a lion because Dr. Abbey is undergoing a soul initiation, called in our culture "a breakdown."

Had it been a lion, Dr. Abbey would have been more concerned with reinstating his stature in society, restoring the brightness of his day-world consciousness and his heroic abilities as a surgeon who rescues from death, takes charge, and helps others. It is the lion who mounts guard over public buildings, not the tiger; the lion who emblematically represents kings and kingdoms, who demands the larger share and comes before all others.

But we may not reduce the lion to a stone representation, as if the king were always a tyrant and a power defined only as heartlessness. Lion lore says that its power comes from the heart as courage, generosity, and faithfulness. If it dominates the animal kingdom, then perhaps

2 M. Ventura, *The Zoo Where You're Fed to God: A Novel* (New York: Simon & Schuster, 1994).

it has been recognized by the other beasts as their king, a recognition accorded the lion not merely because of its roar and ferocity, but because it stands for the hierarchical justice that prevails in the kingdom and that we denigrate with the term "food chain."

To consider the lion in a dream as only the power drive of ego-centric self-importance, or as the drive toward awakening solar consciousness, neglects the eros quality of the lion, that its light brings warmth. For instance, in alchemy, sulfur, sometimes cryptically referred to as "the lion," was both light and heat, both spiritual ideal and physical intensity. The lion of lore not only eats voraciously; it loves hugely. Its locus in astrological physiology is the heart; its home, the house of pleasure and love, teaching and offspring.

The Egyptians understood differentiating the lion. It had different faces and phases: the young lion (of the sun at dawn), the solar strength emerging from the desert night; the midday black lion (the goddess Sekhmet) scorching all things with its overbearing heat and bringing plagues and their healing; and the lion at evening, paws folded at rest. There can be no single interpretation of the dream lion. It must be watched; and this watching draws you closer to the lion's own qualities of courage and attentiveness and devotion. Whether escaped, wounded, appearing unexpectedly, lazing, crouching as if to spring, it is always displaying itself in a scene and bringing a mood. It is a lion *inside an image*, and it is this image as a whole that transmits the lion to our consciousness. The image is its carrier. To take the lion only as such, to see it as only a meaning, lifts it from its habitat in the dream in which its meanings are enfolded.

7

Going Bugs

I want to tell you now about the insects to whom God
gave "sensual lust"... All we Karamazovs are such insects,
and, angel as you are, that insect lives in you too, and
will stir a tempest in your blood. Tempests, because
sensual lust is a tempest–worse than a tempest!
    – F. M. Dostoevski, *The Brothers Karamazov*

Preamble

When I was young and twenty, April in Paris, just after World War II,
I fell far, far up into that anima swoon called, in the 1940s, "love."
I was animated and animalized both at once – as Wallace Stevens says,
"His anima liked its animal/And liked it unsubjugated..."[1] – and I believe now that it was then I first began going bugs. Infested, invaded,
bitten under the skin by winged and soil-loving psychic insistencies;
bugs swarmed through my blood and set my mind a-fever. It was then
I read my first Marcel Proust: anima was definitely a literary affair, so
it is hard to tell now whether Proust made me able to be in love or
love made me able to be in Proust. The worm burst from the cocoon
of adolescent self-spun sleep. I was a seething termites' hill, a hive of
honey bees, a humming drone, and all things traced marvelous webs
of delicately connected implications.

I began then to notice dreams and to be frequented especially by
animals (which seem not to have visited in childhood dreams, though,
statistically, childhood is the age when animals most come into human
dreams, are most kin with the animal soul). These animals pursued me
into the tempests called neurosis, analysis, Zurich. As if to propitiate

---

1 W. Stevens, "Esthetique du Mal," *The Collected Poems* (New York: Knopf, 1978),
321.

them, I began there, in 1960, an animal research group at the Jung Institute. This paper derives from that work and reflections since.

We used to meet each week or two and sort through dreams submitted by analysts and analysands, attempting to compare motifs and behaviors, invent and refine ways of classifying the phenomenology of how the animals appeared and what they did. The group lasted several years. As empirical scientists we did not achieve much. As phenomenological psychology our work attuned my ears to hearing the voices of the creatures and gave me the eye to see the habitual mistakes and cruelties the dreamers make vis-à-vis the animals that come in the night and, especially, how the "dream-I" dreads going bugs.

The collection has grown immensely through the years, from my practice and from seminars all over the country on animal dreams in which participants kindly gave me "their animals." And it has lain waiting, partly because only in the last years could I begin to put into words my devotion to animals – that anima, love, and animals come to my psyche together, indistinguishable – a connection between soul and beast, desire and divinity, anima and animal. The mystery of my devotion is expressed in part by this passage from Proust:

> I feel there is much to be said for the Celtic belief that the souls of
> those whom we have lost are held captive in some inferior being,
> in an animal, in a plant, in some inanimate object and so effec-
> tively lost to us until the day (which to many never comes) when
> we happen to pass by the tree or obtain possession of the object
> that forms their prison. Then they start, tremble, they call us by
> name and as soon as we have recognized their voice, the spell is
> broken. We have delivered them: they have overcome death and
> return to share our life. [2]

The dream of the lowly bug is one such place where they start, tremble, call us by name.

We shall be looking into dreams in order to deliver their bugs from the day-world frames in which they have been fixed, "pinned and wriggling on the wall" (T. S. Eliot). By "bugs" I mean all creepy-crawly things, including spiders, beetles, lice, moths, ants, bees, wasps, flies, larvae, and some creatures not entomologically classified as insects.

---

2 M. Proust, *Swann's Way*, trans. C. K. Scott Moncrieff (London: Chatto and Windus, 1926), 55.

Our history is wholly dark, wholly prejudiced against these varmints. A *locus classicus* of our culture's view going back to the Bible is Goethe's *Faust*, where a chorus of insects greets Mephistopheles, singing,

> O welcome, most welcome
> Old fellow from hell
> We're hovering and humming
> And know thee quite well.
> We singly in quiet
> Were planted by thee
> In thousands, a Father,
> We dance here with glee. [3]

Mephistopheles says: this young creation warms my heart indeed. Lord of the Flies, Beelzebub, the Devil loves the bugs, and the bugs, like demons of the air and the night, and of hiding places in the earth, are his children.

To consider the insect, to entertain its voices, is to listen to the devil. This tradition bedevils our view of them in dreams. Artemidorus (ca. 150 BCE), the author of the first book on dream interpretation, said,

> Whenever ants crawl around the body of the dreamer, it portends death, because they are cold, black, and the children of the earth. Bugs are symbols of cares and anxieties... discontent and dissatisfaction. Gnats... signify that the dreamer will come into contact with evil men... if there are many lice... it is unpropitious and signifies a lingering illness, captivity, or great poverty... if a person should awaken while he is dreaming that he has lice, it means that he will never be saved. [4]

To these curses we might add the traditional tale of Nero who, sometime after he had murdered his mother, dreamt he was covered with winged ants. Think of T. S. Eliot's *The Cocktail Party* in which the remarkable saintly Celia is crucified on an anthill; of Freud's view that bugs are vermin, representing in dreams the unwanted little brothers and sisters who plague us; of Kafka's *Metamorphosis*; Sartre's *The Flies*; and even the Jungian view of the spider as a negative mother or negative self-image because of its eight legs spread in mandala fashion. The words

---

3 Part Two, 2.1.
4 *Oneirocritica*, trans. R. J. White.

themselves bear anxiety. "Insect" means notched, jagged, cut into, emphasizing the sharp, pointy, piercing, as well as the mechanical automaton aspect of the creature. "Bug" means specter, apparition, an object of terror. "Bug" is cognate with to frighten, and also with bow, bend or turn aside; that is, the bug deflects or turns others from their paths. The British tend to use "bug" only for bedbug; other insects are called by their species name or generally "insect." The root of "bee" is probably derived from the Aryan *bhi* (to fear) in the sense of quivering or buzzing" (OED). "Beetle" comes from Old English *bitan* (to bite). "Moth," as early as 1577, means something that eats away, gnaws, wastes, is destructively attracted to a flame. In the popular speech of Western culture (*Volksmund*),[5] mosquito, midge, mite, louse, fly, gnat, flea, moth, cricket, beetle share a common denominator; these terms mean smallness and inferiority, which can be endearing though usually insulting.

"Bug" has crept into computer language when a bug actually crept into Mark II, the first American large-scale digital computer in 1945. Ever since, programmers are obsessed with getting the bugs out by debugging; they attempt to construct bug-proof informational systems. Bugs have long been part of psychiatry, whether as creepy-crawly skin hallucinations, coke-bugs, bugging, obsessional worries, or the place where people who are going bugs can be housed: the bug house.

There are other traditions where the Lord of the Insects is not the Devil but a Trickster. For example, the Navajo Begochidi, "the son of the Sun, who had intercourse with everything in the world."[6] Begochidi means "one-who-grabs-breasts," and details about him are too "dirty" to tell the anthropologist. "He got his name because he would make himself invisible, then sneak upon young girls to touch their breasts as he shouted… He also annoyed men… Just as a hunter was ready to shoot, he would sneak up, grab the man's testicles, and shout… Similarly when a man and woman were engaged in intercourse." Begochidi is a "blond or red-haired god with blue eyes, dressed like a woman. He was in charge of insects, called them at will, and even sometimes

---

5 R. Riegler, *Das Tier im Spiegel der Sprache* (Dresden-Leipzig, C. A. Kochs Verlag, 1907), 223–94.

6 G. A. Reichard, *Navajo Religion: A Study In Symbolism* (New York: Pantheon, 1950), 2.387 ff.

appeared as a worm or insect."[7] Once, when he was caught, hornets swarmed from his mouth, June bugs from his ears, mud beetles from his nose. Hornets stung all the other gods, and then Begochidi swallowed all the bugs back. He could also change himself into any sort of bug.

The tales of this Lord of Bugs present clear insight into the seeming spontaneity of insects, their cheeky irreverence for human intentions, their lordly power over us. We believe that *we* shout at their sting, but perhaps it is *they*, by causing the shout, who shout through us. As for the power of a bug, think only of the crazed state when last you tried to swat a gnat at night or demonically pursued a cockroach around the sink: "A man in Florida pulled out his pistol and shot himself in the leg to kill an (unidentified) bug that was crawling up it."[8]

Let's now hear a dream, first against the background of the usual Judeo-Christian view, and then with Begochidi in mind.

> A pale, young, severely anxious woman at the borders of her sanity, whose love affair had broken up and who was desperately trying to get over it by "pushing him out of her mind," dreams that she murdered a man, and then on a bushy path she was attacked by creeping things all over her body, worms, insects, scorpions. She couldn't kill them or get rid of them. They were even under her skin. She tried to squeeze them out and a yellowish fluid came out of her arm and wrist.

This was her initial dream of a long analysis.

From our usual perspective, the dream presents compensating punishment for her murderous repression. The devil is in her and she is being pushed over the edge because she has pushed love out of her mind, killed her "man"—lover, spirit, animus. By denying the feelings of her body, it takes its revenge by harboring swarms of insects; her flesh crawls. The very instrument with which she pushes, arm and wrist, is going through an alchemical putrefaction, and the yellow that flows out of her may refer to her obsessive thoughts of jealousy, the jaundiced view of the affair in retrospect, and/or the nauseous anxiety about being sick in mind.[9]

---

7 Ibid.

8 S. Hubbell, "Bugs," 79.

9 See "The Yellowing of the Work," in *Alchemical Psychology*, The Uniform Edition of the Writings of James Hillman, vol. 5 (Putnam, Conn.: Spring Publications, forthcoming).

Suppose, however, we were to imagine this emerging yellow as the blond son of the Sun dawning from the double torment of her desire and its murder. The context of the dream is not the past affair but the present initiation into analysis within which the past, the murder, and the love begin to appear in a new light. Will the god of this analysis be Hermes/Mercurius whose first appearance is often as incomprehensible Trickster? Her fruitless attempts to rid herself of torment by murder now appear as the indestructible god whose bugs do not let go of her. Her anxiety about going bugs is the way the new lover, the god of beginnings who does not let her go, begins to vivify her flesh even as he mortifies her will. Then we might say that she is in the grip of the beyond-human mystery of desire as the foundation of life – the mystery of the god who shouts.

Intentionality

> "Close the door! They're coming through the window.
> Close the window! They're coming through the door."

To the dreams:

A young woman, who lived at home and was managed like a wind-up porcelain doll by her mother, began her analysis with this dream:

> (1) I have on a pretty dress and moths and insects keep flying to it like a magnet. They keep flying onto me and eating the dress.

A man of thirty, depressed, immobilized, at times a barfly, dreams:

> (2) Sitting at a bar drinking. Great big insects appeared and started jumping up at me.

Later he dreams:

> (3) I was walking down the street somewhere and saw on the pavement a swarm of black spiders that scattered away from me as I walked along. I stopped to look and as soon as I stood still, they mounted force and came toward me in one spearhead formation.

First we see the movement of the creatures: "flying onto me," "jumping up at me," "toward me in one spearhead formation." They intend the dreamer. Do they attend the dreamer? At least they want the dreamer by closing in on her/him. That they want is generally evident; what they specifically want can be determined only by the image in which they appear. For the young woman, it is her dress (a red one, chosen by her mother to attract young men). But she was shy, slightly anorexic, and red did not suit her feelings. For the man at the bar, the jumping huge bugs interfere with his sitting and drinking.

The bugs can also flee from the dreamer:

> (4) I was walking down cellar steps and to my right saw two large black spiders crawling away from me over a woodpile in my mother's house in the country.

These bugs were going away from her: when she takes steps to go deeper, they leave. But why? Is it because she sees them from the right and the spiders go away when regarded from that perspective? Or, more simply, is it that in her mother's house she and spiders separate or connect only by going away from each other? If I have troubles with my mother, spiders may not want to be with me.

Two further dreams that show intentionality. A man in his thirties finally concludes a long confused dream of many people and motifs with these words:

> (5) ... I'm stubborn and frustrated and pissed off... When I get to my house there is a wasp there that is after me. I go into the house and it is on the screen, but gradually I realize it has worked its way through the screen and is on the inside. I realize I should have set it on fire when it was going through the screen so I think about smashing it with a swatter as it begins to buzz around.

A woman of forty-five dreams:

> (6) I am standing by a well. I notice a fly buzzing all around during the dream. Before me a figure in a black cloak with a hood holds a basket and keeps reaching into it and then into the well. I hear noises like a baby crying, then I realize that there are many kittens in the basket being drowned one by one. It seems like it will never end—and I can't do anything about it. I can't speak or move. The fly keeps buzzing.

These dreams seem to intend something more subtle—if we read the intention of the insect from its effect on the dreamer. In each case the dreamers say, "I realize that..." As the wasp works its way through the screen that is supposed to keep it outside, in the world of people who crowd the preceding part of the dream, the dreamer gradually realizes the wasp is inside. The wasp working its way through the screen and the "I realize that..." are concurrent; so, too, are the wasp's angry, stinging pursuit (of the dreamer) and the dreamer's fiery smashing reaction. The insect reveals its intentions partly through the behavior of the dreamer. Clearly, the wasp's penetration to the inside brings the dreamer to realize his own waspish behavior inside the walls and the screens that are meant to keep out such events, i.e., outside, projected.

Sometimes a dreamer's realization within a dream occurs less as a mental reflection than as an identification with the insect. For instance, the man whose insects jumped up at him sitting at a bar (dream 2) later dreamt:

> (7) I am watching some bugs on the water. Then I am in the water and suddenly I am moving through the water just like the bugs. Like I am a bug too.

He showed me the movement with his arms and legs, swimming like a waterbug. What psychology calls "identification," rhetoric calls "simile." In this case he "realizes" the bug by becoming bug-like, thereby saying the insect is not merely an observable occasion on which I reflect by looking down on it; it is like me, I, myself.

Returning to dream 6: when the fly buzzes, she notices. Does the fly awaken her or is it putting her to sleep ("I can't speak or move")? Although she can't, it both speaks and moves ("A fly keeps buzzing all around during the dream"). The fly carries on the activity of which she is incapable. Because of it and the dream, however, she at least now sees and hears what is going on and might never end. [10] The fly must also be considered the conscious aspect of the dream, inasmuch as psychologists often define consciousness with arousal, activation, intention, alertness. Jung speaks of consciousness in the unconscious as

---

10 On "eternalizing" an image, see J. Hillman, "Further Notes on Images," *Spring 1978: A Journal of Archetype and Culture*, 176–77; reprinted in *From Types to Images*, Uniform Edition of the Writings of James Hillman, vol. 4 (Putnam, Conn.: Spring Publications, forthcoming).

a light in nature.[11] The dream presents this metaphysical idea shaped as a beetle, wasp, or fly, coming to the dreaming mind and disturbing it into awareness.

Often, disturbance comes *suddenly*. This adverb announces a crisis and *peripeteia* in a dream.[12] An initial pattern is invaded, broken, and something else starts, depending largely on how the dreamer acts in the dream. It is as if the dream presents catastrophe theory – sudden breakdown of one pattern as another emerges – and the insect were its catalyst.

How does the dreamer react, not only to the bug but to the suddenness? That is crucial when examining dreams of any animals, maybe even dreams of any kind. The word "sudden" derives via the French *soudain* from the Latin *subitus* ("this has come on suddenly or unexpectedly," "without preparation"). The verb *subeo* (*subitus* is the participial adjective) and the noun *subitum* have curious inflections when the definitions are read with "going bugs" in mind – e.g., "to come or go under anything," "to approach or draw near," "to spring up," "to come on secretly," "stealthily steal into," "to occur or enter one's mind." In an active literal sense, *subeo* also has the meaning of "comes up to, attacks, assails," and then a further meaning of "to submit to," "to subject oneself to," "undergo, sustain, endure, suffer."

Disturbance, even if not sudden, seems inseparable from the bug's intentionality. The creature disturbs the human habit even when the insect seems not malevolent or repulsive but attractive. For instance, a woman early in her therapy dreams:

> (8) I am in the house I grew up in, standing by the open door holding a little girl by the hand ... As I stand there, a large (maybe five or six foot) green and blue and purple and yellow hornet comes to the door and grasps my finger, trying to pull me out. It is very beautiful. I am aware of its little stinger, and its beautiful colors almost glow. I am fascinated by it, but I pull away and don't go because I have to stay and care for the child.

---

11 C. G. Jung, *Structure & Dynamics of the Psyche*, Collected Works, trans. R. F. C. Hull, vol. 8 (Princeton Univ. Press, 1970), par. 388ff.

12 Ibid., par. 563.

The intention is clear enough: to pull her out of the house she grew up in. The insect grasps her finger while she holds the hand of a little girl. Two contrary grips, contrary pulls. She prefers the little girl to the hornet, staying rather than going, pulling her way rather than being pulled its way. Of course, it may be a Green Hornet lover-animus of human size (five or six feet), vivid, glowing, multicolored, beautiful with "its little stinger," coming to the open door of her fantasy. She stands at the threshold, although she will not cross over. Notice that the intention of the insect is countered by her "because I have to stay"—not "I want to stay"—the dutiful feeling of staying within the house "I grew up in," a house to do with the little girl. Remember Dionysus coming to the house of Minyas to draw his daughters from their household duties to follow him to the wildwoods. He took on many shapes, many animal shapes, and some say the women did join him, to go mad; others say they refused him and were turned to bats. [13]

We might compare her hornet with this bee, also from a woman's dream:

> (9) A giant bee is in our backyard. It is looking for me and coming to get me. I see some neighbors outside and scream for help but they won't do anything. [Hiatus] A young couple dressed in Indian costume enter my bedroom in the middle of the night. They open a drawer in my dresser and swarms of bees emerge filling the room.

The outside does nothing to save her from what is coming for her. Maybe these neighbors who do not heed are in fact good neighbors by not defending her against the bee, by not being caught by her anxiety. The opening made by the Indian-dressed couple in her dresser lets the bees emerge inside the intimacy of her bedroom. Perhaps there is a connection between dressing like an Indian and opening up a drawer in her dresser. Does she perhaps dress for neighbors, since her first thought is of them. One thing is sure: the bee has moved from backyard to bedroom and from single giant to swarms. If we look at the dream from the viewpoint of repression of the intimate sphere, then the single giant (perhaps a Queen) bee she avoided returns inside

---

13 W. F. Otto, *Dionysos: Myth and Cult* (Dallas: Spring Publications, 1981), 133–34; Ovid, *Metamorphoses*, 4.1 ff.; Lemprière's *Bibliotheca Classica*, "Minyas."

her drawers. She is suddenly opening up and filled by them. Instead of a one-to-one confrontation with the individual looking for her, she is now plagued by a host of possible torments and excitations. But must the bee be a torment? Perhaps a Queen is looking for her, and the swarm would make an interior hive of drones and workers, pollen, royal jelly, wax, and honey.

The conflict of intentions between dreamer and insect can show in yet another way. A woman dreams:

> (10) There was something in the room I wanted very much but every time I tried to enter I was stopped by a bug. It was big, sort of like a locust, or a cicada, and was sitting on a small table. It would fly at me, making lots of noise, giving off sparks, until I retreated. I was terrified of it and gave up on whatever it was I wanted in the room.

From one perspective, an autonomous complex, firmly established (sitting on a table) and with an energetic charge, frustrates her occupancy of her interior space. Terror of confronting what sits right on her table makes her give up. It would make noise and be shocking. The bug whose intention counters hers is stilled only when she retreats.

We may also look at her dream bug with this passage from Jung in mind:

> To this day God is the name by which I designate all things which cross my willful path violently and recklessly, all things which upset my subjective views, plans and intentions and change the course of my life for better or worse. [14]

Then the bug seems to be acting like Socrates' *daimon*, saying not what she should do but what she should not do. A cautionary *spiritus rector*, it dominates the dream and maybe is indeed a *dominus*, a Lord: "The fear of the LORD is the beginning of wisdom." [15] Only when she can fully respect its intention can she give up "whatever it was I wanted in the room." Not my will be done, but thine. Its intentions remain obscure—why it wants her out of that place—but intention there is!

---

14 C. G. Jung, from an interview in *Good Housekeeping*, December 1961, quoted in E. Edinger, *Ego and Archetype: Individuation and the Religious Function of the Psyche* (Boston and London: Shambala Publications, 1991), 101.

15 Psalm 111:10.

Wound

A man at the beginning of analysis records this dream:

> (11) I dream my hair is falling out. I lift a tuft of hair and find a whole swarm of parasites eating into the flesh and bone.

A young man dreams:

> (12) I am meditating outside. I have been told flies are bringers of consciousness. I am very pleased when one lands on my hand, and stays for twenty minutes. I am proud that I have been so still. I look at my hand—it is covered with blood spots where the fly bit me many times, and I didn't even feel it.

The consciousness is clearly not in his meditative stillness, which turns out to be an anesthesia: "I didn't even feel it." The fly wants blood and bites into his flesh.

An elderly physician dreams:

> (13) I had a small circular wound on the right knee. Its bottom was clear and the wound was not deep. This wound was China, which was plunged in a horrible civil war. In the middle of the wound there was a small circle, which was the capital of China. Suddenly, this circle broke in its center and I could see some movement. I began to press it strongly, and as I pressed an enormous larva leaped out from the capital of China.

From the wound, which is also a raging civil war in a huge, ancient, and populous region, emerges the larva. (I shall omit here discussion of the knee.) The insect lives in the wound, the wound lives as an insect; a living wound, a wounded life.

A forty-nine-year-old woman dreams:

> (14) I was in an old house, in the kitchen, a very large room with a high ceiling. I looked up and saw a round hole in the wall, above my head, and saw huge bugs crawling out. The hole was small for the size of the bugs. I knew instantly that they were termites. They were coming out of the wall and flying around. I screamed for my husband to come and spray them and I began to search frantically for an aerosol can. The termites kept on coming.

We will come back to the aerosol can. Here I want especially to draw attention to the small hole from which the bugs emerge. The hole is in the wall, above her head, that lacuna or vulnerable spot in the protective containment. She instantly names the animals, declaring them termites, that is, hidden saboteurs of solid structures, eating away behind appearances: decomposition, rot, ruin. Those are the human feelings of termites in the house. The termites' intention, evidently, is to come out of the walls and enter her kitchen – the alchemical stomach of the house where the *pepsis* (digestion) goes on, turning the raw into the cooked. Crucial to this emergence from out of the woodwork and into awareness is the small hole (*"la petite tache humide,"* as Thomas Mann calls the spot on Hans Castorp's lung in *The Magic Mountain* from which that entire amazing story flows).

One more such hole, also from a woman of forty-nine:

> (15) There is a small hole in the bare floorboards of my room. As I watch, a green jelly-like blob comes oozing out of it. It is slimy looking and disgusting. It speaks to me in a horrid knowing little voice. It says, "I am the Woman of the Well." It begins to slither toward me over the floor.

This one is from below, not over her head in the high-ceilinged room. But it, too, emerges from the little void, the little wound in the support base of where she lives. And again, what emerges is felt to be disgusting.

The green blob suggests a comparison:

> (16) I lean my head in my hand. A small round hole opens in my cheek. A little salamander drops out onto the table. Almost at once, it starts to inflate like a balloon.

The posture of the head-in-hand is classic in genre portraits of pondering, the moody introversion when the head is heavy. The hand that extends into the world is drawn back from activities, like a magnet to the head, working on its thoughts. Melancholy in Dürer's drawing affects the head with lead, making it too heavy to support. From the tender cheek where love is expressed, where smiles and blushes show, where tears flow – again the hole. The salamander, a crucial symbol of the alchemical renewal of life in fire, presents itself from the wound, announcing its importance by inflation.

Not only do the wound and the insect appear together in the same place, but the wound seems irremediable, a permanent wounding.

> (17) I'm with a teenage boy and girl. We're driving around in a fast sports car trying to get away from whoever is chasing us. [various incidents]... suddenly there is a swarm of yellow and black bees. I am unafraid and I pass through the swarm; two sting me in my throat and the stingers are stuck in my neck. The boy and girl tell me to pour milk on my throat. We try this. I drink the milk, but the stingers won't come out of my throat.

Again the bug in the body.

A woman, age twenty-seven, dreams:

> (18) My inner arms are covered with hives. In the hives are small worms, squirming about. I pull the worms out, cast them off, brush them away, but there are so many and their number is increasing.

The dreamer explains:

> At the time of this dream there was a lot of difficulty in the relationship between myself and the man I've been living with. I was constantly thinking about this situation; it was "under my skin"; it was "infesting my mind."

Of course the word "hives" means both homes of insects and an irritating nervous inflammation. The inner arms are particularly affected, those soft surfaces that embrace, hold and hug. Whether what is worming into her consciousness, despite her efforts at riddance, is a sense of ageing or sin or decay, or lowliness, the shadows of love are emerging as "the difficulty in the relationship."

A twenty-seven-year-old man of charm, talent, and airiness dreams:

> (19) I am walking in a garden when suddenly I see a huge butterfly flying around crazily and then it does a backward flip and lies motionless on the ground. As I approach it to see what has happened to it, it suddenly flips back up and bites me in the calf.

The flip side of the butterfly is its hugeness and craziness, and that it has a bite. Until then, this dreamer could have assumed that the psyche was only a delightful, esthetic, many-colored gossamer delicacy, but now it bites him in the forward-striding calf (familiar place of wounding in the Tarot). Perhaps it has found his vulnerability: his calf-likeness, his milk-seeking, calf-love emotions.

Sometimes the wound is in an animal other than the human. For instance:

> (20) I am tending my cat. He is covered with fleas. As I look closer, I see the fleas have turned into white worms that are coming out of a deep wound in his lower stomach. I am frantic. The veterinarian says the cat may have to be put down. I won't let that happen. I prepare health foods and salves and vitamin E and determine to save my cat.

In this example, the totem animal or animal soul carrier, the *familiaris* of her daily life and habitual affections, is infested, beginning a putrefaction of what she holds close and dear. The region of the eruption is the lower stomach. She does not look into this specific place where the problem is emerging but is determined to deny the wound and the bugs with more generalized health measures: "health foods" and "salves."

Another dream shows a similar motif of the bug-infested animal and its putrefaction, but the sense of it is carried further by the dreamer's own understanding:

> (21) I was walking on the sandy beach. I came upon something very dead and decaying—a large St. Bernard dog. I looked closer. Its belly was wide open and filled with luminous larvae or eggs—like bubbles glistening in the sun. First I felt grossly repulsed. Then I looked again and the dog was my father. Then I looked back again and the eggs had wiggly little bugs or crabs in them that hatched and crawled en masse off into the sea. I felt good about it then. The old body had given new life to these creatures. It looked beautiful instead of gross. The sun on the dog and the waves.

The parallel with the carcass of the dead lion in which is a hive of honey bees (Samson's story in Judges 14:8) suggests the solar component of the bugs, that they bring or are the new light, and that the dog (or the lion) or the saintly, savior father provides only the body for what is going on. The bugs in the body of the old dog may be occurring in the turmoil and ugly repulsion felt in regard to an actual affliction in daily affairs. But the actual situation is merely the belly that bears the bugs, the body that we are familiar with and attached to. Until we take a close look, we cannot see that the dog is not the main concern but the hatching. Psychic life breeds invisible in the belly of the concrete, and it will out.

The bug-in-the-wound states that the wound has bug consciousness. If ontogeny recapitulates phylogeny, then insect-ridden body parts could refer to neurovegetative responses, i.e., the sympathetic and parasympathetic systems. In actual insects, these primary adaptations are called tropisms, meaning the turning reactions of an organism to external stimuli—moisture, pressure, sunlight, season, temperature, salinity, wind, elevation, etc. Insects are particularly sensitive to these general cosmic factors. They turn as the world turns, at one with the world. Do bugs have a cosmic knowledge, indicative of their accord with the order of things?

When the symptom presents itself as a dream bug, [16] then we might speculate that the symptom could be lodged in the vegetative system which, like the insect, is not susceptible to understanding or willing. Suicides reach their statistical peak in June; heart attacks at 3 a. m.; duodenal ulcers in spring and autumn.

The bug-in-the-wound motif gives a wider implication to the analytical notion that the symptom attempts to cure the condition that required the symptom. The symptom reattaches us to the tropisms of the cosmic parade. The sympathetic and parasympathetic nervous systems reflect our sympathy with all things, the presence in the body of its concord with an ecological cosmos.

Moreover, the bug modes of being in the world—despite the rigidity of insect behaviors, their limitations by the tropisms that adapt them—are infinitely differentiated. Six hundred and forty thousand species of insects, each with habits, forms, patterns, displays; each a slightly different ecological affirmation. This vast variety allows us therapists to view the complexity of symptom formation, the display or presenting complaint the patient brings, as a specific form of adaptation and orientation, requiring from us the attentiveness of the entomologist. To chart the ecological significance of the patient's bugs, we must look bug-eyed at each dream image, fantasy, behavior,

16 See Jung's fundamental essay on the interrelation of symptoms, complexes, and dream images in *Experimental Researches*, Collected Works, trans. R. F. C. Hull, vol. 2 (Princeton Univ. Press, 1973), par. 858–61.

complex, with our antennae outstretched, feeling forward with the as-
siduous persistence of an ant.

This cosmic sense is severed early in our lives. A sign of this "Fall" is
the relation to the insect, for children often love bugs, play with them,
eat them, capture nightcrawlers and beetles, keep anthills under glass,
spiders in jars. Children often are not fully severed from the minute
and concrete relation with the cosmos. The symbiotic connection between complex and vegetative nervous system – or, in my reading,
between insect and plant – shows in these two dreams.

A woman in her twenties dreams:

> (22) I begin to make an arrangement of some clay pots. I take
> some plants out of glasses, thinking they are dead and I'll throw
> them away. To my surprise they are not dead but have grown
> roots. There are insects (pinkish with beige spots, flat like sliced
> almonds) on the leaves, which I begin to pick off...

The growth of the roots and the presence of the bugs are concurrent,
just as the image seems not to distinguish between picking off bugs
and leaves. That the plants are "not dead" is stated by the presence of
both roots and bugs. The destructive aspect, if we label the insects so,
displays life as much as do the roots. The next paragraph of her dream,
however, shows that the "positive mothering" voice would separate
the roots and the bugs into positive and negative aspects, leading to a
me-centered ego therapy.

> ... X [a motherly, kind woman supervisor] tells *me* to forget about
> the plants, because the bugs are on *me* and extremely dangerous
> (will kill *me*). Must get a spray for *me* immediately. [italics mine]

A man in his thirties dreams:

> (23) Getting ready to leave the country. The concierge and her
> husband ask if I have checked the plant that is mine but kept in
> their area. I take a look at the plant. It appears healthy enough.
> But underneath there is clearly something wrong. I dig under and
> discover hundreds of beetle-like bugs crawling around. I also hear
> the sound of teeth chewing on lettuce. The concierge suggests I
> take the plant out of the pot and start all over. But that will surely
> kill it. Anyway the sound comes from inside the plant. I can't
> figure it out. I just sit there with my hand in the dirt watching

the horrible bugs crawling everywhere, wondering what this means and what to do.

The dreamer is left with his hand in the dirt – not leaving on his trip, sitting still and wondering, defeated. The symbiotic relationship between plant and bugs has brought him into a like condition, planted there, his mind crawling everywhere, trying to figure it out. The sound comes from inside the plant, an internal gnawing beyond reason and will. Whether the bugs are chewing at his business worries (lettuce as money), or chewing up his youth (lettuce as his salad days), or chewing into his sexual potency (lettuce in the gardens of Adonis referred to quick-wilting feebleness),[17] analysis would have to determine in time. But the buried facts are come to life, discovery has begun, and the initiation of a change in his motion and attitude are the wounding bugs in the vegetation.

Eradication

"Quick, Henry, the FLIT!"

You will notice that the "dream-I" again and again tries to rid itself of the insects. For example, a young man dreams:

(24) Green caterpillar on my leg in a garden restaurant. I lit a match and held it under the creature and it became like charcoal.

Right thereafter he dreams:

(25) Lying on my bed, I see insects on the ceiling. One was green and the other was blue. They seemed to be dancing or fighting. I took a broom and crushed them and wiped away the spot so that the ceiling looked all right again.

Another young man dreams:

(26) Beetles and roaches come into the room where we are. It is the upstairs family room. My father, brother, and I fight the beetles

17 M. Detienne, *The Gardens of Adonis: Spices in Greek Mythology* (Hassocks: Harvester Press, 1977), 67–68: "Whether Adonis takes refuge or is hidden by his mistress, it is always in a bed of lettuce ... mythical significance of the lettuce: sexual impotence and a lack of vital force."

with lots of powders on the floor and make a very irregular mess. They don't seem to die. Probably takes time. My mother and sister interfere with our work. It is hard to work with them around.

A woman reports this dream:

(27) I'm gardening out in the backyard with my husband and children. A few limp damp weeds get pulled, dragged up, and I track a few into the kitchen on my shoe. One weed that I pick up reveals itself as a bee and I stalk it, trying first to kill it with a brush, then I get a large kitchen knife and cut it in half, after which I feel safe.

Let us note the different sorts of extermination: fire, crushing, powders, knife. Dreamers defend against the insects in different ways. For example, the kitchen knife that cuts the bee in two: she feels safe when she can dissect problems with sharp practical distinctions.

The insects crushed against the ceiling are swept out of the young man's uplooking attitude, restoring it to the status quo ante of blankness. Jung calls this move "the regressive restoration of the persona."[18] By crushing the insect, we exercise the will and strengthen the heroic stance. By setting fire to the bug, the dreamer cruelly tortures what tortures him. Here we see an answer to Jung's question about torture in the alchemical work.[19] Is the subject the torturer or the victim of it? Jung asks. In dream 24, the source of the suffering lies in the means the dreamer uses to rid himself of the bug in the garden. Yet this same torture ignites the alchemical process, that "work in fire," that *opus contra naturam*, which turns sheer green nature into the nigredo of ignorance of mind, powerlessness of will, and darkness of heart. Nonetheless, the caterpillar, symbol of transformation *par excellence*, releases in the imaginal ego of the dream the transformational reaction of fire, the Promethean act. To side with the dreamer against the invasive caterpillar for the sake of igniting the ego into action or to side with the poor caterpillar against the cruel "dream-I" misses the complexity of the alchemical process. Or, in Patricia Berry's language, there is always a *telos* in a defense, and a defense woven into every aim.[20]

18 C. G. Jung, *Two Essays in Analytical Psychology*, Collected Works, trans. R. F. C. Hull, vol. 7 (Princeton Univ. Press, 1967), par. 254–59.

19 C. G. Jung, *Alchemical Studies*, Collected Works, trans. R. F. C. Hull, vol. 13 (Princeton Univ. Press, 1968), par. 439–40.

20 P. Berry, *Echo's Subtle Body* (Dallas: Spring Publications, 1982), 81–95.

The eradicating powders (dream 26) indicate a dry and white defense; shall we say abstraction? – for powders result from a formulaic, conceptualized and objectified process. In alchemy they result from the *calcinatio* (the drying over heat to remove moisture). Little wonder that the dreamer works well with father and brother and that mother and sister interfere. The bugs do not quickly succumb, for their inner moisture, the *succus vitae* of their emotionality, is not fully susceptible to male abstract understanding.

These four images of eradication also show the insect and the defense or attack against it interlock into a pattern similar to what Berry calls "simultaneity."[21] By reversing the image, we discover that when I whitewash my ceiling, bugs appear. When I align myself with father and brother against sister and mother, roaches appear. (Or, when I intellectualize, roaches appear.) When I burn bugs under the table, I sit relaxed in a garden restaurant. When I feel safe, I am cutting bees in half.

The power of these insights can be reinforced by "eternalizing the image":[22] when*ever* I feel safe, I may be cutting bees in two; when*ever* I am relaxed in the garden, under the table I am blackening the green bug on my leg.

We have yet to understand why the bugs raise such anxiety that eradication becomes the automatic response. This automatic step from fear to eradication leads to a further one into the world – pesticides. If we could better account for the psyche's exterminating reaction – and let us remember that the dream shows the psyche's reactions laid bare – and alleviate the fear of insects in the psyche, then we might more sensibly manage the acting-out of panic in the overkill fantasy of insecticides. This overkill may have its source in four frightening fantasies attributed to insects as their qualities.

Multiplicity. A colony of hornets has three thousand members, a queen bee can lay four thousand eggs a day and a bee hive maintain fifty thousand bees. Large ant colonies may consist of half a million ants. Moths can be so numerous that they can blind a coastal lighthouse with their dusky thick myriad fluttering. In a single tomato plant

---

21 Ibid., 59–60.
22 See above, n. 10.

24,688 aphids have been counted, and an acre of soil, depending on where and when, may bear in it from one to 65 million insects. Of the species of the animal kingdom, by far most are insects: 250,000 *kinds* of beetles alone.[23] Our language speaks of clouds of gnats, swarms of flies, plagues of locusts, heaps of ants.

Imagining insects numerically threatens the individualized fantasy of a unique and unitary human being. Should the bugs take over, we become mere bits of crawling, leaping, fluttering matter. Their very numbers indicate insignificance and worthlessness as individuals. Usually, bug dreams are interpreted as signs of fragmentation and the lowering of individualized consciousness to an undifferentiated, merely numerical or statistical level. The invasion of insects in a dream indicates psychotic dissociation and the loss of centralized control. Eradication, then, is an "anti-psychotic," whereas the source of the psychosis may lie not in the multiplicity of the bugs but in the defensive unity of the eradicator.

The issue here is more how we regard multiplicity than how we see insects, for once we imagine multiplicity through the single lens of a unitary human being, and conceive wholeness as oneness, the insects become the active embodiments of the Many against the One. That swarm, that heap in itself, shows unity and multiplicity at once. The anthill is also a community, the active embodiment of *Gemeinschaftsgefühl* (collective feeling), and the crowd of insects demonstrates wholeness, not as an abstract ideal but as a busy, buzzing body of life going every which way at once. The swarm redefines wholeness as cooperative complexity. Remember Apuleius: the ants help Psyche by differentiating what looks like a numerical heap into different particulars. They teach Psyche how to resolve the problem of wholeness into what William James called "eaches."[24]

Monstrosity. Bug-eyed, spidery, worm, roach, bloodsucker—terms of contempt characterizing supposedly inhuman traits in people. To become an insect is to become a creature without the warm blood of feeling, as depicted by horror fiction and films. Nature corresponds to these fantasies, having generated seven-inch spiders that eat birds,

23 See S. W. Frost, *Insect Life and Insect Natural History* (New York: Dover, 1959).
24 W. James. *A Pluralistic Universe* (London: Longmans, Green, 1909), 194.

beetles as long as eight inches, a Brazilian moth of nearly a foot across, centipedes extending a foot in length. Insects in dreams suggest the psyche's capacity to generate extraordinary forms almost beyond imagining and that these inhuman monstrosities show the reactive potential of the psyche beyond its humanistic definitions. The bug takes us out of ego psychology, out of humanisms. Isn't that the horrifying point of Kafka's *Metamorphosis*?

The fact that the monstrous comes in such minute forms – for even the life of a twelve-inch centipede can be extinguished by a human foot – and that we fear it so, shows to what extent the human world has separated itself from the non-human cosmos. What is man (or woman)? A little less than angel, lord of the universe, crown of creation, who wakes in terror from a dream of an ant.

Autonomy. They shall be crushed, burnt, and poisoned because they do not submit. They have other intentions, and even compete with me for my apples, corn, and roses, walk uninvited through my kitchen, nest under my eaves. They represent the autonomous nervous system's persistent symptoms. They bug me. They are autonomous.

Their autonomy not only eats wounds into me, stings me into rage, or reveals my rot and holes; it also drives me crazy. In German, *spinnen*, the activity of the spider (*Spinne*), means delusional fantasies, as does *Grillen haben* from *Grille* (cricket). The "me" believing itself in possession of autonomous free will is relentlessly pursued by the imagination (or unconsciousness) on which it rests, in which it nests, so that "I" am driven to exterminate whatever threatens its delusion of autonomy. The radical freedom of the bug from human control makes it the Great Enemy to whom is attributed all the ruthless traits used by the pesticidal ego to maintain the delusion of its autonomy.

Parasites. "One who eats at the table of another," from *para* (beside) and *sitos* (food). Little Miss Muffet was frightened away when the spider sat down beside her. Not only do bugs invade your realm, they also live off your property and share your body, thriving on your vegetative roots and your pet's flesh, as in the dreams of insects in the roots of a household plant or in the belly of a household animal.

The fear of being eaten up by one's complexes may be yet more terrifying than the other fears: disintegration into myriad parts, infestation with discarded filth (the return of the repressed), affected by monstrosities. The parasite is a biological amazement. Microcosmic organisms can enter a host and thereby radically alter its behavior, for instance, rabies. A huge human under the influence of a tiny bug becomes a rabid personality. The fear of alteration of personality by an alien power accounts for the panic sometimes associated with vermin dreams (bedbugs, chiggers, mosquitoes, ticks) and is witnessed by the insect-like shapes given to aliens in science fiction. We may read the fear of parasites in three ways. First, through the lens of compensation. The overly controlling ego is being sapped by the intention of the bugs who attempt to alter the usual personality in order to restore a more moderate relation between it and the cosmos. Second, through the lens of ego-psychology, the parasites present the hungry unlived life that also needs food at your table, and it is the job of the day-world ego to examine these needs, deciding what it will feed and what it will eradicate.

Third, from the viewpoint of a homeopathic archetypal psychology, the parasitical bugs reflect a parasitical personality. They show us our own face. If, as Jung said, the unconscious turns the face to you that you turn to it, then a parasitical invasion brings home to the host specifically how it depends in tiny hidden ways upon other psychic organisms, how it is influenced by complexes, how we use their blood to sustain our ambitions. The complexes, upon which we depend for our daily personality and from which we draw our energetic compulsion, show up in the dream as parasites, showing us up to be one among them, feeding off life's banquet by taking care of number one, whether in workplace, family, friendship—or feeding off the dreams themselves, interpretation as a parasitical blood-sucking act, taking all, giving nothing back.

Mystery

> The bug slides
> out from behind
> the radio dial
> where all winter
> he lived
> eating music.
> — Bill Holm, *Boxelder Bug Variations*

This last section of this phenomenology shall approach an almost inexpressible theme by returning to some of the same dreamers and their dreams subsequent to those we have already observed.

The young man who sat in a garden restaurant and set fire to the green caterpillar (dream 24) and who also crushed bugs on his ceiling and then whitewashed the spot (dream 25) later dreamt:

(28) A frog is sitting on the wood stove in my cabin. It has a crown and when I look close I see this crown is an insect, perched there with spread wings.

The man who tried to smash the wasp coming through his screen (dream 5) later dreamt:

(29) A bee is sitting on part of my bedroll and I start to flick him off. He keeps buzzing around me and I see that he has sacs on his legs filled with honey.

Despite the attempt at eradication the insect survives and surprises, even crowns the work or has sacs filled with honey.

An anxious woman in her forties dreams:

(30) Right in front of me in the middle of the street a young mother and three little girls are crouching by a low fire. They are burning insects. They sizzle and crackle and soon they die in the heat. But in the middle is a very big butterfly cocoon, a really tough creature. One of the girls tries to burn this too, but she doesn't succeed. It keeps coming out of the fire, staying alive.

If indestructible, does this mean eternal? The insect's "forever-ness"—witnessed in our common conviction that they are the ultimate survivors—states that the bugs are the keepers of the flame because, perhaps, they keep through the flame, the corrosive exterminating powders of our rage. They show the tough autonomy of the will to live, which is also an impersonal faith in life, as if a tropism permeating the cosmos.

> Kill me if you want to
> Black ant said
> Even if I die … still, I am black
> Even if I die … still I am black and I will be here.
> My blood will seep into the ground
> My intense black blood seep into the ground.
> Black forever.[25]

The cosmic connection of bug and world, of which we have already spoken, appears in this rather astounding example from a forty-two-year-old woman:

> (31) A huge praying mantis, maybe twenty feet high, says to me, "Are you a citizen?" I wake up screaming, "No!"

Has mantis (king of all creatures, according to Laurens van der Post's Bushmen) come to her dream requiring political awareness? If so, what is she specifically denying? What horror does this scream acknowledge? Is she being shocked into cosmic citizenry, asked to become a citizen of an ecological civilization in which bugs are not put daily into holocaust?

Two further examples of mystery—from a young woman musician:

> (32) I looked at a book and saw sawdust coming out of it. I watched it and was surprised to see a bee come out. It was making a hive or enlarging.

Even if reading and mental work, page by page, are for her as dry as sawdust, inside the book a bee is enlarging. But what is actually enlarging: the book, her, or the bee itself?

From an unmarried academic researcher:

> (33) A white man from the city is being held by some other men from a traditional culture (Indians, etc.). He is naked. One of the others reaches into a trough of water and fishes out some large black spiders, which he puts on the man's penis. Honey or treacle

---

25 *Proteus: Poems by Kaji Aso* (Boston: Gallery Nature & Temptation, 1977), 12.

has already been placed on the penis to attract the spiders. There is a sense of ritual about it, an initiation.

Some of the mystery here has to do with the spider-fly relation (a penis in much folklore and many languages is a flying creature and, of course, lives inside a "fly"). If the spider embodies the power of the dark natural mind that can unfurl a fantasy system out of itself that holds all things together in an inescapable network and the fly acts the puer role of the ever-conjuring, ever-escaping lightweight gadabout, then an initiation of the penis by the spidery realm may have to do with connecting the penis to and holding it within some regular order. But why the honey? What makes the spider come to a treacle-covered penis? Is sweetening, even sentimentalizing, the phallus the first step in the initiation of his phallic consciousness by the "salve" of Demeter, Lady of Bees and goddess of the earth's crops and harvests?

The bug indeed carries a secret. A trainee dreams:

> (34) I see two or three white mealy bugs on a healthy green plant and I get alcohol or something to kill them. They are very handsome, perfect.

Here, the urge to eradicate (perhaps with alcohol) moves her, yet her dream mind does perceive the handsome perfection in the bug. The white bug and healthy green plant are not in conflict except when she thinks of alcohol and of killing.

Dreams may show insects in terrifying or destructive modes, such as we have already seen, but the atmosphere of the dream gives them another aspect, and the dreamer another tolerance. For instance, a forty-five-year-old professor dreams:

> (35) I went to my neighbor in the village where I come from to buy some fruit. He lived in a room which was primitive (like a cave). He showed me the fruit—tangerines—and said, "This is all I have." I agreed to buy them. In the room there were ants—millions of them—and black spiders crawling all over me. The spiders seemed to be black widows that would stick to me. (I was not afraid at all.)

The multiplicity of the insects does not disturb him, nor that they crawl on him and stick to him, nor that the spiders are notoriously deadly. The neighbor in the cave in his memory was a simple, natural man "unreflective but industrious" who always "made do and got by," no matter the circumstances. The fruit in the dream gave off a wonderful smell: tangerine as vivid, earthy, easy to eat, and festive. It seems that the bright orange globe and the black bugs live in the same terrain and that the professor is, in Jungian terms, "integrating the shadow" by letting himself be infested by the creatureliness of earth. The dream shows both the life in the new nigredo (as the dark birds return from below in the *Rosarium* toward the end of the opus[26]) and the motif of re-birth ("village where I come from"). There is unreflected, unanalyzed life in the cave of the bricoleur-trickster who, like Begochidi, is both solar and insect at once.

In the case of the man who swims in his dream like a waterbug (dream 7), we saw that dreams can use identification to bring the dreamer to assimilate the insect, to realize it as oneself. Here is a further example from another dream:

> (36) I am standing at the entrance to a crypt or cave. Inside is a strange creature: the body of a large insect, like a grasshopper. It is very delicate, beautiful and the shine has hints of color. I am amazed that the insect has my face. The contrast between the soft skin and the hard carapace strikes me. Although the face is beautiful in its gentleness, I realize that it is a little sad, possibly because the carapace is so hard and armorlike.

To see one's face in the bug, to be a bug, here, does not have the Kafkaesque horror. Rather, beauty, gentleness and sadness are revealed. "I am an insect" takes on a very different feeling from the pejorative senses of louse or bug. In the beauty of finding that she and the insect share the same *figura, visage, ansikten* perhaps will come a new outlook that sees the beauty of the world and that one's way through it requires, perhaps, the face of softness and hardness both, for that is how the face of the insect is, apart from her judgment against the carapace.

Animal dreams frequently show the mystery of integration of one complex by another by the assimilation of one animal by another. A cat swallows a mouse; a rabbit, on closer look, becomes a cat; or

---

26 C. G. Jung, *Practice of Psychotherapy*, Collected Works, trans. R. F. C. Hull, vol. 16 (Princeton Univ. Press, 1966), fig. 9.

a black snake eats a red one, etc. There are, however, questions to be raised about integration. What happens to the former substance? Where is the red snake or the rabbit now that it has gone into the other animal? Is it overcome, simply gone, no longer a necessity of the psyche? Could integration also mean loss of differentiation, assimilation as simplification?

A woman scientist with extrasensory gifts dreams:

> (37) Walking along a lane, I become aware of a huge dark brown butterfly, about a foot long, flying upward, at my right shoulder. It ascends toward the right and is overtaken by a bird, which swoops down and eats it. The bird then flies higher, and a still larger bird, looking like a dove, captures the smaller bird and eats it, then itself flies upward. Tone of dream: wonder at the order of nature.

In the margin of this written dream beside each of the creatures I had penciled: soul, ideas, spirit. My rubrics assimilated the dream into my schema of soul versus spirit: the lane (vale of soul-making), the butterfly (dark brown and foot-sized has an upward intention). As it ascends, it is seized and devoured by a higher level hunger, which in turn is captured by a similitude of the dove, emblem of holy spirit's love. But it is not for sure a dove. The tone of the dream is not the downward feeling of anxiety about or sympathy for the lost butterfly and swallowed bird. Instead, the tone is "wonder" (the beginning of philosophy, says Schopenhauer) at the order of nature—a distant, wise, objectified reflection from the viewpoint of above, of the upward flying, all-consuming spirit. Is my reflection on the dream also a bird's view?

Finally, a dream from a man in his thirties—who had earlier dreamt (dream 23) of the bugs chewing the lettuce in his potted plant—states what this long essay wishes it were able to say:

> (38) I am walking with my wife. We notice a lot of ants, and we get interested in them, even getting down and looking at them from eye level—like being one of them. Seeing things as they do.

Perhaps there is a cosmic push in the intention of the bugs. That is, if Navajo lore says that insects are at the primordial beginning of things, and Hindu lore says all the world is spun in the web of Maya, and Bushmen lore gives kingship over living creatures to the praying mantis, then perhaps the movement of dream insects announces a new beginning, and, in Jung's language, they would be the small persistent instigators of individuation, its instinctual image, smaller-than-small in appearance, bigger-than-big in effect. They may be the animal compulsion in the sensate body of the world beyond human feeling, that brainless, bloodless insistence upon moving out and moving on.

A twelve-year-old boy in sixth grade dreams:

> (39) I am ice-skating (playing hockey) with my best friend (Ray), and another friend and two fellow hockey players and we're just playing. All of a sudden a big swarm of roaches come from the team benches and totally cover the ice, but we just keep playing and occasionally sweep up a few with our sticks. I can't remember the score, and I don't remember the exact place either. This is the first type of dream like this I have ever had.

He keeps playing, though his arena is covered with roaches. Some strange invasive element is coming off the benches, entering the game, and for the first time. He no longer knows the score. How long will his twelve-year-old, best-friend kind of playing last?

A young woman dreams:

> (40) ... I went up to my hotel room for a last look around before leaving on a trip and saw that cloudy murky water had risen to about eighteen inches in the room. Dead roaches were floating on the water and sticking to the walls. I thought, "A place like this is all right to stay in for a day or two, but you have to move on because it gets like this."

A musician, who came to analysis because he couldn't "get anything going," dreams:

> (41) I am lying out in a deck chair in the woods, when all of a sudden I see I'm right on top of an anthill. I get out of that chair fast. I wake up with my heart beating.

The urge to get away from bugs occurs often enough, but does the bug urge the get-away, as if the prompting to get out of the deck chair (dream 41) or off the bar-stool (dream 2) were not merely human reactions to the bug but the intention of the bug expressed in the human response, autonomic, inexplicable, compelling? Is perhaps the urge "to move on" an expression of a primal life instinct, the bug as *matière vivante?* Then the *opus contra naturam* of spiritual disciplines–zazen, meditation, the dark night of the emptying out, "teach us to sit still"–actually aims at overcoming going bugs. Their incessant pullulation out of the holes and through the screens, flapping toward the light or burrowing into veins of blood are styles of desire desiring to live. When we fantasize that only insects will survive a nuclear fire and the winter that follows, what cosmic potency are we attributing to the bug? No wonder our fear of its minute force.

And this force is ancient. It has been argued, perhaps established, that insect life is older in the chronology of the planet than plant life, that there are insects capable of life in frigid, arid, stony ground and in saline cavewaters void of sunlight and vegetable matter. That insects and plants can look alike, science calls "camouflage" and "mimicry," constructing a paranoid fantasy of bug behavior. Moths, beetles, mantises, etc., are so steadily menaced and so wily that they must disguise themselves as twigs, sticks, leaves, buds, pods, blossoms.

Perhaps they did learn or selectively breed to adapt. Perhaps, however, they like to dress this way or, perhaps, the plants have put on the insects' clothing. Or, perhaps, the bug and the plant share a common habitat and climate, and both present themselves in a manner fitting to it. Suppose the bug doesn't know it's not a plant, doesn't follow our classifications into "animal" and "vegetable," never read Linnaeus, as if its dress, its mask, its body habits were so vegetative that mimicry is not only the one kingdom of the other, or of each other, but of a third factor that requires them to accommodate with one another in a sympathy of all things, a cosmic ecology. Perhaps it is love that attracts these life forms to each other and inclines them to look alike.

Whatever the speculation about the mystery in their force and our fright (speculations beyond television's "nature" themes of ruthless competition, insatiable consumption, and paranoid defenses against predators–all of which tell as much of our way of looking at insect life as about insect life itself), one theme repeats often enough in dreams: the bug and the soil. They appear in the dirt, under the earth, in the toilet bowl. The fly buzzes over the manure pile, the scarab rolls its ball of dung; crabs in the pubis, lice in the scalp, parasites in the entrails, maggots in the rotten meat. Especially the hair and the lower body are affected. Karl Abenheimer interprets spiders and centipedes into anal symbolism, a move which repeats the idea of the bug as the evil outcast, smelly, sulfuric, of the Devil.[27]

The low evaluation corresponds with the bugs' underground surreptitious concealment. Hidden, buried, interior, appearing at night through small openings in day-world structures, these attributes suggest the underworld. Maybe it is not enough to say insects in dreams are the return of the repressed. Maybe they refer neither to the morally repressed (evil), nor the esthetically repressed (ugly), nor the primordially repressed (death), but to the chthonic gods, especially Hades, who emerges through—and whose intentions live in—those holes we feel as wounds.

If the bite of the bug is an underworld wound, then a pesticide is a theological instrument, a chemical Christ who harrows hell in the words of Hosea and Paul (1 Cor. 15:15), "O Thanatos, where is thy sting (*kentron*)?" in order to rid the world of Thanatos and Hades, imagined as a black figure with wings. *Kentron* literally denotes a sting, such as that of bees, scorpions, fiery ants, etc., while the same word provides the root of our "center," meaning originally "prick," "goad." The goad in the center of the deeps is both the presence of death and the cosmic urge of desirous life to live, like Karamazov's "sensual lust," like Hades who is also Pluto's riches, and also Dionysus's *zoe*. The Christian revolution, which recentered the cosmos in an upperworld – and an upperbody, resurrected Christ—removes the sting both of desire and of death. We re-enact the conquest of Christ over Pluto with our aerosol can of bug spray, swinging that censer in secular ritual, ridding each our own Garden of underworld demons.[28]

---

27 K. M. Abenheimer, "Re-Assessment of the Theoretical and Therapeutic Meaning of Anal Symbolism," (London: Guild of Pastoral Psychology, 1952).

28 On Christianism's victory over the underworld's sting, see my *The Dream and the Underworld* (New York: Harper & Row, 1979), 85–90. J. G. Frazer, *Folklore in the Old Testament*, 3 vols. (London: Macmillan and Co., 1918), 3:424–38, reports many cases where the Church and various religious orders tried and executed or excommunicated insects as vermin. For instance, St. Bernard, by excommunicating the flies that buzzed about him, laid them all out dead on the floor of the church. Vermin were dealt with by the Church authorities, domesticated animals tried by civil authorities. Frazer (438) explains this, saying, "It was physically impossible for a common executioner, however zealous, active and robust, to hang, decapitate ... all the rats, mice, ants, flies, mosquitoes, caterpillars ... but what is impossible with man is possible with God, and accordingly it was logically ... left

A Simple Conclusion

If the dreamworld is the return of the repressed (Freud), turning the face to us that we unconsciously turn to it (Jung), then it appears so stinging, buzzing and persecutory when our cultural consciousness treats our symptoms as vermin, our complexes as parasites. Yes, we want to rid ourselves of the underworld, using the nice white powder of destructive abstraction available from any pharmacy and/or physician, and in any session of ego-psychology. A source of the pharmacology industry lies in the fear of going bugs. That we need an ecology movement, animal rights advocacy, and a world wildlife fund begins in our dreams.

The fears aroused by bugs ascribes to *them* attributes of *our* eradication—autonomy, monstrosity, toxicity, proliferation. Poison spreads by human hands through the rivers and soils; kinds of toxins multiply, acres and acres of profligate overkill, Bhopal and Seveso, monstrous underworld infestation hidden in the underground aquifers, buried in the food chain. The "problem," as it is called, has become so autonomous that science, government, agriculture and industry cannot bring it under control. As prophesied, the bugs are winning, although not so much out there as in our eradicating minds that mimic the "enemy." By fighting going bugs, we have become the killer bees, fire ants, and black widows.

How we got here is too long and sad to tell. But briefly: animals were mere property in Rome; soulless for Scholastics; mindless machines for Cartesians and Kantians; carriers of bestiality, flesh, and sin for Christians; and lower levels of evolution for Darwin; while insects, in particular, suffered Christ's harrowing of the underworld in the first generic pesticide.

This history is embedded in our reactions in dreams. The dream ego is also the historical ego going through its conditioned responses. That

---

to God's ministers on earth to grapple with a problem which far exceeded the capacity of the magistrate and his minister, the hangman." I would contend the reason to be less logical: vermin present the theological problem of the underworld and had to be eradicated as demons rather than as animals. Nonetheless, records show that the bugs got a "fair trial" (even if they always lost): against the prosecuting priest, another priest took on their advocacy as having been created by God before humans, and therefore they had their rights to fields and crops.

figure we call Ego—were we Amerindians we might it call Roach-Killer, Fly-Swatter, Bee-Burner, Ant-Crusher—rides the back of a beast that it considers soulless private property. What we call the "progress" of Western civilization, from the ant's eye level, is but the forward stride of the Great Exterminator. Who is the parasite who lives on dead carcasses? Who is the white maggot embedded in insatiable consumption, chewing the leaves of the plants the world over, breeding ever new hybrid varietals that bugs will avoid and only it can enjoy?

The dreams we have reviewed show something in the dreamworld also suspected and predicted for the world at large: the bugs mysteriously survive. They withstand the fire. They seem to bear an indestructible life—annoying the eradicators who continually alter the formulae for their poisons. "Yet we've never been able to completely exterminate even a single insect species...They are the most diverse and powerful forms of life on earth. Their biomass outweighs that of humans."[29]

The dreams show something further, not suspected or predicted: bugs have something to teach us. They demonstrate the intentions of the natural mind, the undeviating faith of desire, and the urge to survive. They bring the community consciousness of a swarm and hive, a *Gemeinschaftsgefühl*, a cosmic sympathy, deeper than a social contract. They conjoin and enjoy the contrary elements of earth and air, show amazing capacities to conform and transform, and are resolute in their persistence to draw a dreamer out of the shelters of human habitation, the sheltering limits of human habits. At the end, we feel that they want us, these winged creatures with their astonishing eyes. They come to us in dreams, which is what angels are supposed to do. Startling, terrifying, sudden: is this the only way angels can now enter our world, which has no openings for their welcome?

At least we may consider this angelic interpretation, the bug as strange angel, almost small enough to fit its definition of beauty dancing on a pinhead (the very instrument we use to fix bugs in classificatory death). To survive as they survive, we must utterly transform the shapes of our thought, as they risk all in their transformations. Our minds cannot go far enough out on a limb. This angelic view calls us

---

29 R.D. Hall, in C. Dreifuss, "The Fine Art of Watching a Bug's Life...," *The New York Times* (2 January 2007), D2.

to look again, to re-spect who they are, what they are, why they are in the dream, and further, how to meet them, even care for them – these miraculous shapes and behaviors, each intricate appearance, a superb archaic ability, faultless, pious, fierce, comical, grave, intense, seeking us out while we sleep.

For archaic psychology in cultures the world over, the *divine* is partly *animal* and the *animal* partly *divine*. Theology says the divine is a *tremendum*, but a *tremendum* can come in small tremulous ways, a mere tremor, a shake, brush, shrug – the swift reaction to an insect. Because we are one of the very largest of the animal species, we expect only the larger to be more tremendous. That God must be as large as Behemoth is one more biblical anthropomorphism. Actually, *behemoth* means merely "animal," so what Job saw may have simply been his animals in a new, larger light so that they could be restored to him and he to them. Just look. Watch the animal and see the divine in self-display. Study the shiny shell and veined wings, the feeling feet, the determination. Study the head, the coat, the motions. Study the eye, each its own kind, like a bead, a dot, millionfold like a fly's.

Archaic cultures also kill animals on the altars of the gods. Of course: like unto like. By taking the animal to the altar, we are not ridding ourselves of it nor making it more pure and holy. It goes to the altar to feed the animal in the god, the divine that is partly animal, thereby keeping the god alive, and alive there in that *temenos*, the altar. The altar is an animal's keeper, keeps the god from roaming, its dreadful power tethered to a concentrated location. Get back, stay there behind smoking candles and grillwork. Don't cross over suddenly. The altar is a cage, each cathedral a great zoo. And the god who disdained Cain's sacrifice of grains wants Abel's animal meat, just as do wasps, maggots, and flies. We keep the gods alive with flesh, our animal flesh, the animal of our meaty imagination, infested and buzzing with stinging winged things. So, of course, the bugs in our dreams pierce into us, bite and draw blood, reminding us that we, too, are meat – and decaying. They eat their way into our reluctant recognition, force us to remember them. What else is incarnation but the god driving himself, herself, into and under our skin. God, a bedbug, crab, chigger, tick. The incarnation – the mystery of a louse. The gods become diseases;

ourselves infested by gods, forced to religion by bodily sensations; the religious instinct, the religious insect.

All is not lost. Much is recoverable – if only at moments, suddenly. Our dreams recover what the world forgets. Forgotten pagan polytheism breeds in animal forms. In those animals are the ancient gods: the Celtic horns and salmon, the Viking bears, the Egyptian pigs and river horses, crocodiles and cats, the Roman wolves and eagles, and Navaho Begochidi. The old gods are still there in our dreams – those zoological cathedrals, where there is a mansion for the insects of Beelzebub and Mephistopheles. The animals may go on like gods, alive and well and unforgotten, in the icons of our dreams and in the vital obsessions of our complexes and symptoms, the little bugs indestructible. Sing praise. *Gaudeamus*.

8

The Elephant in The Garden of Eden

The Dying Animal

A psychological lecture on Ernest Hemingway feels distasteful to say the least. Hemingway could be offended. He said to Aaron Hotchner: "What these shock doctors don't know is about writers and such things as remorse and contrition and what they do to them. They should make all psychiatrists take a course in creative writing so they'd know about writers."[1]

I follow Hemingway in this. Psychology cannot explain writing and cannot account for the writer. Hemingway detested psycho-biography. He suppressed Lawrence Kubie's psychoanalytic essay on him and threatened to cut his own mother from support if she gave an interview about her son to a journalist for *Cosmopolitan*. He detested the reduction of a man to an idea, of life as it is lived to reasons "discovered" after the fact. Remember: psychiatric accounts are *a posteriori*. Psychology explains actions *after* they occur with supposed reasons supposedly operative *before* the actions occurred.

The psychological explication of a text by means of personalistic psychobiography not only dilutes the true medicine of depth psychology by purveying patent explanations. Hemingway's fictions show Hemingway's machismo, multiple marriages and unfaithfulness, bi-sexuality, impotence, cruelty, lies, deceits, boastings, mother complex, *ad infinitum*. Even worse than the watered-down simplistic psychology is that biographical criticism avoids its own task of literary analysis. Rather than lay itself on the line by challenging a work as literature, it subverts the work by undoing the man.

---

1 A. E. Hotchner, *Papa Hemingway* (New York: Random House, 1966), 279–80.

I shall abstain from connecting Hemingway's life with his books. I shall try to keep distinct Hemingway, a character in the fiction of his life, from the characters Hemingway wrote into the life of his fiction. Nonetheless, I am a psychoanalyst and one who pretends to some knowledge about writing. And, I pretend to an idea drawn from the study of books by Hemingway and about him, an idea that appears in one of Yeats's late poems:

> Nor dread nor hope attend
> A dying animal;
> A man awaits his end
> Dreading and hoping all;
> Many times he died,
> Many times rose again. [2]

"Many times he died! Many times rose again": is that not Hemingway, the man himself, his characters, his reputation: counted out and coming back? The chronicle of his woundings, illnesses, accidents, batterings: how hurt he was himself? [3]

However, the motif in Yeats's poem that I wish to elaborate on is not death and resurrection but "dying animal." The dying lion, bull, buck deer, buffalo, or marlin—the great animal and the great death. This death link between man and animal—man as dying animal who achieves an action beyond hope or dread, the boxer's achievement of pure execution like the moment of truth in the bullring where reflection becomes one with reflex action, where art and death join — recreates the originary bond of man with animal, consciousness recognizing its animal soul, hunter and hunted fused in a *participation mystique*.

From this perspective of the animal soul, the cult of experience of which Hemingway is accused takes on a different look. "Experience" can no longer be conceived as merely trying this and that, going where the action is, doing things just to do them. Nor is experience the introspectively examined life. Rather, it becomes a physical knowing of the animal self through exposure to pressure. Experience yields knowledge of the animal's patterns and responses, its tendencies

---

2 "Death," in *The Collected Poems of W. B. Yeats* (London: Macmillan, 1952), 264.

3 For a full chronology of Hemingway's wounds, illnesses, accidents, and surgical operations, see "Appendix I," in J. Meyers, *Hemingway* (New York: Harper & Row, 1985).

to fear, to desire, to run savage or cut loose and leap free. The fish line as *axis mundi* so that self-knowledge becomes knowledge of the tug, the feel in the lines that run between the human hand and the invisible animal soul in the deep.

"In the worst part when I was tiredest I couldn't tell which was him and which was me...Then I began to love him more than anything else on earth," says boy David in "Bimini"[4] after fighting and losing the superb fish in a struggle that was his bloody initiation into manhood. Fusion with the dying animal moves Hemingway's stories and his language backward and inward to an elemental reality behind the modern guns and modern travel and modern words, and the characters in their modern relationships, to the archaic physical rituals that surround the dying animal of which the human is but one kind.

Elemental realities present themselves in the fusion as well as in truthful prose, as if Hemingway's language itself is given by fusion with the animal. Beyond dread and hope, cleansed of trivia, essentials bared by exact remembering, it is a language ritualized into thing beyond metaphor but not beyond morality. Rightness of word is at the same time rightness of action—"the devotion of a priest...the guts of a burglar," traits which Hemingway considered requisite for a writer.[5]

Let me remind you of Hemingway's appreciation, in his writings and writings about him, of the animal soul. I use the word *soul* following Hemingway himself, as he wrote of it in the *Eden* holograph:[6]

Only bible punchers could say the word now without embarrassment. But its passing from the vocabulary of the writer like himself, he knew, left a gap that no other word would fill. A word would be found, he was certain but not by him on this day when all he felt was the strangeness of the gap in his vocabulary. Even more strange, however, was his discovery in thinking about it that the loss of the word "soul" was not a handicap to him as a writer. He realized that the good prose writer always loses it; even in the old days they lost it although it remained current in the vocabulary of reflective men. He saw in fact that the writer *had* to lose it in the act of writing. But the loss of the word was not the loss of the presence that it named, a presence that had to be met and

---

4 E. Hemingway, *Islands in the Stream* (New York: Charles Scribner's Sons, 1970), 143.

5 Hotchner, *Papa Hemingway* (above, n.1), 200.

6 Hemingway Room, JFK Library, Boston.

known and named again and again as the writer moved in the garden of his work like Adam in Eden. The writer had to be a "priest
of God" in his work. (19:24)[7]

Hemingway here confirms a psychological truth: the presence of soul
is known mainly in the feeling of its loss. Workers in the arts must
perform their "soul-making" without the easy reliance upon the word
itself. The reference to Adam returns us again to the animals, for his
only task in the garden was naming them.

Legends of Adam, the primordial man, say that he spoke with animals. He knew their language, and that's why he knew their names. So,
too, Hemingway, another sort of primordial man; he too, according
to Hotchner, spoke with a black bear blocking a Western highway, a
circus gorilla to the amazement of its keeper, bulls in Spain, his dog in
Cuba.[8] The animals listened to the sound of his animal voice. But now
to *The Garden of Eden* and its elephant.

Tracking the Elephant

The Garden of Eden, begun in 1946 and published only in 1986, displays
Hemingway's late, purified prose.[9] The book leans forward into our day
of photorealism, of hard light and concealment on the surface, of yuppie
physical narcissism—French food, experimental sex, suntan wealth, good
clothes, fast cars, athletic prowess, hairdressers, androgynous liberated
feminism, newspaper success. It is a book that leans into our time also
indicating a remedy for those physical narcissisms through recovery of
a deeper physicality, an animal sense of self.

---

7 F. Scafella, "Clippings from *The Garden of Eden*," *The Hemingway Review* 7/1 (Fall
1987), 27. I am following Scafella for numbering of file folders and page numbers
within each file folder.

8 A good graduate student combing the sources would find page after page of
the motifs of hunter and hunted and of the dying animal. The student would also
find examples of that particular ability, which we in psychoanalysis have to teach
to patients as "active imagination," that is, talking to one's animals. This seems a
habit rather natural to Hemingway's characters. For instance, the old man, in *The
Old Man and the Sea*, talks to the marlin and the sharks and to the little bird that
rests on his skiff, much as Colonel Lambert, in *Across the River and into the Trees*, in
his hotel room talks to the portrait of the girl.

9 E. Hemingway, *The Garden of Eden* (New York: Collier-Macmillan, 1986).

David, a budding writer, and Catherine, his wealthy new wife, are a couple of Light, utterly sun-struck, young, bright, clean, rich, and with bleached silver hair. Like a painting by Hopper or Hockney, morbidity is in the light itself. The story is variously of a girl becoming a boy; of a man being "laid" low by a devil-woman; of a woman destructively envious of a man's writing; of what happens to women with men writers; of a writer's survival despite his inability to withstand his need for serving woman. The relations between working and loving, between surviving and serving, between losing self to woman and finding self in father, between fiction and life remain crucial and therefore ambiguous.

Traveling the Mediterranean coast and enjoying its sensuous offering, David one day breaks off writing a narrative of life with Catherine to begin a story he had long intended to write but never could. "The necessity to write it... had come to him." (*Eden*, 93) That same day Catherine introduces Marita, the new lover, to him; and David, while writing the new story that had been waiting for the time to be written, becomes ever more tightly wrapped in the slippery, fast-moving *ménage à trois*.

The new and necessary story is about his boyhood, his hatred for his father, and the tracking and killing of a mammoth elephant. This great beast, its rumbling stomach, its odor, skin, and padded pressing feet weight the latter portion of the book, truly a subplot, like a leaded keel below the light Mediterranean skiff plying about in the banter and breeze of Dufy-like scenes of halcyon blue, quick light touches, sudden storms. Overtly, the book tells what happens between the three. Covertly and essentially, the book tells what happens within the book, within David's writing, that shift from present narrative with Catherine to remembering Africa, the father, and the elephant—a narrative that Catherine discovers, stealthily reads, vengefully incinerates, and which David recovers in his mind and sets down again, while Catherine at the close of the book vanishes into distant places, repentance, and possibly insanity. The book concludes with these two paragraphs:

> He found he knew much more about his father than when he had first written this story and he knew he could measure his progress by the small things which made his father more tactile and to have more dimensions than he had in the story before.
>
> David wrote steadily and well and the sentences that he had made before came to him complete and entire and he put them down, corrected them, and cut them as if he were going over

proof. Not a sentence was missing and there were many that he put down as they were returned to him without changing them. By two o'clock he had recovered, corrected and improved what it had taken him five days to write originally. He wrote on a while longer now and there was no sign that any of it would ever cease returning to him intact. (*Eden*, 247)

What saves David is the story of the imaginal elephant — and my present essay elaborates that thesis, altogether missed by the critics. Kenneth Lynn [10] calls the elephant story "an interpolated yarn," while John Updike [11] hardly mentions the hunt and the elephant in his *New Yorker* review of the book. For him the theme is marginal, only incidental to the man-woman affairs and androgyny as they reflect Hemingway's reconstructed biography. Lynn reduces the novel to Hemingway's alleged "sexual duality," [12] a charge that locates Lynn in the mindset of the nineteenth century—pre-Weininger, Adler, Freud, and Jung. Updike and Lynn both ignore the book's own statement that the Africa story is regarded by the author as "completely real" and the Riviera *ménage à trois* as "unreal and false." (*Eden*, 174) The elephant hunt and the author's reflections on the writing of it become a parable for the mystical integrity of writing itself, which is the soul of the book. Hemingway, via David, anchors this soul below the conscious intricacies of human relations in the African depths of what Jung calls "thinking in primordial images." [13]

This is the story of the elephant hunt: David, when a small boy, perhaps eleven, treks with his father and an African, Juma, hunters both.

---

10 K. Lynn, *Ernest Hemingway* (New York: Simon and Schuster, 1987).

11 J. Updike, "The Sinister Sex," *The New Yorker* (30 June 1986), 85–88.

12 Lynn, *Ernest Hemingway* (above, n. 10), 541.

13 "... there is a thinking in primordial images, in symbols which are older than the historical man, which are inborn in him from the earliest times, and, eternally living, outlasting all generations, [that] still make up the ground work of the human psyche. It is only possible to live the fullest life when we are in harmony with these symbols... (C. G. Jung, *Structure & Dynamics of the Psyche*, Collected Works, trans. R. F. C. Hull, vol. 8 [Princeton Univ. Press, 1970], par. 794). On the tendency to literalize the primordial unconscious in the "dark continent" (black Africa), see my "Notes on White Supremacy," *Spring 1986: An Annual of Archetypal Psychology and Jungian Thought*, 45–46; also Jung's descriptions of Africa in the chapter on his travels there in his *Memories, Dreams, Reflections* (recorded and edited by Aniela Jaffé, trans. R. and C. Winston [New York: Vintage, 1965]).

One night, David and his dog Kibo come close upon a huge old bull elephant in the moonlight. David tells the two men. They begin tracking the beast. As they go on, they are led to the remains of a dead elephant, this one's friend, which had been killed for his tusks by Juma some time before. The sight of this enormous skull and whitened bones, and the murder of friendship between animals, associates in David's feeling with his dog; whereupon, under pressure of the exhausting trek ("Tiredness brought the beginning of understanding" [*Eden*, 182]), a shift takes place in David's affection from hunter and father to hunted and elephant: "His father waited for him to come up and said very gently, 'He rested here. He's not travelling as he was. We'll be up to him anytime now.' 'Fuck elephant hunting,' David had said very quietly." (*Eden*, 181) He has begun to identify with the dying animal. "My father doesn't need to kill elephants to live, David thought ... Kibo and I found him and I never should have told them ... I'm going to keep everything secret always. I'll never tell them anything again ... Never, never tell them. Try and remember that. Never tell anyone anything ever. Never tell anyone anything again." (Ibid.)

David's tracking the elephant to its death moves Hemingway's story and this essay on it into a literary *topos*, for the dying elephant appears as well in poetry (Charles Stein, Gianfranco Pagnucci) and in William Kotzwinkle and George Orwell. For a reason we still shall have to uncover, the elephant's death is essential to the writer's life as a writer.

Kotzwinkle's early stories collected in *Elephant Bangs Train* take the reader inside the elephant as it dies, an imagination of feeling he superbly accomplishes again in his *Doctor Rat*. There, animal after animal species rises up against humans only to be put down and slaughtered. Here is the death of the elephant:

> Something has struck me in the belly. Too old for the mustering ... too old ...
>
> I lie on the great plain with death inside me, with death sunk deep into me.
>
> The smoke is drifting over us. We lie in a heap, the quivering elephant nation. The mightiest bulls are fallen beside me, their tongues hanging out, their eyes staring into the sand ... My breath is leaving me. My breath is departing. I'm sorry for the young ones, for the newborn calves. They barely tasted the sweet leaves.

My breath goes further... I cannot call it back. The path is black. This is the great fear. The plums, the plums... [14]

This is from Orwell's story "Shooting an Elephant":

When I pulled the trigger I did not hear the bang or feel the kick... In that instant, in too short a time, one would have thought, even for the bullet to get there, a mysterious, terrible change had come over the elephant... An enormous senility seemed to have settled upon him. One could have imagined him thousands of years old. I fired again into the same spot. At the second shot he did not collapse but climbed with desperate slowness to his feet and stood weakly upright, with legs sagging and head drooping. I fired a third time... He trumpeted, for the first and only time. And then down he came, his belly towards me, with a crash that seemed to shake the ground even where I lay...

His mouth was wide open—I could see far down into caverns of pale pink throat. I waited a long time for him to die, but his breathing did not weaken. Finally I fired my two remaining shots into the spot where I thought his heart must be. The thick blood welled out of him like red velvet, but still he did not die. His body did not even jerk when the shots hit him, the tortured breathing continued without a pause. He was dying, very slowly and in great agony, but in some world remote from me where not even a bullet could damage him further. I felt that I had to put an end to that dreadful noise... and poured shot after shot into his heart and down his throat. They seemed to make no impression. The tortured gasps continued as steadily as the ticking of a clock.

In the end I could not stand it any longer and went away. I heard later that it took him half an hour to die. [15]

And now Hemingway, as David writes it:

They found him anchored, in such suffering and despair that he could no longer move. He had crashed through the heavy cover where he had been feeding and crossed a path of open forest and David and his father had run along the heavily splashed blood trail... David could only see his stern and then his father moved ahead of him and he followed and they came alongside the elephant as though he was a ship and David saw the blood

---

14 W. Kotzwinkle, *Doctor Rat* (New York: Knopf, 1976), 218–23.

15 G. Orwell, *Shooting an Elephant and Other Essays* (New York: Harcourt Brace, 1945), 10–11.

coming from his flanks and running down his sides and then his father raised his rifle and fired and the elephant turned his head with the great tusks moving heavy and slow and looked at them and when his father fired the second barrel the elephant seemed to sway like a felled tree and came smashing down toward them. But he was not dead. He had been anchored and now he was down with his shoulder broken. He did not move but his eye was alive and looked at David. He had very long eyelashes and his eye was the most alive thing David had ever seen.

"Shoot him in the ear hole with the three oh three," his father said. "Go on."

"You shoot him," David had said.

Juma had come up ... and taken the rifle from David without speaking and pushed the muzzle almost into the ear hole and fired twice jerking the bolt and driving it forward angrily. The eye of the elephant had opened wide on the first shot and then started to glaze and blood came out of the ear and ran in two bright streams down the wrinkled gray hide. It was a different colored blood and David had thought I must remember that and he had but it had never been of any use to him.

His father had known how he had felt about the elephant and that night and in the next few days he had tried if not to convert him to bring him back to the boy he had been before he had come to the knowledge that he hated elephant hunting ... The elephant was his hero now as his father had been for a long time ...

There was no more true elephant, only the gray wrinkled swelling dead body and the huge great mottled brown and yellow tusks that they had killed him for. The tusks were stained with the dried blood and he scraped some of it off with his thumbnail like a dried piece of sealing wax and put it in the pocket of his shirt. That was all he took from the elephant except the beginning of the knowledge of loneliness. (*Eden,* 199–201)

We are left devastated by these deaths because they are ritual murders without propitiation of the spirit of the sacrifices. They are one-sided rites, incomplete, sacrilegious. Compare the three slayings with this song of the Mbuti elephant hunters of the Congo rainforest:

Our spears have gone astray, Father Elephant!
We didn't want to kill you.
We didn't want to harm you, O Father Elephant!
Not our warriors ended your life,
Destiny decided that your hour had come.

So don't come back and trample our huts,
O Father Elephant.[16]

Why does the dying of the elephant *not* leave one feeling unable to bear, to go on, utterly emptied out? Instead, its death strengthens the heart with compassion, angers the temper with rage, and, for David, gives the silent lonely honor to stand against the father—"Fuck elephant hunting"—and to go on now with an elephant spirit, with a power that can withstand the devastation wrought upon him once by father and now by Catherine—"fuck your lawyers." (*Eden*, 226) The dying old bull is both the dying of the need for support and the finding of imaginal support, from the base of familial memory to the ground of imaginal language, from David as boy-son to David as man-writer, of personal father to archetypal father, of personal suffering to suffering at the species level. The dying elephant weighs us with an immense sadness. We recognize in it the huge beauty, the divinity, of that animal vitality that carries us through life as if larger than life—a magnificence, a power, a grace equaled only by the obsessive enormity of our rage to kill. As it dies, it transmits to the witnessing reader its qualities of an animal heart larger than human.[17]

Why an Elephant?

Why was the elephant the instrumental animal in David's recovery of his writing, his father, and his integrity? Why an elephant and not a great fish, a bull, buffalo, or lion—animals central to Hemingway's other stories?

Some elephant tales from my practice may begin to answer this. A young woman in and out of clinics, diagnosed as schizophrenic, scattered, unable, desperately sensitive, recurrent menstrual troubles, open to everything and closed off at the same time. She sees me for a month or so while her trusted analyst is on vacation. She is falling apart, running around, acting out. She paints pictures of her "insides"—what

---

16 P. Hamm, ed., *Welches Tier gehört zu dir? Eine poetische Arche Noah* (Munich: Hanser Verlag, 1984), 509.

17 See E. Cox, *Familiar Ground* (New York: Avon Books, 1986), 78–80, for another vivid scene of an elephant's tortured death and its effect on character in the novel and its readers.

she sees there and feels. Pink tufts, clouds, scissors, wavy jagged lines, faces, separated limbs, thorns. One day, in the midst of the scatter there appears a large pink elephant. It begins to dominate the pictures. It becomes less pink, more gray, brownish even. She likes its thick legs; she too has thick legs. She likes its skin. "Pachyderm: thick-skinned," I remind her. She slows down and holds together.

Another woman: this one is overweight in mid-life, mid-divorce, mid-love with an indecisive married man. Things look hopeless: where to live, what to live on; battles over children, changing lawyers, secrecy, hiding, feeling rushed, pushed, running scared. Decisions, decisions. She awakens one morning with an elephant dream too long and entwined to recount here, but the elephant came from an egg in a nest on an island and it had wings though it was not flying. (She knew no Hindu mythology where a comparable motif appears.[18]) She felt the combination of nest, egg, wing, elephant as a spiritual strength. Her divorced isolation had become a sheltering place, giving her an ability to bear and go on while the bulk of her body and weight of her troubles, and her gray-mooded obstinacy, had received backing from the elephant in the dream. She felt her luck might change.

In other dreams collected from here and there, I have seen elephants in procession as in a circus or parade, or as told of Dionysus's return from Asia and Hannibal's march through Europe. The elephants in the dreams sometimes balk and refuse to be driven further. They may all lie down, waiting, or move majestically, rhythmically forward. The images of elephants in procession, like those in line imaged on a carved ivory tusk, bespeak the forward-going sense of psychic process, the lumbering inevitability of one's time as fate into aging, as if destiny, or what Jung's psychology calls the "process of individuation," were an instinct that can indeed halt, balk, sit right down still so that one feels blocked and old and immensely tired. Yet that elephantine heaviness appears in dreams and symbolic images as a supporting base. The same power appears in both the block and the movement through the block, a movement that requires learning the sensitive art of the mahout, how to speak into an elephant's ear and

18 H. Zimmer, *Myths and Symbols in Indian Art and Civilization* (New York: Pantheon, 1946), 104–106.

read the sounds of its internal rumblings, following its grasp of the world through the nose.

Beyond these presentations in contemporary dreams, the elephant receives lengthy attention from writers on animal lore in antiquity—Aristotle's *Historia animalium* and *De natura animalium*, Pliny the Elder's *Naturalis historia*, and Aelian's *De natura animalium*, among others. The qualities of this great beast are generally only praiseworthy, much as the whale in the contemporary imagination. Again and again, the elephant is associated with the majesty of kings and gods. For the Romans, the elephant appeared in triumphs and represented victory, and the chariot of *fama* (fame) was drawn by elephants.[19] Also, in Roman symbolizations of geography with animals, the elephant stood for the continent of Africa.

In India, as Heinrich Zimmer writes, "in their function of bestowing the life-giving ... waters, elephants are akin to ... demons of divine earthly energy ... the majestic appearance, irresistible strength, and gentle calm temper of the elephant, its grandeur and intelligence, were virtues inherent in the Indian ideal of ... character."[20] "... the Buddha is more than once still called an elephant."[21] Asian, African, and our Western imagination saw in the elephant wisdom, patience, invincibility, long memory, pity, chasteness, moderation, peacefulness, tactile sensitivity, old age—a host of beneficent senex qualities—elephant as Old Wise Man or reliable kindly old parent. Lore said elephants live two hundred to three hundred years.[22]

But the lore gives lesser place to their fury, their ravening appetite, their musth madness, justifying their rages as reactions to betrayals and wrongs. Though the Romans used them for war, and for bloody spectacles, the elephants' compassionate gentleness remains the dominant

---

19 H.H. Scullard, *The Elephant in the Greek and Roman World* (London: Thames & Hudson, 1974), 235–36.

20 H. Zimmer, *The Art of Indian Asia: Its Mythology and Transformations*, ed. Joseph Campbell, 2 vols. (Princeton Univ. Press, 1983), 1:161.

21 Zimmer, *Myths and Symbols in Indian Art and Civilization* (above, n.18), 103 n.

22 Scullard, *The Elephant in the Greek and Roman World* (above, n.19), 45, 215, 223. In popular American political symbolism, the Republican (Grand Old Party) emblem maintains the senex tradition versus the Democrats' donkey, the humble, of-the-people, brother ass.

theme, as for instance the elephants that refused to do battle against their own kind at Raphia (Polybius).[23]

Aelian described them as particularly pious and said that gods loved elephants. "At a new moon elephants were said to pluck fresh branches and wave them gently to and fro in honour of the goddess...They also do obeisance to the rising sun, raising their trunks like hands."[24] And they revere death: "An elephant will not pass by a dead elephant without casting a branch or some dust on the body."[25] Their legendary concern with death, bones, and burial is attested to by many eyewitness accounts retold by Iain and Oria Douglas-Hamilton[26] and by Cynthia Moss.[27]

Also relevant for Hemingway's account of David is the elephant lore regarding labor. Baron Cuvier says that they are "beasts of draught and burden,"[28] and Thomas Bewick, in an eighteenth-century bestiary, writes, "The Elephant, when tamed is gentle, obedient and docile: patient of labour, he submits to the most toilsome of drudgery... he receives his orders with attention and executes them with eagerness, but without precipitation. All his motions are orderly, and seem to correspond with the dignity of his appearance, being grave, majestic and cautious."[29]

Love of work, yes; but love of women as well. Topsell's bestiary (based on Conrad Gesner), which collects masses of lore, observations, and anecdote, states, "At the sight of a beautiful woman they leave off all rage and grow meek and gentle."[30] He recounts tales of elephants making gifts of fruit to women, stroking their faces and their bosoms.

---

23 Ibid., 139–40. (For a continuation of this idealizing tradition, see the virtues attributed to the elephant symbol in Jungian interpretive writings by L.Fierz-David, *The Dream of Poliphilo* [Dallas: Spring Publications, 1987], 56–58, and M.-L. von Franz, *The Problem of the Puer Aeternus* [Santa Monica: Sigo Press, 1981], 17–18.)

24 Scullard, *The Elephant in the Greek and Roman World* (above, n.19), 226.

25 Ibid.

26 I. and O. Douglas-Hamilton, *Among the Elephants* (London: Book Club Associates, 1975), 239–42.

27 C. Moss, *Elephant Memories* (New York: Fawcett Ballantine, 1988), 270–71.

28 Baron Georges Cuvier, *The Animal Kingdom*, trans. W.B. Carpenter and O. Westwood (London: Bohn, 1963), 117.

29 T. Bewick, *A General History of Quadrupeds* [1790] (London: Ward Lock Reprints, 1970), 191.

30 E. Topsell, *History of Four-Footed Beasts and Serpents and Insects*, 3 vols. (London: Cass and Co., 1967), 1:164.

Another passage from Aelian states, "The young show respect for the old. They give place to them in feeding and drinking; they never abandon the weak... they help the old out of pits when they have fallen in." "Where," asks Aelian, "I should like to know, did an elephant ever belabor his sire with blows?"[31]

One god that bears an elephant shape, Ganesha of Hindu myth and cult, is called "The Lord of Obstacles" who "breaks a path for the devotee."[32] At the outset of undertakings of every kind (including obeisances to other gods), he is invoked first. Often, his vehicle is the rat, the marvelous survivor, wily and determined, who finds his way through ruins to hidden resources.[33] Neither Ganesha nor his rat is by any means ascetic. The elephant god is joyful, jaunty, potbellied; he loves humankind, earthly prosperity, and the good things of life. Asian, African, and classical tales tell of his huge appetite for sweets, jeweled refinements, delicacies, and for the scents of flowers. Compare David, his tastes for pleasure, and his resourcefulness at work.

At the core of the Ganesha myth is father-son conflict and reconciliation. Courtright considers it a myth of initiation. Siva cuts off his son's head, which, when restored, is that of an elephant. "Ganesha becomes the embodiment of restoration... a powerful reality whom all gods and powers must acknowledge if their undertakings are to be successful."[34] "The theological message of the Siva-Ganesha, father-son pattern can be summarized in this way: submit that you may be saved, be destroyed that you may be made whole. The sacrificial violence is not the tragic conclusion but the necessary beginning of a passage into a new order... the God who breaks you makes you; destruction and creating ultimately spring from the same source."[35]

Furthermore, because "a central recurring theme in Ganesha's character is that of mediation,"[36] we can understand the *ménage à trois* as inherently necessary to the mythical substructure of Hemingway's narrative.

---

31 *De natura animalium* 6.61 and 7.15.

32 Zimmer, *Myths and Symbols in Indian Art and Civilization* (above, n.18), 133.

33 Ibid.

34 P. B. Courtright, *Ganesha* (Oxford Univ. Press, 1985), 97.

35 Ibid., 122. (Cf. Zimmer, *Myths and Symbols in Indian Art and Civilization* [above, n.18], 109, where elephant = son and son = "living copy of the father": "the father's essence in another individualization.")

36 Courtright, *Ganesha* (above, n.34), 250.

The elephantine bulky strength emphasized in Hindu myth—elephants as caryatids of the universe,[37] the whole world resting on their backs—does not find confirmation in actuality. "A full-grown Indian elephant weighs as much as 64 humans, but it can only pull as much as twenty of them."[38] A big draft horse can carry farther and longer (in proportion to its weight) at least twice as much as an elephant. They are actually lightweights in that their foot pads carry only six hundred grams per square centimeter compared with a skinny fashion model whose high-heel talons press down two kilograms per square centimeter.[39]

Evidently, the elephant's power is less empirical than mythical, fertilizing the imagination. In Hindu myths they also symbolize with clouds; and in the animal symbolism of Kundalini Yoga the elephant appears twice, below and above. First, at the lowest chakra (*muladhara*) at the base of the spine and/or genitals, where the gray elephant refers to the seat of the strength, the generative root in earth, community, family, and body. Second, the white elephant in the throat chakra (*visuddha*) refers to the supporting power of word, mind, images, the reality of utterance, the utter reality of the *vis imaginativa*.[40]

Contemporary research continues the lore, investigating elephants for their mental abilities and language. By means of complicated laboratory tests in a German zoo, it has been shown that elephants possess excellent memory, absolute pitch, can learn whole vocabularies of visual signs despite inferior visual acuity, i.e., they can read, showing little fatigue over long tests with six hundred choices lasting several hours; in fact, they improved performance toward the end.[41]

---

37 Zimmer, *Myths and Symbols in Indian Art and Civilization* (above, n.18), 105.

38 F. Kurt, "The Elephant in the China Shop," *Swissair Gazette* 9 (1987), 15.

39 Ibid.

40 See H. Zimmer, "The Chakras of Kundalini Yoga," *Spring 1975: An Annual of Archetypal Psychology and Jungian Thought,* 134, and C. G. Jung, "Psychological Commentary on Kundalini Yoga," *Spring 1976: An Annual of Archetypal Psychology and Jungian Thought,* 131.

41 B. Rensch, "The Intelligence of Elephants," *Scientific American* 196 (February 1957), 44–49.

The Fathering Imagination

In sum, the elephant is a bringer of weight and bearer of weight, whether in the world or in word; the strength and endurance of substantial virtues. To have an elephant in one's dream or in the life of one's fiction is for the imagination itself to be imbued with long-lasting value. It is for imagination to be as accurate as an elephant placing its foot, as accurate as the grasp of its trunk; an imagination as unforgettable as Orwell's memoir, and unforgetting like David's memory returning complete, like Hemingway's esthetic discipline of "exact remembering,"[42] which locates the reports of life in the "blue" "high country" (*Eden*, 147) of imagination. "I'm a reporter *and an imaginative writer* and I can still imagine plenty..." Hemingway wrote in a letter to Maxwell Perkins (16 November 1933).[43]

The elephant: a power slow to anger as was David, yet well able to kill, as was David ("All I want to do is kill you," he says to Catherine after her destructive act [*Eden*, 233]); slow to gestate and slow to die, with a patience that pushes a path through obstacles. The elephant provides a vegetative digestion equal to the enormity of its appetite for the sweet things of the green world, and a thick-skinned resistance to the arrows of fortune. It lumbers forward with gray depressive strength, growing long in the tooth for the imaginer's art, and, in its processional aspect, declares the inevitability of movement greater than any creature walking the earth.

Even more unbearable than the protracted and bloody dying of the elephant written by Kotzwinkle, Orwell, Elizabeth Cox, and Hemingway is *the arrest of movement*, the image of the beast stopped, wedged, boxed, sunk in sand, no longer able to go forward or even support itself—the destruction of its essential meaning.

Many of the qualities attributed to it by lore—wisdom, continence, loyalty, carefulness, as well as the power of the *vis imaginativa*—were considered in folk medicine, astrology, and traditional symbolism to belong to Saturn, the senex, the god of lead, aloneness, slowness, and

---

42 R. B. Jones, "Mimesis and Metafiction in Hemingway's *The Garden of Eden*," *The Hemingway Review* 7/1 (Fall 1987), 10 n7.

43 E. Hemingway, *Selected Letters 1917–1961*, ed. C. Baker (London: Granada, 1981), 400.

dignity, the old man or woman, the archetypal parent among the classical gods. Saturn was emblematically represented as riding an elephant,
and the notion persisted throughout antiquity that the elephant's adult
life began at sixty, the precise age at which one put on the *toga senilis* in
Rome or becomes a "senior" in Japan.

So, when we read again those last paragraphs of *Eden* – David's memory returning, the chaste (not abstinent) devoted and sensate affection
for Marita, "the small things that made his father more tactile and to
have more dimensions than he had in the story before," the final word
intact – this increase in dimension, in tactile sense, would be gifts of the
elephant. David can say, "He was fortunate just now, that his father
was not a simple man," because David was no longer a simple man.
These increases in regard to his father suggest further reflection: this
dying elephant had made it possible for David to find his father, to
no longer "belabor his sire with blows," to reconcile with his father's
nature and to love him, as if the shift in affection away from father
to elephant in the earlier chapters allows a shift back to the personal
father at the end. "He found he knew much more about his father than
when he had first written this story..." Especially the knowledge of
feeling. David writes,

> All morning writing he had been trying to remember truly how
> he had felt and keep it untinctured by how he had felt later... his
> feeling about the elephant had been the hardest part... the feel-
> ing had begun to form but he had been too exhausted to remem-
> ber it exactly. (*Eden*, 174)

The physical ordeal of "exact remembering" the elephant in the act of
writing recapitulates the physical ordeal of tracking the elephant.

We can imagine Ganesha's presence in moving David forward
against all obstacles and Hemingway forward in continuing the narrative from 1946 until the end, and Tom Jenks, his editor, forward
in digesting the mass of material into elegant form. This presence,
however, is below the surface (and thus unnoticed by the critics).
"In fiction," said Hemingway to Arnold Samuelson, "it's what you
leave out that counts. Nine tenths of it has got to be beneath the
surface. That's what gives dignity to a story."[44] Invisible plodding.

---

44 A. Samuelson, *With Hemingway* (New York: Random House, 1984), 178.

Five hundred words a day. Hemingway writes of David,

> He wrote it in simple declarative sentences with all the prob-
> lems ahead to be lived through and made to come alive. The very
> beginning was written and all he had to do was go on. That's all,
> he said. You see how simple what you cannot do is? (*Eden,* 108)

> The difficult parts he had dreaded he now faced one after an-
> other... (*Eden,* 128)

"That which is creative must create itself," said John Keats, which
in this context suggests that what now fathers David is his shaping
imagination, pursuit of it, and loyalty to it. Parents carry the parenting
image until imagining itself begins parenting. David previously hadn't
the power to write the story of the father and the elephant, for his own
generative strength was held captive in the father.

In the imagination of the subplot the boy has been initiated. He has
left the father and returned to him. He has left simple resentment and
found complex affection. He is no longer estranged from the fathering root, holding back from essential action, postponing, substituting.
Woman also now shifts in his universe from wealthy supporter of his
work to intimate partner in it. David finds the fathering capacity in
his imaginative memory, which he nourishes daily in the Africa of his
mind, that high plateau where boy, father, and elephant meet. The fiction of the father cures fixation on the father. Waters of love released;
memory cured by imagination, that impersonal steadying force below
the human. The positive senex can bear the whole world of disaster
and personal suffering by transmuting that world with the digestive
capacity of story.

The digestive capacity of story compares with what I have called,
borrowing Keats's phrase, "soul-making": soul-making as story-making.
By soul I mean that perspective which deepens events into experiences, makes meaning possible, has a religious concern, is communicated
in love, and reflects a special relation with death. Further, soul refers to
the imaginative possibility in human nature that recognizes all realities
as primarily metaphoric and mythic. Scafella concludes his penetrat-
ing and compassionate study, saying,

> Part of the *mystère* of David Bourne's art and Hemingway's vision is
> that each works from beyond personal feelings... out of an inner

core of being which...he [David Bourne] would call his "soul" if they had the word, is what he writes for and from. Therein is the central quality or *mystère* of David's work, the origin of the garden itself...The soul is the origin of the compassionating mood at the heart of the garden into which David goes as he writes...[45]

Hence the elephant. And hence a "dying" elephant, for death is the translation of life into soul, world into underworld or the imaginal isles of the blest, as the Greeks called that psychic reflection after life, which gives life a raised value, an intensity unattended by hope or dread, the truth of mortal and immortal in any moment, a divine energy in this heavy earth, not beyond, above, or elsewhere, but in the plump mackerel tinned in aromatic juice and a bottle of Tuborg beer (*Eden*, 237–38) with which David begins again on that first day after the disaster by fire. Born again in the flesh—round-bellied Ganesha, bringer of good luck.

The elephant, by performing this translation in his slow and agonizing dying, teaches the writer, here David (also Hemingway?), Orwell, and Kotzwinkle, the art of imaginal translation: life into story, personal fury and blood transmuted into compassion and a moral vision that in turn transforms life. After shooting the elephant, Orwell left the Burmese colonial service;[46] the death of the elephant in his story so affected Kotzwinkle that he wept and rededicated himself to his writing;[47] David in this story becomes "intact." In each of the three cases the act of writing, of being a writer, is tied with the dying of the elephant, as if a calling rises like a ghost from the soul of the falling beast. It is as if only the power of the living word is equal to the power of the dying elephant.

Here I refer to an equivalence between the *muladhara* and the *visuddha* elephants, between life and word, that mirroring interplay of nature and imagination. By transposing the Kundalini model of the psyche to writing, writing becomes a spiritual discipline of the soul—like David's long hours of sitting alone in a special room, his *fanum*, sanctuary, which no one else might enter. Writing kills natural, unreflected life, animal life, the grounding support from below (the *muladhara* of community,

---

45 Scafella, "Clippings," "Clippings from *The Garden of Eden*," (above, n.7), 29.
46 P. Stansky and W. Abrahams, *The Unknown Orwell* (New York: Knopf, 1972).
47 Private communication.

family, locality). As the dying elephant leads to writing, writing leads to shooting the elephant, arrest of movement, which long has been the narrowest definition of art. And the writer is carried in the vehicle of his work to his death, as if each book chiseled another chip of the gravestone. The act of writing as a daily trek [48] in which the increasing exhaustion reports the slow slaughtering of life's vitality. Writing as addiction to suicide. Hemingway's intense need to be among and write about animals, as well as the way he lived and died by the hunting gun, epitomizes the relation between beast and word.

When Henry James, remote indeed from the style and nature of Hemingway, in four different letters to Hugh Walpole (1909) [49] compares himself with an old elephant, we can read this as an internal recognition of a similar experience. Old James, who had become a wholly imaginational beast in the jungle of his language, in the reality of *visuddha*, was perhaps drawn, in his emotional attraction to Walpole, to the physical elephant below.

Each of us reading these tales of the murdered beast awakens to the moral monstrosity of human affairs; [50] we feel cleansed of the wrong and the false, and we are filled with immense pity. This moral sense, this pity have their source not in the chastened, converted heart that Christian humanism attributed to Hemingway because that heart still hopes. "Nor hope nor dread attend..." Below that heart is the heart of the beast that in these stories is also the slain beast. We have been witnesses to a murder exceeding any human crime, the ultimate transgression: the gratuitous killing of another species, which is, at the same time, a god.

The elephant god requires that it be remembered first before any other god, reminding that the way to the gods is via the elephant. After its dying fall, the only possible way to the gods is by recapitulation of that death in story, thereby opening to a recognition of the religious function of literature, writing as a ceremonial invocation of the animal,

---

48 See Jones, "Mimesis and Metafiction," (above, n.42), 811.

49 L. Edel, *Stuff of Sleep and Dreams* (New York: Harper & Row, 1982), 317–19.

50 "The inclusion of this incident [the incineration of a trapped elephant] is the necessary look at what we are capable of. If we know our capability for violence, we can choose not to act on it...There are echoes in this... of Germany and the war, and of people putting *people* (not elephants) into boxcars—a reminder of what we allow ourselves to do." (private letter from Elizabeth Cox)

each book a mystery novel translating the reader to another time and place, *in illo tempore,* the garden of Eden.

Hemingway was aware of the book as religious mystery and said so. The holograph records this unpublished conversation about writing between David and Marita. (He allowed her into the sanctuary of his writing room, sharing his stories with her so that she had become his *soror mystica* – but only after he had concluded the elephant tale, only after he had become an initiate, or son of the elephant.) David says,

> "It's a *mystère.* But you know about it."
>
> "It's a true *mystère,*" the girl said. "The way they had true *mystères* in religion. Have maybe."
>
> "I didn't have to tell you about it," David said. "You knew about it when I met you."
>
> "I only learned with the stories... It was like being allowed to take part in the *mystère.* Please David I'm not meaning to talk trash."
>
> "It isn't trash. But we must be very careful not to ever say it to other people. I mustn't ever and you be careful too."[51]

David as little boy in the story swears not to tell anyone anything ever again. That David, hating his father, is locked into stubborn secrecy. This David, loving his mistress, transforms secret into mystery through the act of writing – "the guts of a burglar" into "the devotion of a priest." Therefore, the radical change in David, his rededication, and our own emotion – animal as theophany, story as mystery, reading as participatory ritual.

Finally we may appreciate further what is implied by the title of Hemingway's twenty-year opus, published posthumously, the author in the land of the dead, the isles of the blest. *The Garden of Eden* at first level connotes from innocence to corruption, the boy-girl couple in paradise, like paintings by Memling, Cranach, or Dürer, thin twin bodies lascivious, the release of evil and their fall with the entry of a third, the fascinating tempter who is the subtle ambiguous redeemer, for the biblical garden was a *ménage à trois,* a perfect couple that became an unholy triangle.

---

51 Holograph 29:49, from Scafella, "Clippings from *The Garden of Eden,*" (above, n.7), 21.

There is, however, another vision of that garden: the animal in the evening, walking to and fro in conversation, man and woman and God and beast. This second vision sees not merely expulsion and the usual moral progress from innocence to experience, sees not merely paradise barred from return by the flaming desire to return. This other vision imagines the garden as ever there at the level of animal intelligence and in the images of animal presences. In the tactile dimension of divine earthliness, the empty bleached hedonism becomes a full-bodied sensuousness that can recognize and find words for each animal as it passes; a garden to be entered any evening when the bright mind cools, ourselves seated upon the elephant, swaying, sniffing the flowering ground, great foot lifted, paused in air.

9

You Dirty Dog!

Nature is in the doghouse, an outcast from our corporate, capitalist, consumerized, commodified cosmos, despite Al Gore, the Sierra Club, Earth Island, the Green movement... In response to this hard fact of rejection and exploitation of nature – trees, soils, oceans, rivers, creatures – has come a soft idealization and sentimentalism to retrieve the dog and take it back into the family lap.

I want, rather, to play with the idea of nature in a different way. Neither as rejected nor as sentimentalized. I prefer to look at nature up close and personal, by means of something most familiar and least conceptual: the dog.

Before we go to the dogs, let's remember we have no clear consensus at all about the word "nature." Lovejoy and Boas have found at least sixty differing meanings of the term.[1] This is another reason I prefer to turn to dog, for "dog" gives us a word with a bark, with hair and teeth and feet. So let's unleash the dogs.

Melancholy

Curled near the base of a ponderous geometric stone a sleeping dog lies by the feet of Dame Melancholy in Albrecht Dürer's early sixteenth-century etching. Among symbols of the measuring intellect and the passing of time we find a bony, half-starved dog as an important part of an enigmatic cosmology. How does that sleeping dog fit with this depicted state of soul: abysmal dejection, darkened visage, and the intense distant stare of inspired visionary. There is madness here, riches

---

1 A. O. Lovejoy and G. Boas, *Primitivism and Related Ideas in Antiquity* (New York: Octagon Books, 1965).

of imagination, even terror. This becomes our first question: the dog-gedness of depression, depressive doggedness.

Dürer's image places the dog within a wholly psychological field altogether different from the familiar dogs of the day world: the sportsman's hunting dog, the courtesan's frilly dog, the breeder's triumph on show, the willingly harnessed dog pulling its load and the brave rescue dog, the children's romping playmate and the household's favorite and faithful companion. From Dame Melancholy's *familiaris* might we learn something else, something deeper that depression takes us toward?

An animal (*hayyah*) says the *Zohar* is "the highest grade of angel." Which specific kind of angel is the dog? Angels, from *aggelos* in Greek, are bearers of messages; what angelic message does the dog bear? What essential intelligence is embodied in that hairy coat, behind those soft eyes and black muzzle of that angel we call a dog?

I understand "angelic essence" to mean the deepest and highest intention that the animal brings into this world, offering the world necessary qualities specific to each kind of animal. That is the first importance of these creatures, each of them, all of them. That is why they had to be saved as seeds on Noah's ark and why for early peoples and still many today, gods first appear as animals.

Animals in the Psyche

More narrowly in terms of human lives, each kind of animal backs a style of human behavior, showing us in their display our traits and our sustaining natures, which we have named "instincts." We meet animals out there, in the bush, in the streets, but they also live in the psyche transmitting behavior patterns. Human nature consists not only in the community sitting around the campfire but also in the beasts in the surrounding jungle. Each of our souls is comprised of tigers of wrath, vultures of greedy hunger, owls of attentive stealth, and parasitical vermin sucking life from anything we fasten upon. Hogs, skunks, and cocks of the walk inhabit the soul's menagerie. All our behaviors, even our faces, as caricaturists have shown, betray some animal trace. The *canidae* (dog, wolf, jackal, fox, dingo) are present in our very structure. Those incisors in our mouths are "canines."

Animal traits in human habits are quite specific. To help sense "dog-ness," study the cat. These two carnivores, which we nourish in the bosom of domesticity, never could get along with each other according to the legends. They are not fungible—it's not a cat cuddled in Dame Melancholy's lap, else we might read her as a witch. Cats bring with them something magical from far away, from Egypt and the night, fundamentally heathen, pagan (no cats anywhere in the Bible).

Cat and dog tend to divide along a comfortable fault line in our thinking: male and female. Mister Dog and Miss Kitty. Social evolutions follow this fable when they suggest that dogs were domesticated by nomadic hunter/gatherers, a mainly male activity, while cats belong more to settled agriculturalists (along the Nile), protecting the stored crops against mice. More a world of women. Thus, dogs' feet hold up in long cross-country treks; they ford streams and follow scent. They need exercise and they love chasing, while life with cats is more indoor, intimate, and societal, including those traits transferred in terms like "catty," "pussy," "wild cat," "alley cat," etc. (Puppy love is boys only.) Cats seem never to be fully on "our side." Will a cat heel, take a leash, sit up on its haunches, or dance on command? They prefer to watch, from a distance, on high. A cat climbs a tree; a dog digs a hole. The way up and the way down are not one and the same. The dog, however, enjoys its "almost human" qualities: e.g., Rin Tin Tin, Lassie, the shepherds and police dogs, the St. Bernards, and all the guardians with their straight-forward un-catlike qualities of courage, loyalty, obedience, responsiveness, and sociability.

Our language, too, shows the animal in our behaviors, and the dog particularly in melancholy: "the hangdog look"; "dog-tired"; "you cannot teach an old dog new tricks"; "a dog smells his own dirt first"; "it's easy to find a stick to beat a dog"; "dog-eat-dog"; "the dog returns to its own vomit"; "helping lame dogs over stiles"; "if you lie down with dogs, you will get up with fleas"; "thrown to the dogs"; "scratch like a dog at a door till it opens;" etc.

In depression, the mind goes on a hunt to find a cause, digs up old bones that have been chewed many times before—past sins, omissions, and regrets. Regurgitations as meditations and one feels oneself to be ugly and smelly, and full of blame. Like a dog, the mind chases its own tail, obsessively seizes on a misery, shakes it like a terrier, and won't let go—compulsive repetitions of complaint, like a dog barking and barking long after the postman has passed.

Traits shared by the dog and depressed person were long noted and incorporated into common proverbs. They also belonged to "diagnosis by analogy," the use of images for grouping and understanding sufferings before modern times. *Acedia*, that melancholy sloth and silent obsessive despair afflicting monks in monasteries, was sometimes indicated by the dog (as in Dürer's engraving). Old Saturn, god of winter, darkness and cold—and melancholy—, could also be seen in the horny old goat; the lonely moose in a wintry swamp, his head burdened by the huge weight of its processes; the elephant, its gray, somber bulk like the very body of depression; the camel, which could continue on for days in a deserted condition. Emblems of sadness each, speaking our feelings more vividly than can psychiatric concepts.

We carry them with us. The animals have not been left behind in a different kingdom separated from us by a wide chasm. That famous old story may not be true: it says that once we humans and the animals were all together in a peaceable kingdom, until slowly a rift appeared in the earth, and gradually the animals were all on one side, the humans on the other of an ever-widening gap. At the very last moment, the dog leapt the chasm to be on the side of the humans.

What is not true is that we are far from them, but what may indeed be true is the special place of the dog at our side, perhaps as their representative, their ambassador with a particular mission. From what country? With what mission? Let us pursue further.

Here we come upon the first message from our dog. Humans touch nature via depression. They drop into slowness, the muteness of animal, vegetable, and mineral being, the bafflement of mind's inability to find words. Depression restores us to the dumb animal, the futility of explanation, of language itself.

We find nature in our mutual wordless relation with the dog. This is Benjamin's defeat of *Überbenennung* (over-naming). This is Kafka's dog; and Wittgenstein's "Whereof one cannot speak, thereof one must be silent" or bark or whine or howl or, most famously, whimper.

In the depths of his despair, Ernie, the focal figure of Schwarz-Bart's excruciating novel of Jewish persecution, chooses to become a mad dog, "tears...running down his cheeks while he barks hoarsely...

barks, barks endlessly..."[2] Not dumb, not truly mute, but absolutely wordless must nature remain. "When we divert the current of feeling that flows between ourselves and the animal into words, we abstract it forever from the animal."[3]

Phusis kruptesthai philei (Nature loves to hide), said Heraclitus. Where does it hide? How does nature hide? In wordlessness. We know it best by living with it, closely.

Ancestors

Did that primordial dog leap the chasm to escape its own shadow? To leave its ancestral wolf behind? Can it leave the wolf behind? Is a dog still not susceptible to the call of the wild?

One of the indelible terrors left from childhood is the curled lip and bared teeth of the sudden dog jumping at you or throwing itself against a chain-link fence. The pack of running dogs in an empty lot, the collie nipping at the sheep's trotters, the baying of dogs in the neighborhood setting off one another with their cries and howls, the chasing Doberman, the ferocity of bull terriers, pit bulls, Rottweilers, even a yapping Jack Russell... Our fondness for dog's endearing sweetness may not deny the fear they can also evoke. Like all things under the sun, they, too, are shadowed.

An important alchemical tract[4] depicts a dog and wolf fighting. The scene is by a river, but in this image the chasm is bridged, possibly because there is a recognition, as the text says, that they both "are descended from the same stock ... and full of jealousy, fury, rage and madness."

Full of misery too. Again we find traits of Dame Melancholy in the ancestral wolf. The Norse *Prose Edda* describes a mythic figure, Hel, sister of the wolf Fenrir, as "queen of a far-flung land of weeping and wailing; her courts are exceedingly vast and her portal wide as death. Her palace is called Sleetcold; her platter is Hunger; her knife and fork Famine; Senility her house-slave and Dotage her bondmaid; at the

2 A. Schwarz-Bart, *The Last of the Just*, trans. S. Becker (New York: Atheneum/Macmillan, 1960), 289.

3 J.M. Coetzee, *The Lives of Animals* (Princeton Univ. Press, 1999), 51.

4 N. Barnaud Delphinas, "The Book of Lambspring," in *The Hermetic Museum*, vol. 1 (London: John M. Watkins, 1953).

entering-in, her doorstep is Pitfall; Bedridden is her pallet and Woeful Wan its curtains."[5] That wolf, her brother, could snap the chains of all physical fetters. And he had a ferocious, voracious appetite. Hungry as a wolf, we say. Watch even a small dog rip into its meat; hear a big dog gulp its food, slurp its bowl of water. They wolf down their food.

If the matted hair of the mythical wolf still lies under the dog's silky sheen, then terrible traits still lurk, archetypally, in dog's ancestry. Does the family pet take well to the new baby? Protective or jealous? How far will a dog go when inciting its fury with a tugging game? Watch the hair stand up on the back of its neck; the snarl and growl. Why has training a dog and daily living with it so much to do with submission and mastery? Is it not possible that somewhere in the dog's subliminal habits, the household is reducible to a wolf pack with hierarchy of power? The study of dogs should also include wolves and jackals and the feral dogs that have been betrayed by their human keepers.

Dog carries its ancestors: that is a second message. Wolves, dingoes, jackals; the snarling, howling mad dogs of war and mad dogs of the noonday sun. Nature is packed with ancestors, all of whom have been eating one another through millennia, a never-concluding feast in which we participate daily, sustaining our lives with dead meat. Eating is ancestor commemoration, and consumption; eating is evolution; eating one another is the principal activity of nature's life.

Cynicism

Our dog has even whelped a philosophical school. The hangdog look, banishment from polite society to the doghouse, and a nose-to-the-ground way of living appear in cynicism (from *kuon*, dog in Greek), an asocial, amoral, and anti-intellectual lifestyle stripped of civilized defenses against death.

The Cynics flourished from the early fourth century BCE right through to Rome, and the mainly anecdotal accounts of them emphasize canine qualities. In propounding primitive nature over and against civilized custom, they justified eating the flesh of any animal, even human, professed laziness as a virtue and identified themselves with

---

5 B. Branston, *Gods of the North* (London/New York: Thames & Hudson, 1955), 170.

their physical bodies and their needs. In a dialogue with a Cynic, the interlocutor says, "Your food is what you pick up, as a dog's is; your bed is no better than a dog's."[6] Another says, "My costume consists of a rough hairy skin, long hair, a threadbare cloak, and bare feet."[7]

These bare feet are declared sturdy enough to take the Cynic everywhere freely through city and town, like a vagrant dog in the hurly-burly of the streets and alleys that were the preferable "home" of the Cynic – not the cloistered academic school of the traditional philosopher or the remote cave of the ascetic.

He could boast of being unconstrained by law, by marriage, by care of children, military service – no leashes of any sort, fully autonomous and performing every act (of "nature") unashamedly in public, "both the works of Demeter and those of Aphrodite," (digestive, whether vomit or defecation, and sexual promiscuity). Xenophon[8] has a Cynic say, "If my body ever has sexual needs, I am satisfied with whatever is at hand." Another text, commenting on Oedipus, reports that the Cynic claims there is nothing wrong with incest since it is natural to roosters, asses, and dogs.[9] Cynicism today still refers to the dog for its attitude, as when tough guys supposedly say, "If you can't eat it and can't f... it, then piss on it."

The dog becomes the exemplar of direct, practical, unrepressed natural life, without artificiality, quite literally the "raw" preferred to the "cooked." Nonetheless, the ancient Cynic considered himself "watchdog of mankind to bark at illusion"[10] on the side of humans who are poor, weak, and oppressed. His calling was to this world and this life, not to another world or afterlife.

Here is the third message from our angelic dog. Keep a cynical eye toward idealizations and ideologies, wide-eyed wisdoms, grand illusions and delusions of grandeur, love of romance and romantic love. Follow the ways of nature, nose to the ground, keeping on track.

6 Lovejoy and Boas, *Primitivism and Related Ideas in Antiquity* (above, n. 2), 142.

7 Ibid., 145.

8 *Symposium* 4.40.

9 Lovejoy and Boas, *Primitivism and Related Ideas in Antiquity* (above, n. 2), 135.

10 I. G. Kidd, "Cynics," *The Encyclopedia of Philosophy* (New York: Macmillan, 1967), 285a.

Unclean

The deepest question still lies curled asleep, starved for an answer. Why unclean? Is it only the daily evidence of dogs copulating at length in public, the pack following a bitch in heat, humping the leg of a visitor and snuffling under women's skirts? Is it only their slobbering jowls and rank odor when wet with rain, the fleas they give home to, their excrements tracked on your shoe?

Or is the dog considered unclean merely in contrast with the cat's fastidiousness, or because a dog imports into domesticity the wolf's wildness? Or maybe unclean because the Bible so often says so? After all, the dog and the raven violated Noah's law of continence on the ark, says Jewish legend. Why does Greek folklore place garbage at the crossroads where Hekate rules, she whose companions are dogs?

For a clue, look to the bone. Of course every dog loves a bone and every "good dog" will run and fetch anything bone-like, and gnaw a bone happily all day long. The dog's desire for the bone has commanded an entire industry to produce bone-shaped fakes of pighide, cowhide, plastic, rubber—and we forget the corpse from which all true bones come. From bone to corpse to graveyard. Raven taught dog the art of burial, but dog knows the art of retrieval, digging up what is hidden and buried away and laying the truth at your feet—if only the truth of what is concealed in your carry-on at the arrival terminal.

The one with the finest nose for the dead is the ancestral jackal: "In ancient Egypt, where this animal nightly prowled among the tombs, the god of the dead was Anubis, the jackal, and, this deity … is closely associated with decay and decomposition."[11]

Imagine! A close relative of Anubis asleep at the foot of your bed. The dog's delectation with bones ranges far wider than Egypt. In the Aztec calendar the sign of the tenth day was named "dog" and "regent of this sign is… the god of the dead."[12] This god fed on the hands and feet of human corpses. In Siberia, on the Chukchee peninsula, the inhabitants "give their dead to be eaten by dogs and picture the 'Lord of the Underworld' wearing a dog-skin and riding a sled drawn by

---

11 P. Dale-Green, *Dog* (London: Rupert Hart-Davis, 1966), 85.
12 E. Herzog, *Psyche and Death: Death-Demons in Folklore, Myths, and Modern Dreams*, trans. D. Cox and E. Rolfe (Woodstock, Conn.: Spring Publications, 1983), 47.

strong dogs."[13] Sven Hedin reported from Lhasa (Tibet) that "special dogs are kept, and they destroy the dead bodies with astounding appetite. In many temples the corpse-eating dogs are regarded as holy, and a man acquires merit by allowing his dead body to be eaten by them."[14] From Mongolia, this report: "At the burial place... the corpses are thrown directly to the dogs... Such a place makes a horrifying impression; it is covered with heaps of bones among which packs of dogs, living entirely on human flesh, wander like shadows... The dogs of Urga are so accustomed to this food that they always follow the relatives of the dead as they carry a corpse through the streets of the town."[15]

Perhaps, however, these habits are simply manifestations of the dog's angelic essence, necessary to its calling, a display of its archetypal nature. Dare we speak of a dirty angel?

And a fourth message: Nature is loving bones. Stripped to essentials, the lasting structure and economy of movement. Go toward the marrow, that inmost character as presented in a well-composed obituary, a Haiku, a portrait of an old face, a wintry tree, or a clearly dissected analysis such as done by a forensic pathologist. This, too, is following nature.

A Dirty Angel

It is this association with death, dog as death demon, ravening on death, muzzle deep in the virulent flesh, that I suggest lies at the root of our fear of dogs, our condemnation of them as unclean, and their moping companionship of our loneliness. The death demon may approach via depression (Churchill called his bouts of melancholy "the black dog"), via our fear of their growl and sudden spring or our disgust at the dog's nose for filth.

The dog's association with the underworld and death occurs widely in folklore, in stories of revenants, hauntings and uncanny intuitions, and in the myths of many cultures. Most well-known for our tradition is the twelfth labor of Hercules, his most arduous of all, it was said:

13 Ibid., 44.
14 Ibid.
15 Ibid.

the retrieval of the Hound of Hell, Hades' guardian dog, Cerberus. To wrestle this terrifying creature into daylight means more than overcoming death and hell as in the Christian example of Jesus's descent, which aimed to do away with the underworld and overcome death (1 Cor. 15:55). Hercules' struggle is also about the dog.

The Greek myth repeats the motif of the dog crossing over a chasm. This one between death and life, the dog furiously resisting leaving his hellish aspect. Cerberus is also, of course, Hercules' "own" dog, the death-loving propensity in even "the greatest of all humans" and in every human. Unlike the other monsters with which he had to deal, Hercules did not slay Cerberus. Hence bringing the dog to heel was the last major task, if Hercules was to be the founder of so many Greek cults and cities, as well as culture hero, healer, and personal savior.

The ghost of Cerberus in every dog provides its archetypal urge to guard and protect. A Jewish legend says that the dog barks when the angel of death approaches, and a dog warned blind old Isaac by barking that the food his son Esau had prepared for him was unclean dog meat. The animal that brings death knows when death is near and can protect from it. Even its excrements are protective. They "are used in tanning the hides from which the Torah scrolls are made, as well as the Mezuzot and the phylacteries."[16]

This twofold potential shows in Anubis, who, as jackal, desecrated the body and as embalmer preserved it. Likewise the dog, sacred to Asklepius, the healer who worked the line between life and death. In his temples of healing, to see or be touched in a dream by a dog was to be healed. The dog was the god in animal form.

The distinction so decisive in our culture between life and death, this world and another world, between clean and unclean is supervened by Anubis and Asklepius. If the dog is necessary to healing and preservation of the soul, then the unclean belongs with the clean; rot and despair are necessary to preserving the soul. Yes, the angel is dirty. Hence "dog" in some Arabic alchemy is a code word for the spirit hidden in matter.[17] The way down is the way up. That persistence,

---

16 L. Ginzberg: *The Legends of the Jews*, vol. 3: *Moses in the Wilderness* (Baltimore and London: The Johns Hopkins Univ. Press, 1998), 6.

17 Muhammad Ibn Umail, *Book of the Explanations of the Symbols* (*Kitāb Ḥall ar-Rumūz*), trans. S. Fuad and T. Abt (Zurich: Living Human Heritage, 2003), 149–50.

nose to the ground, relishing the offal of decay, the fever and fret of the rutting male, the bitch in heat, the unwavering melancholy stare, constellate the healers. The dog's obsessive scratching opens the door. Uncleanliness is next to godliness.

Nature is also *thanatos*, bringer of death. That is a fifth message from the dog. If nature loves to hide, the hidden is entropy, that slow and steady metamorphosis of dust to dust. To our human attempts to prolong life, to discover the genetics of aging, the dog says: preservation of life depends on the dirty angel, the angel with a love for earth. "Get down!"

So, finally, when we walk our dog for our health or for its, when we make sure it gets its shots on schedule, wears its flea collar, when we groom it for "best in show," when it travels with us on family outings, or rides mascot in the pickup, we are engaged in apotropaic defenses against the death demon. A dog's companionship holds off our madness; our faithfulness, his. For it is the owner's commitment to staying alive—that Herculean task in all things human—that develops in the dog its latent virtues, and also may account for why that primordial dog leapt the chasm. Those virtues—loyalty, bravery, command, and a certain sweet affection that radiates from your dog are as much potentials in the owner's character as in the dog's. A mutuality of natures. The dog becomes *familiaris* (the old word for household soul carrier) because owner and animal are familiar in soul, angel to angel, each knowing how deep the soul can delve, how dark the passage.

10

Human Being as Animal Being
A Correspondence with John Stockwell

John Stockwell: You speak now of "ensouling the world." How does this relate to concerns that people have about the destruction of nature and the extinction of species, about cruelty to animals and killing them?

James Hillman: According to prevailing Western (or Northern) consciousness, the world is merely matter, not alive, and without soul. What difference does it make what we do with everything that is not human—it is already dead. Strip-mining is good, according to this view, because it helps humans in whom the soul is exclusively located. You can see that the idea of *anima mundi*, as the soul in the world, upsets this prevailing attitude. Cosmology has to change if you want to liberate animals from their Western predicament. And the first step in changing cosmology is returning the soul to the world, thereby releasing soul from entrapment in human subjectivism.

JS: What has polytheistic consciousness to do with this? Is there some relationship to a possible way of life that would retain room for the variety of species to survive?

JH: Support for variety is not the crucial aspect of polytheistic consciousness. After all, Noah's ark also supported variety. More significant in this consciousness is that wherever you look into polytheistic religions—Egypt, Eskimo, India, Mesopotamia, tribal societies—you find that animals are divinities. Anything one does with them must be with their accord, else one is alienated from them (as we are). Polytheistic consciousness implies religious respect for animals—*all* animals.

JS: A bioregionalist is a person who seeks to base his/her living upon the characteristics of the natural place, attempting to live *here* in *this* place, situated within a watershed, and that within a bioregion defined by its specific mix of fauna and flora and, often physiographically. A reinhabitant is even more concrete in this practice.

When I read several of your essays on city life, taken from talks given for the Dallas Institute of Humanities and Culture and the Center for Civic Leadership in Dallas, I found in them much about which a bioregionalist or reinhabitant would be enthusiastic. It can be seen that if it were possible to take an attitude toward the urban environment that would tend to ensoul, and then *actually* ensoul those objects – the freeways and towers, and so on – then a fundamental transformation of our attitude would be accomplished. It would be a transformation that would play back beneficially into our relationship with nature and other species. I wonder, however, whether to suggest this project does not, in fact, lend additional status to certain of the main sources of the destruction of nature, namely those freeways and towers, with the result that the immense pressure they exert upon natural place is ratified rather than resisted and relieved. So much additional construction of towers going forward while we undertake the immense task of ensouling the massive constructed world might be thought to continue to entail concomitant destruction of nature. Would it not be better to resist such construction and, if possible, bring down much that has been constructed, and in cities to approach the ensouling of the world in relation to visions of the city at a more human scale?

JH: While I am in sympathy with both bioregionalism and reinhabitation as you have described them, we have to face a very simple fact: contemporary consciousness is thoroughly urbanized and technologized. Nature is no longer adequately imagined as the Great Mother who sustains us; instead, she has become a very fragile, endangered old lady, a senile case who has to be protected and preserved. The twentieth century seems to have ended the rule of Nature and replaced it with the rule of Technology. So, the issue today is double: both maintaining what we can of nature and extending the soul into technology. Here I follow my friends Robert Sardello and Wolfgang Giegerich, who are attempting to revision the urban and the technological in terms of the incarnation, the word becoming flesh, the flesh of the material world, actual things – from ashtrays and flush toilets to nuclear bombs. As long as the sacred and the soulful are exclusively and sentimentally limited to natural things, then all other things like freeways and towers, become Satanic or soulless. This division will kill us; it is the old Christian division between the realm of Christ and that of Caesar. Every effort has to be made to face the realm of Caesar, the cities, and to rethink them in terms of the *anima mundi*, which encompasses all things, constructed and natural. Once we can see with an animated eye and read buildings for their psychic import, and trust our eyes, we will not have such extreme opposition between urban and rural. It is not that freeways and towers as such are wrong but the arrogance, paranoia, and speed they embody. They merely concretize and exhibit massively those qualities of soul that appear as well in human beings and in natural objects. We need desperately not to harden the lines of confrontation between advocates—developers and conservers—but, rather, to soften the frontiers in our thinking about where the soul is located. Until we recognize soul in man-made things, and not only in snail darters and whooping cranes, we condemn freeways and towers into being forever monsters without souls. Of course, they cannot help but have a deleterious effect on their environment and will continue to be erected as Satanic demonstrations.

JS: In several of your books you have characterized the turn to the East, the return to the land, the return to the primitive, and the turn to animals as wrongly chosen directions. You say that these ways fail to recognize that which is most alive and resourceful in our Western consciousness, namely, the archetypes/divine persons of first the Greek experience and then other Western experiences still alive in our own. You add that in turning toward animals, there is a risk of barbaric animality. As I understand what you are saying, it is because the absence of imagination, of images, psyche, the imaginal—the failure to give their due to the divine persons who *are* alive in our experience as Western people—is connected with the harm that is visited upon nature. We are like Ajax slaying animals *because* we are not sufficiently imaginal.

Our idea, however, as advocates for animals, is to turn toward the animal through caring, through appreciation, through respect and reverence for other living species, even through a recognition of our shared identity with other species. We turn toward animals as toward others having rights. We turn as humans do to one another, in the common community. We also turn as shapeshifters, exploring empathetically and imaginatively, and then ethically, this larger sense of kind. We *return* to animals, seeking to critique our present in terms of what we once were and, hopefully, will continue to be, even more so.

Will you comment?

JH: When I made those remarks against returning to animality, I meant only one thing: our becoming nonverbal, grunting goofs—"Animal House." I was using the term "animality" in the usual, insulting sense: dumb, brute, wild. I was addressing that style of simplistic therapy that has given up on language as expression of soul and calls crawling and screaming "reconnection with the animal body." When patients are urged to wriggle like a snake or hug like a bear, they are encouraged to be as ugly and violent as only humans can be. These therapies do not notice the beauty of actual animals and that reconnecting to the animal means getting to a more sensitive, more artful, and humorous place in the psyche. Thus, these therapies I was condemning in the name of finding the animal soul actually re-enact our Western tradition's contempt.

Besides, giving up on language betrays our own human nature. I think that the human form of display, in the ethologist's sense of "display," is *rhetoric.* Our ability to sing, speak, tell tales, recite, and orate is essential to our lovemaking, boasting, fear-inspiring, territory-protecting, surrendering, and offspring-guarding behaviors. Giraffes and tigers have splendid coats; we have splendid speech. Returning to animality, in your sense of "animal," I therefore heartily endorse, as you know, for instance, from my recent seminars with Gary Snyder, Gioia Timpanelli, and Robert Bly, and also from my lectures on the subject going back to the sixties, all of which have been aimed at evoking the animal as psychic presence. I have been trying to foster self-recognition of *human being as animal being.*

JS: Bioregionalists and reinhabitants have noticed that indigenous peoples, who resided in their natural region usually for a long time, had become shaped by their place into people whose relationships with the natural world were respectful and more reciprocal than we find ours to be. Immigrants, most of us, by contrast, were shaped physiographically elsewhere than where we now are. Our escalating assault on nature derives from our being transients, from our being in a place we do not recognize, and from the compensative efforts we make to live as if we were in that other place we came from. We modify the geography we do not recognize, try to shape it like the old, or simply root it up or pave it over, so that at least we can fantasize the old defensively against the earth voices of a place unfamiliar to us. Re-inhabitants seek instead to recognize place as *this* place, with its spe-cific character; they seek to live here. The animals, plants, rocks, and waters of this place are specific. Considering now San Francisco Bay, the life of indigenous people in this place, under its influence, shaped by it, gave rise to divine persons, Kuksu and possibly Coyote among them, who are exquisitely appropriate to nature and the potentiali-ties of human life here. Attempting to approach these local figures through the imitation or even enactment of the rituals of peoples for whom these figures were alive, is one way of tuning in to the actual nature of this place, of learning to see, even to see *through* the pave-ment. They are figures of regulation, offering the suggestion of limits within which to live.

Acquaintance with these local persons is held by reinhabitants to be a highly important factor in contending with those forces that are destroying this place. The recommendation to turn away from the attempt to become acquainted with these figures appears to recom-mend giving up this means of finding out where we are. Ajax, slayer of animals, mistook the scene. Hercules does not appropriately relate to where he arrives, in the Underworld. It would be held that Dionysus, for example, is disoriented in Shasta (Northern California), though perhaps less so than Ajax, and offers not much contact with the ac-tual place. By knowing him one rather knows Greece, which is just the trouble, for the Greeks and other figures of the immigrant tradi-tions are perhaps present as pioneers and forty-niners too, even if we can agree that the eternal nature of a god does not permit him to be other than his character, though it be changeable, indicates, no matter where he is.

By attending to the persons of Western consciousness, it would seem, what one gets are visions of the City on the Hill (San Francisco) or the Athens of the West (Berkeley). But are these notions sufficiently ecological to remain humane? At the very least, the persons of our Western imagination would seem to be well advised to themselves be-come reinhabitants through acquaintance with the ancient figures of this place. Being precise in their mythic structures, however, can they be so polytheistic?

JH: "To see through the pavement"—what a lovely metaphor! Who could be against it? Yet I hear the voice of Gaia in your question. You see, from the perspective of an archetypal psychology, every position presents the voice of a "god," an imaginative trope that governs the viewpoint. The emphasis on geography and physiography, on earth, plants, rocks, etc., seems to bespeak the perspective of Gaia (who today is tending to replace old Yahweh with a new and fanatical monotheistic consciousness). The danger of this perspective—which is, nonetheless, very appealing—is that it, too, becomes a literalism; i.e., Dionysus has meaning only in Greece, whereas if you live in the Pacific Northwest, you must see through the literal pavement into the literal Native American myths and styles, for they once literally inhabited that soil. Reinhabiting could become a kind of *imitatio Christi* transferred to an imitation of pre-white culture.

I do not want to offend you, or Gaia, or the Native Americans of the Pacific Northwest, or those who follow the path of reinhabitation. Yet, psychologically, wherever we move, we immigrants, we sons and daughters of Europe, mainly, speaking English with its roots in Northern Europe and Latin and Greek, with our civilization's customs, dogmas, and laws, and our Bible, we see through the pavement only according to our own tradition. Our eyeballs and ears were made in Palestine and Athens, in Rome, Florence, and London—even if we study Zen, change our name into Sanskrit, or chant Native American songs. Because of our background, we can never hear the rocks speak without the distortions we bring with our hearing, in our unconscious baggage. My task has been to unpack the immigrants' trunks, to insist that the settlers look at what they are transporting with them from Palestine and Rome in their attitudes in which lies history. Dionysus and Gaia, and especially Christianity, continue to affect what we Americans do and say. Anyway, even if I am all wrong, doesn't it take centuries for a settler to hear the earth of a place, to become soil-soaked?

JS: In your essay, "The Animal Kingdom in the Human Dream," you write, movingly:

> We know the record of extermination. The animal kingdom, from the caveman through Darwin on the Galapagos and Melville on the whaler, is no more. Insecticides lie on the leaves. In the green

hills of Africa the bull elephants are brought to their knees for their tusks. *We long for an ecological restoration of the kingdom that is impossible* [emphasis added].[1]

Please elaborate. Is the protection of nature a lost cause? But we and nature live on in dream and imagination?

JH: The protection of nature is noble; it isn't a lost cause. It is an act of devotion to Gaia, let us say—and also to Dionysus, who was called *zoe* (life). However, whether nature, in the Romantic sense of Wordsworth and Rousseau and the Hudson River school of painting, can continue—that I surely do not know. I do think that "nature" is already pretty well gone, except in our sentimental nostalgia. "Nature" seems to be under a two-pronged attack. We can distinguish between the attack on actual soil and wetlands, actual species and forests, and the attack on the Romantic idea of nature as locus of Beauty, as God's veil, or as a nourishing Mother. I think we can protect plants and soil without having to subscribe to the Romantic idealization of nature. And I think we can protect plants and soil without being moralistic—our Duty, their Rights, our Guilt over ancient abuses... Reasons for this protective work? I can suggest three:

a) it is a devotion

b) it is practical common sense to maintain the eon-old biosphere

c) it extends the idea of soul, and the experience of animation, from our subjective personalism so that the individual human is less isolated and sick.

Of course, protecting plants and soil is also probably good for the plants and the soil—but I am confining myself to reasons why self-centered Western humans might support this protective work.

JS: In that same essay ("The Animal Kingdom in the Human Dream") you write of an "aesthetic and ecological perception" visited by events constituting a "momentary restoration of Eden," and that for "that short eternal while" there is "an original co-presence of human and animal."[2] How do you see the image of the Peaceable Kingdom? To which divine person or persons does this image belong?

JH: Could you move the "Peaceable Kingdom" from a utopian ideal, from becoming a project (which requires "execution" and must be

---

1 Above, 55.

2 Above, 32.

achieved by will power) to a psychological experience readily available? The phrase you quote bespeaks an experience anyone can have when playing with a cat, when close to a horse's breathing, when hearing a bird call. An extraordinary chord of communion that, I believe, must also be sensed by the animal, maybe even the bird. The temporary infatuation with the new animal pioneers (Jane Goodall, the Kalahari couple, and the observers of elephants, tigers, wolves, etc.) invites anyone to that psychological experience of the Peaceable Kingdom. It occurs most frequently, however, right at home, in bed, dreaming. And I believe, too, that this sort of experience gives us a very ancient sense of the animal as a divinity.

JS: How do you view the activity and thinking of the animal rights/liberation movement? Could you recommend directions the movement might profitably take?

JH: I must decline saying anything specific about the animal rights movement because I don't know enough. I'm generally leery of programs and movements wherever they tend to obscure psychological insight. (Christianity is a good example of an excellent program that results in psychological unconsciousness regarding the program's own shadow.) However, the idea of Rights is too Lockean, too secular and legalistic. It seems like another anthropomorphism—imagining animals as underprivileged people who must be included in the social contract. Perhaps they want to be; I just don't know. Does anyone? However, if the cosmology shifts and we imagine them ensouled, if our perception shifts and we see their beauty, if our humanism shifts and we recognize our own inflation, then the dignity that rights would grant to animals would already have been restored. I prefer to go at this issue, not by extending our humanistic constitutional rights but by re-visioning secular humanism itself.

JS: If you were asking yourself questions about our relationship with animals, what question would you consider was the most important? What answers would you initially propose?

JH: My answer will probably surprise you, and even disappoint you. Most important is bettering the human-animal relation in dreams. Everything comes to a head there: our derogatory Cartesian Christianity, our meat addiction, our insecticides; all our alienation from animals and arrogance toward them show up nightly in dreams where animals are feared, attacked, eradicated—so that the ego can awaken in the morning as a self-centered hero ready to enter the campaign of its daily business. Hercules, slayer of animals. I have found people with the strongest sympathy toward animal causes who still act as animal terrorists in their dreams. A change in consciousness may also begin in dream, when the dreamer allows the fierce black dog to approach or the snake's fang to pierce his or her skin. A great emotion is released, a transformative recognition, upon dreaming of a skinned pony, a drowned bird, a fish lying belly up. When these images are taken deeply to heart—as something going on right inside my own psyche, my soul—the rest follows. I haven't even mentioned the marvelous dream animals that come to teach the dream ego, or save it, or impress it with beauty and power.

11

Animal Presence
A Conversation with Jonathan White

Jonathan White: Let's start with where we are. What influence does this boat[1] and these waters have on the contents of your seminar, "Come into Animal Presence"?

James Hillman: Well, the first thing I feel is that this boat doesn't disturb the world it's in. I don't know if that's because it's old or funky or wood or what. But there's no slickness to it. And because it doesn't disturb the world it's in, it makes the feeling right. Getting the feeling right is very important in the primitive world, the wilderness world, or what I would rather call the world of tribal people. Tribal people spend an immense amount of time making sure the feeling is right, either by sweats, rituals, dances, or feasts. There are anthropological studies that say tribal people spend about thirty percent of their time doing what we would call working and the rest of the time preparing and performing rituals, dances, and ceremonies. Why do they do that? They do that so their feeling is in right relation with the world they're in. And we do none of that, we don't even think about it. So, this boat provides the right contact for the feeling. That's the first thing.

JW: I often think of the spring maintenance on the *Crusader* as a form of ritual. It's a tremendous effort to keep an old wooden boat in good shape, but that's only a small part of the whole project.

JH: No, it isn't a small part of it, and that's the point. It's not the talk, and it's not the people, because you can have talk and people anywhere. In our culture we forget the importance of place. You go somewhere to hear a talk on the Greek gods and goddesses and you find out it's in the basement of a church with fluorescent lights, hideous folding

---

1 This conversation took place aboard the schooner *Crusader* in Chatham Strait, Alaska.

chairs, and no windows. The place is absolutely ruinous, and you're supposed to talk about individuation or beauty or something.

I've talked about animal images in dreams for thirty years, and given seminars in many, many places, and this is the only place where it's really appropriate. Because the animals are right here. You have to be careful you don't say something stupid because the animals are listening. You can't interpret them; you can't symbolize them; you can't do something that is only human about them. Their presence is felt.

If the boat is ignored, or just treated as a vehicle to get you here, the whole relation wouldn't work. How do we know that the whales, coming as close to the boat as they did on this trip, don't also appreciate it? How do we know that? We don't know that. The main thing is, we don't know any of that—how they perceive us, how they pick up our vibes. We know their sensitivities are extraordinary, that their hearing and communication methods are physiologically beyond ours in many ways. So how do we know they don't pick up the boat as well, and that your attention to the boat is not just keeping it in ship-shape and comfortable but something else.

JW: As we prepare the boat for the season, we do it with much of the memory of the things that happen out here each summer. There's a sense in which the adventures of every season are always present. The atmosphere seems to contain them.

JH: Suppose that, instead of the word *atmosphere,* we used the word *soul?* Suppose this boat has soul—the way people used to say, "This boat really has soul," or, "That old woman, she's got soul," or the way blacks use the word for *soul brother, soul food, soul music.* So this boat, it's a *soul boat.* I think that if the seminar participants and teachers who come on board bring their souls, it adds soul to the boat. You don't want religion, or "new age," or something that's going to make it... well, you don't want to lose the animals.

JW: I'd like to hear you talk more about the whole idea of preparation, of getting the feeling right.

JH: Getting the feeling right in relation to animals, let's talk about that. In order to go about a hunt, or to fish, or to bring the quail closer, you learn the quail songs or the buffalo songs so you can draw them in. You need those songs in order to be successful in the hunt and to feed yourself, your tribe, and your community. The hunters had to get their feeling right, or the quail and the buffalo wouldn't come; they wouldn't allow themselves to be hunted. When you're preparing the boat for a trip, you are also getting your feeling right, which is different from management.

Management is information: making sure the connections are right, that you've got everybody's addresses right, and the tickets, and the fuel. All of that is the management of a successful thing. But if you're sitting, looking out, thinking about the portholes or the lines, or you're walking through town and you see something that would go wonderfully on the boat, like a brass fitting or whatever, then your soul's engaged. It's like a writer who gets a thought and, wherever he or she is, puts it down in a notebook. Or painters who see something that moves their vision, and when they begin to paint, it comes into the painting. I think that's what must happen if your mind is meditatively on the boat. The boat becomes a vehicle for soul, like a book for a writer's soul or a canvas for a painter's soul. And that's tremendously important. It makes the whole activity more of a ritual. And then you're also not fighting the boat, "Oh, this thing, I've gotta fix that, oh I don't want to ..." You couldn't write a book that way; you couldn't paint a painting that way. You work fourteen hours a day, but it's because your soul's in it.

JW: In *Trail to Heaven*,[2] Robin Riddington writes about how the Dunne-za or Beaver Indians, a tribe from northeastern British Columbia, hunt. Part of their preparation is to wait for a dream, and, when it comes, the dream instructs them on how to proceed. The actual event of finding and killing the animal is understood as a re-enactment of the dream. So, when the hunter returns to the village to tell the story, it's the dream he tells.

JH: That's the whole difference between soul and management. If you were thinking about management, you would come back from this trip and say, "Well, that was a successful trip, nothing went wrong. We had one little problem with the toilet, but it all worked pretty well, and everyone was happy and they wrote a little note saying they were." It was a clean job: management. Close the book. But the dream would be something else.

---

2 R. Riddington, *Trail to Heaven: Knowledge and Narrative in a Northern Native Community* (Iowa City: Univ. of Iowa Press, 1988).

And the dream has an echo that goes on in memory, in resonance, and in other souls. The best thing that could happen from this trip, for me, would be that the animals benefit. Not only that the people benefit, that the ten people all learn something, fine, they can learn something. But if something happened in the soul of these people that can reach the animals, that would be the best thing of all, because these animals have done so much for us for thousands of years. They've brought us food, they've brought us dances, they've brought us wisdom, they've brought us technical skills. Who taught us to make a halibut hook? See, this is the way people think, "Oh boy, some smart guy named Joe Jones, he invented the hook so that we could catch halibut more quickly this way than that way. What a good idea." So we call it the Joe Jones hook.

But originally the people who lived with halibut and whose life depended on them watched the halibut, and it taught them how to make the hook. So we owe the halibut for the instrument to catch it. And we owe the deer for the way to hunt it—walking stealthily, walking downwind. They taught us all those things. We owe them so much.

From the dreams we've been working with on this boat I've tried to point out again and again that the animals come in our dreams as guides, helpers, and saviors; as teachers, again. We still are inflated to think we're saving them, but they may be teaching us about saving. What happens to our hearts when we see them wounded or hurt? That's a turning point, when the animal is hurt. They teach us something through their woundedness; that they're threatened and endangered and wounded. They're beginning to convert the world! The animal rights movement and the efforts to save endangered species have all sprung up in the last thirty years, but they've changed our consciousness enormously. The images of dead elephants, whales, seals, and birds affect us deeply. The spotted owl is saving the forest. Take it as a myth, don't take it as a law.

JW: Most psychologists tell us that when animals come into our dreams, they come as representations of some aspect of ourselves. But you're saying they come into our dreams for their own sake—to teach us something.

JH: Yes, they teach us something, but they're not part of us. They correspond with part of us. The bear dream that one man had corresponds with his own earthy, shaggy nature, and therefore he can feel an affinity. But that bear is not his own shaggy nature. That reduces the bear to just a piece of himself and insults the bear—it interprets the bear away. The presence of the bear in the dream corresponds with qualities of the human soul but is not reducible to it.

JW: How do you know when an animal is in your dream to teach you something on its own account or when it has appeared because its qualities correspond to something in your soul?

JH: I think they go together. I wouldn't want to make it an either/or. I would rather say the animal in the dream is a presence that corresponds with some interiority of your own self—your own wolf, for instance, or your relation to Wolf, whether it's insatiable appetite, or constantly tracking and pursuing, loneliness, or pack intelligence. And at the same time it's a presentation of the divine wolf, the wolf god, the wolf totem, the wolf ancestor, who may be bringing you to more intensity in regard to those qualities.

So the question is: What does the wolf want? Why did it bother to come to me? Is it trying to remind me of my own wolfishness? If the animal is an ancestor, then it's going to bless those qualities. It's going to give them an archetypal background. My loneliness, my constant trekking and feeling an outsider, is blessed by the wolf's appearance. That's a nice thought.

Or take the fox. My cleverness, my sneakiness, and my trying to raid everything that happens and getting into all the chicken coops—instead of saying, "This is my psychopathic shadow, this is my sex complex," the fox comes and says, "This is part of nature, this is where we connect." Then you have more respect for that part of yourself and you begin to try to live it right.

JW: By acknowledging the animal's presence on its own account, we are saying that the unconscious is not just a private place where everything that happens is ultimately about our own ego. The animal demands our respect and attention, and I imagine this way of looking at it is part of what it means to "get the feeling right" in relation to the world around you.

JH: "Morality," "being right," and having the "true" sense of things—those words that are moral words in our world—come out of religious texts or from priests. In the tribal world, those words come out of the behavior of animals. In that world, you're not going to be able to eat if you don't do it right. Morality is like a craftsman's morality. You have to have a "true" line or a "right" angle. Those words, *true* and *right*, are craft words, skill words.

JW: You've talked about animal presences in dreams, but what about actual encounters in the wild? For instance, over this last week we've been with whales, bears, salmon...

JH: Eagles, seals, orcas. My goodness, it's remarkable how many animals we've seen on this trip, and how close we've come to them!

JW: And porpoises playing off the bow! Nobody really knows why they do that, but they sure look like they're having fun.

JH: Yes. What I tried to say yesterday had to do with corresponding emotions. If we feel moved by the porpoise leaping and playing on the bow, as we all did, then our emotion is corresponding to the animal. Do you remember how everyone on board was imitating the movements of the porpoise—jumping up and down, laughing, being playful? Those emotions tell us the truth about something. When we're afraid, emotions give us significant information about fear or desire or anger or insult. Your emotion is corresponding to the act, the external world. That's called the significance theory of emotion. Your emotion is telling you about the significance of something. You look at a big dark forest and you feel melancholy. It's telling you something about the gestalt there.

So why not imagine that there's a correspondence between the joy we're feeling and what the porpoise is feeling? When you hear the whales blow or see them leap and turn over slowly, you get this heartfelt beauty and sadness and wonder. Why couldn't that correspond to something the whales feel about themselves? That they, too, are depleted; their environment is noisy; they can't communicate as they used to; and they're not appreciated. Who knows what goes on in the whale's soul? But why not read it through our own feeling? You see those eagles, you have a certain feeling of awe and terror—you don't feel warmth in your heart.

JW: No, it's more like respect.

JH: Respect, right. Amazement when they're flying up high, and respect. So why not read those emotions the way tribal people did? We would call that anthropomorphism; we use that term way too much.

The reverence that people feel, the excitement when they see the actual animal, is much more powerful than the talk or the dream or the poem, usually, because it's so unfamiliar to most of us. It's synergistic. It brings together the two, the word and the physical thing.

JW: Last night we were talking about some of the physical and spiritual challenges imposed by the need to kill in order to live. It's interesting to consider that the spiritual challenge of killing can be so intense for a culture that it can outweigh many of its other material concerns. Some ethnologists suggest that the spiritual problem of killing and eating large animals in the Far North may pose a more difficult problem than dealing with the extreme cold.

JH: The Inuit people told Rasmussen that the tragedy of their life was that they were always eating other souls.

JW: Richard Nelson and Paul Shepard, among others, suggest there may be no better way to feel our connectedness to nature than to kill our own food. Although Ursula Le Guin acknowledges the necessity of killing, she says hunting is something we should outgrow. She believes she can get the same sense of connectedness by watching a sparrow fly or an old cat walk across the room. Is there something unique that we gain, and that we can't get any other way, from killing an animal?

JH: We need to be very careful, very reserved talking about killing. Our American civilization rests upon killing—animals, trees, Native Americans, Africans, Mexicans, and of course directly or indirectly people and life all over the globe. I think Le Guin is right about her cat, but she may be avoiding the issue of killing. Shepard and Nelson are saying that to eat, we kill. It's better to recognize this fact concretely than to deny it with supermarket-packaged meat. Nature eats nature, and we are no exception, so let us have rituals that remind us. Hunters like Nelson and Shepard are asking us to restore the sacramental feeling to the necessary killing that sustains life. And not only killing animals: carrots, wheat, cherries from the tree, are all killed that we may eat them. Maybe, if we were more ritualistic, more directly concrete about the killing that goes into daily eating, we might be less extravagantly mad in those other killings—the twenty thousand murders an adolescent will have watched on television; the Vietnam, Iraq, and Panama bombings; and so on. There is a horror with bloodletting, and only the most serious and communal rituals can encompass this horror—like what goes on in surgery or when an animal is slaughtered and dressed for winter eating.

Practically, I don't see how we can even begin to kill, each of us, the food we need to eat daily. But we can stop for a moment when buying food, preparing food, and eating food to thank the Lord. But the Lord is not an abstraction in Heaven; the Lord we need to thank is the animal itself—a little belatedly of course—who is giving itself to our delight. Sometimes I think, I've eaten tons of meat by now. I owe the animals one helluva debt. When and how will they ask me to pay up?

JW: Are there other ways to approach this inevitable death and killing?

JH: Well, I think we can be closer to the killing of animals.

JW: What do you mean by that?

JH: We put our pets away, or put our sick horses down, and nobody sees it or knows anything about it. We don't bury our animals, we don't hold them dead in our arms. We know nothing about butchering or slaughtering any longer. We see road kills, but that's about it. The wounded, dead animal evokes a tremendous feeling.

What else can we do? We can take trips on the *Crusader*. We can move to places where one is with the animal and watch it. We can be much less involved with pesticides and insecticides and allow ourselves to get in quandaries about things like that.

For example, I have chickens, and raccoons come in night after night and steal the chickens. In the springtime, raccoons feed their young. This is the time when they need the chickens. But I don't want them to take *my* chickens. So I'm caught in a quandary. What do I do? That, magnified, is exactly what the Masai or the tribes of northern Kenya feel. They want to keep the wild animals away from where they're grazing their cattle. It's the same problem worldwide: what is the relation between my territory and theirs? What do I do, slaughter a chicken once a week and throw it out where the raccoons will get it. Or do I start feeding the raccoons, which would then set up a whole other system of them going into the garbage?

This is a neighborhood problem because it involves alley cats and street dogs as well as humans. It's an important problem because it gets us all thinking about these issues of living together. I don't have an answer—think locally and feel globally, or whatever they say.

And it means the loss of the human's position. We have to give up more territory. If I want to keep raccoons in the world, I have to give up something. So when I left, I closed my chicken house. I give my chickens away to the guy I got them from. It wasn't right to let them get slaughtered, either. So I gave up my territory. I don't think that's the only solution, but you have to come to some terms.

When I said people should take trips on the *Crusader*, I mean people should have more direct contact and thereby feel the wonder, which is the beginning of the feeling of religion. Swedish ethnologists have said that religion began with the circumpolar people's experience with bears. That was the first feeling of religion and the beginning of doing things to propitiate the animals—to dance, to sing, to worship, to think about the bear.

We're usually taught that religion begins with burial, with death and wonder about the afterlife. But my theory is that religion grew out of the human relationship to the animal. That keeps you earthed, rather than thinking about the afterlife and beyond. I think that's a very important thought.

JW: In *Pan and the Nightmare* you describe how Pan, the goat god of nature, died with the rise of monotheism: "What had soul, lost it; lost was the psychic connection with nature...When Pan is alive, then nature is too, and it is filled with gods, so that the owl's hoot is Athene and the mollusc on the shore is Aphrodite... how better to participate in them than through their concrete natural presentations?"[3] Later you say that to restore our relationship to nature, both "in here" and "out there," we must start in part from Pan's point of view. "But," you say, "Pan's world includes masturbation, rape, panic, convulsions, and nightmares. The re-education of the citizen in relation to nature means nothing less than a new relationship with the 'horrors,' 'moral depravations,' and 'madnesses' which are part of the instinctual life of the citizen's soul."[4] Isn't this proposal in direct opposition to everything our modern culture prides itself on? How would one go about this process, and where would we find support for such a reeducation?

JH: You bet those remarks in my book on Pan oppose "modern culture." Psychoanalysis from its inception opposes modern culture.

---

3 J. Hillman, *Pan and the Nightmare* (Putnam, Conn.: Spring Publications, 2007), 26.

4 Ibid., 80.

Analysis is subversive. It's mainly on the side of what Freud called the *id*—at least as I understand it. This is because an analysis starts with psycho-pathology. It says, come along with me and explore Hell—the horrors, peculiarities, and cruelties that exist in your nature and all nature. You see, remembering Pan means remembering that nature is wild, hairy, savage, frightening—a nightmare. Pan was, after all, the god of nightmares. As children of nature we are each children of Pan. We are already creating Hell in our civic life, in our foreign policies. So the task is to find rituals and times and places and mentors who can give to wildness its due rather than have wildness take us over and turn us into adolescent savages, as in William Golding's *Lord of the Flies.*

JW: In *News of the Universe,*[5] Robert Bly says that each time a human being's desire-energy leaves the body and goes out into the hills or forest, it whispers as it leaves, "You know, one day you will die." Bly says we need this whisper in order to be grounded. Is this the reality of seeking a relationship with nature? Is this part of the danger and the fear, that ultimately we are facing our own mortality in the act?

JH: That's a very deep thought from Bly. I think he's right on. Alone in a field or at the seashore we do feel closer to the natural boundaries set by death. We feel closer to the mystery of life and death than when actually at risk crossing the street or riding in a fast car, when death may be literally just around the corner. Then we feel fear and panic but not mystery. So we go to nature, the field, the seashore, or these Alaskan waters to feel more alive by feeling the death that nature insists we not forget. Nature seems to want us to remember death. Is that why it's so hard to get out of the house, out of the car, off the boat? I may be "dying to get out of the house," but, in fact, getting out of the daily routine brings you face to face with the whisper Bly hears.

JW: How do we gain access to these natural boundaries if we live in the city?

JH: Some people are doing it by watching animal movies. There's a tremendous amount more of that on television now than there was when I was a kid, or even thirty years ago. You can also get access to those feelings by engaging in the life and death of your pet, as I

5 R. Bly, ed., *News of the Universe: Poems of Twofold Consciousness* (San Francisco: Sierra Club Books, 1980), 281.

said earlier. Or leaving the city for periods of time. But I don't have a real solution.

JW: It's tricky, I think. Although I'm up here five months of the year, it's not my home. There's a sense in which I feel like a guest.

JH: Yet it is your neighborhood.

JW: Yes.

JH: I don't know why you have to give up either of those positions. Maybe the feeling of being a guest is an important one in the world. Suppose we're all guests. In his biography, George Santayana gave a tribute, or a memoir: "To my host, the world." He was a guest in the world. You treat everything with great respect if you're a guest.

JW: It has always struck me as odd that our culture fosters such extreme positions in regard to the environment. On one hand, we have the greatest leaders in conservation and the most devoted protectors of wildlife in the world and, on the other hand, we're the most consumptive and ecologically destructive. What do you think accounts for these two extremes?

JH: These two positions seem diametrically contradictory, but they stem from the same psychological ground. Neither group feels it is nature. The first group is the good shepherds, the caretakers, basically moralists, and moralists are always above what they are judging. The second group is the conquerors, Promethean and Herculean in their ability to overcome nature. But both groups stand apart, forever doing something *to* or *for* or *with* nature. If you feel yourself to be nature, no different from it, then you simply are like a tree or a squirrel in the tree, and you move along without an attitude of one kind or another. Of course, this is a very romantic view, but why not? It's no more mad than the two ways you just described in your question.

12

Let the Creatures Be
A Conversation with Thomas Moore

James Hillman: People have animals in their lives, that's the first thing. These are either animals they live with – dogs, fish, a bird in a cage – or they are animals they remember – images from their childhood, fantasies, animals they saw in the zoo, or crushed on the road. The question for a psychologist is, why are these animals so important?

Thomas Moore: And it seems people are fascinated, too, by films and books about animals.

JH: True. Look at cats: something like six of the ten current bestsellers are about cats. What's going on? Plus *The Black Stallion*, and *Bambi*, and all the Disney animals. And what are animals doing in dreams? Lots of people, especially children, dream of animals – bugs, spiders, snakes, horses.

In most societies the animals were once gods. They weren't representations of gods; they *were* the gods. There was a divinity in the animal. I think we still feel that, especially in dreams. People occasionally have a dream in which an animal talks to them or saves them. A polar bear swims through the ice to rescue a dreamer or a man gets on the back of a horse and is saved. Being saved by an animal makes the dreamer feel that there's something special or holy about them.

Animals were gods because they were eternal. The American Indians saw the buffalo that appeared in the spring as the same buffalo that had disappeared in the fall. The animals went down into the earth and then came back up again, like the sun. We see the same sun rise every morning; they see the same animal always returning. That absolute perfection – that the animal is always the same – is a divine quality. So of course if you kill one to eat it, you have to propitiate it, to go through a ritual.

TM: Because it is more than human.

JH: But in our culture animals have become less than human.

TM: I remember an uncle of mine, when I was a child living on a farm, who knew animals very well. He was able to make little noises and the animals would respond and do what he wanted. It was almost magical. I think that like many people he felt animals can do many things that humans can't. We rely on them to know what the weather will be like, for instance. So there's a feeling that they are in fact more than human.

JH: But if you look at our Western tradition, we've had 2000 years in which animals were degraded. In Rome, they were property and you could do anything you wanted with them. It was a special law; they were like slaves. In the Christian world, animals did not have souls. By the sixteenth or seventeenth century, animals were machines. The Cartesians said that animals didn't have sense—they didn't even have sensation. It wasn't just that they couldn't think and therefore they were inferior. According to the Cartesians they couldn't feel. So it didn't matter if you kicked them. The noise they made was no sign of being in pain because they couldn't feel pain. One Cartesian argued that when he played his organ it made more noise than his cat did when he kicked it. Did that mean the organ hurt more? Animals were machines.

Why couldn't we allow the world, as in Japan or Egypt or even Greece, to be a continuum in which all things belong together? One Japanese critic said the only reason the West eats so much meat is because in our culture there's an ontological difference between animals and men. And so we can kill them with impunity. But in a culture where there's no ontological difference you have to ask the animal's permission. Otherwise it would mean genocide or fratricide.

TM: The classical scholastic approach was to look at the animal soul.

JH: But the soul was inferior because it didn't have reason. A great deal of Western psychology in the last one hundred years has been devoted to showing the ability to reason in animals. An octopus can go through a maze; whales sing; dolphins have an extraordinary language. In fact, we're now beginning to try to understand ourselves by watching animals. Psychoanalysts say that when people dream of animals, they reveal their animal nature. If you dream of a pig, it shows you that you're piggish.

TM: It seems like a way of protecting yourself from the animal. If you can say the animal is there because you're piggish you don't have to stand apart and look the animal in the face.

JH: Right. You don't have to take the animal as other. It's part of you, so you deal with your piggish nature. But what about the pig? Where did it come from? It would be very different for, say, an Egyptian who dreamt of a pig. He wouldn't immediately say, "that's my piggish nature." He would say that he was visited by a pig—just what a little child would say. A child will come in in the morning and say, "There's a pig in my room" or "I saw a wolf last night, don't let the wolf come back tonight." Neither the Egyptian nor the child would say, "This is my piggish self" or "I'm being wolfish."

TM: Isn't the presence of the animal without interpretation what comes through in Christian iconography and the sculpture of other religions, where you are face to face with a boar or an eagle or a snake? In the Aesculapius cult there actually was a snake in the temple. You can't say this is a symbol.

JH: No. And that's so important, because you were healed by the appearance of the god in snake or dog form. The dog came into your dream or your night vision and licked your wound and you were healed. No one took your dream down in the morning and then said, "That dog is a symbol of your underworld, your dark, doggy nature. You've been cut off from your instinct and therefore you dreamt of a dog, but now that you've found your instinct again, you're better." To them, it would have been a genuine appearance by the god in animal form. That's so distant from the way we think. We look at them chiefly as representing our lower, instinctual nature.

TM: Which has to be bridled in some way like the animals.

JH: Or let out for a good run or fed well so you have a nice healthy instinct. There are even case studies where the images get more and more humanoid, and therefore the therapist thinks the case is getting better and better until the animals have been done away with. The Navaho, by contrast, would say that the world begins with bugs, creeping creatures. They're the lowest level of things, not in the sense of inferior but in the sense of providing a foundation. Yet when we dream of bugs, we think we're going "bugs" or crazy.

I've collected dreams with animals in them since 1958. One of the major motifs is the dreamer trying to eradicate the animal. Another one is the dreamer seeing the animal as more dangerous than it turns out to be. But rapprochement with the animal is crucial.

TM: We could take the animal's point of view in the dream. If you're not taking the dreamer's position, often there's no indication of danger.

JH: Even in a dream where it seems the behavior of the animal is dangerous you still have to see what the dreamer is doing to make the animal pursue him. An American Indian goes out hoping an animal appears to him. Being chased by an animal needs to be seen in a much wider cultural context than our Western tradition. It could be a demon that needs to be released like the frog in the fairy tale. Or the fox that stops a young boy on his way through the forest and turns out to be the king in disguise. Being pursued or held up or questioned by an animal means that animal has something to tell you. It wants something. It may want to bite you just to get under your skin, or to make you aware of your animal nature.

TM: It may bite, it may sting. But that doesn't mean that the proper reaction is to run away or exterminate it.

JH: We pay a terrible price for this extermination. My own little fantasy is that if we could change the dreams of Americans in regard to insects we would have much less toxic waste. There are statistics in California on how much money is spent on insecticides and pesticides. And there are studies indicating that if these chemicals were not used, the crop loss would be less than the money spent on spraying. Of course, some of our fruit wouldn't look as if it was made of wax. But the fear of the bug—the fear of a crawling thing—gives us overkill. If you live in another culture, like India, you live with bugs all the time. To the Bushmen, according to Laurens van der Post, the chief of the animals is not the lion or the elephant but the praying mantis. And to the Navaho, as I said, the world starts with an insect. In Hindu mythology insects are extremely important.

TM: What's behind this fear of insects?

JH: They have an autonomous life. They go about in their own way. They have an autonomous psyche. And we have the feeling that insects will win out and take over the world. We are afraid of that autonomy—it's beyond the ego's control. You can't talk to an insect, you can't make it change its mind, you can't pet it. The more independent the animal – snakes, for example – the more anxiety associated with them. Yet that is also a key aspect of divinity. To the ancient Egyptians the fact that the animal was autonomous was evidence of its sacredness. To us it means the animal is somehow demonic.

One side of our attitude toward animals is anxiety. The other reveals itself in excessive sentimentality.

TM: I was impressed in my childhood by my uncle who had no sentimentality about animals. They lived in their world, he lived in his. At the same time he would probably defend his horse with the same vigor that he would defend himself. So there's sentimentality toward animals on one side and distrust of animals on the other. These attitudes tend to go together.

This brings to mind another polarity, the blending of man and animal in religion and mythology. I was struck by the image from Greece of Chiron, the great educator and healer who was half horse and half man. In a sense our whole history of medicine goes back to that horse-man.

JH: This is a tough one. There are also images like the Minotaur where you have a bull's head and a human body. If you look at Greek images of the Minotaur, or some of Picasso's drawings of it, you get this terrible feeling – it's so sad it makes you cry – of being caught inside that bull's head. It's as if everything that goes through your own mind gets trapped in that bull and can't get out. That's an image of a monster, which is quite different from Chiron. Why are certain things monstrous? Why is the animal-human combination in some cases monstrous and in others divine?

TM: In popular culture we have films of men and women turning into wolves. And there's a great deal of sympathy for them while at the same time you see all the "beastly" things they do.

JH: In one way it belongs to a destiny to be lost or caught in an animal, to enter the animal's totem. I don't know if you ever read *The Last of the Just* by André Schwarz-Bart about the Jews during the Occupation. It's one of the great books of the postwar period. There's one long chapter about how he becomes a dog. He lives life as a dog. You don't know whether he's imagining it or whether he is a dog or whether he is "as if" a dog. But it's part of a destiny, like Lucius's destiny to become ass.

There's a shamanistic tradition in which to become the animal is part of the experience. That we really need to understand. The American Indians took animal names so often—Sitting Bull, Running Deer, Black Elk. Is it to take on the power of the animal?

TM: Would it also be to have some of the animal's autonomy, so you're not just operating out of reason?

JH: You can yield to that autonomy. You can let the animal speak through you. But that autonomy, of course, is divine.

TM: That makes it a little clearer why getting rid of the animal is a secularization of psychology, because then you reduce all behavior to that rational part.

JH: You lose the otherness.

TM: Maybe that was expressed by philosophies that said every human being had an animal soul, and even by modern philosophy, which talks about the human being as a symbol-making animal.

JH: The way we define ourselves defines the animals. If we define ourselves in terms of our senses, then we begin to see the animals as gods. They know everything about the senses. But we define ourselves as *homo rationalis.* That means the animals are inferior because we define ourselves in terms of what they don't really have.

TM: Do you think the argument religious people have with evolutionary theory is that it connects them with animals? Isn't that how they usually put it—"We're not monkeys?"

JH: It's partly what the monkey symbolizes. In each major culture the monkey carries the shadow of the culture. In the Middle Ages monkeys represented drunkenness. In Jewish religion they represented lasciviousness. The monkey in India is a redeemer, but he's also a crafty trickster. Even Heraclitus remarked, "We are to the gods as the monkeys are to us." If we were closer to the horse than anything else, Darwin would probably be widely accepted.

TM: What do you think about symbolic studies of animals? I've noticed that more books are coming up about animals in mythology and religion.

JH: If study is a way of getting closer to the divinity of the animal, then I think it's important. It's like trying to know the nature of the god. The paths of revelation are many, and one of them can be through study. It's only when study becomes knowing that it doesn't work.

TM: As we talk we're not making much of a distinction between the animal we look at and the one of the imagination.

JH: I don't want to make a big distinction between the two. If we think they're different then we've divided the world into subject and object. I would rather think that the animal out there is also a psychic fact. When you look at a Chinese or Japanese painting of, say, a duck or a heron, is it an absolute copy of nature or is it a psychic image? There's no difference. If I go to the zoo and watch a tiger, it's like being with that tiger in a dream.

TM: Would that apply to pets?

JH: I think the pet has become an anthropomorphized animal, a little freak. It's completely in the human world. That's no longer an animal as totem or fetish or *familiarus* or tribe member. It's like having a dwarf or a eunuch, as in the Middle Ages. I don't think it's the same as with your uncle. He didn't have pets. Those were *animals*.

But there are different ways of having pets. Some people's pets put them in touch with the animal world. I can think of one case in particular where the animal was the representative of the spirit world. It gave signs that were very important; the animal actually had second sight or something. It was the mediator to the other world in the shamanistic sense. The other world may not be so remarkable. It may be just what's on the other side of the wall where the cat goes out at night. Maybe that's one reason why people have pets. It's related to a religious activity. Whether they know it or not, they are still in the cult.

13

Now You See Them, Now You Don't
A Conversation Between the Author and the Artist

James Hillman: This book [*Dream Animals*] began in Hartford, when...
Margot McLean: ... you came to my exhibition.
JH: *The Metaphorical Forest.* I saw the way you painted animals—I remember especially the cheetah.
MM: It was a quite small painting in the midst of a large competing environment. It is interesting that you remember that one.
JH: It was the tenuous reality of the animal, that it was there and not there, much like the animals in our dreams that can be so terrifying, so startling, and yet are "only dreams." You seemed to have caught in a painting something I had been working on, teaching about, trying to put into words for thirty years.
MM: But I wasn't painting dream animals. These paintings that I have been doing since the mid-eighties are not pictures from my dreams. They are more about the real animal in an unreal world. The animals are in another place. And yes, on a deeper level, these paintings are a kind of acknowledgment.
JH: For their sake?
MM: Well, not only for their sake, for our sake too. We are animals and these animals are tied to *our* bodies. That's why I gave many of the paintings anatomical names: to emphasize this connection of brotherhood-sisterhood.
JH: And common fate—what happens to them, happens to us. Their extinction is ours too.
MM: *Yes,* of course, their extinction is on my mind, like it's on everyone's, I suppose, or ought to be. But these paintings were never *significantly* about extinction. It has been amazing how quick people are to react, "Oh, endangered species." That has become a disturbing phrase

to me these days because "endangered species" has fallen into the just-another-category syndrome and has lost its emotional foundation. Besides, these paintings are not just about endangered species, they're about species. No, these paintings are not messages to "warn" of impending disaster or loss; but, rather, they are images of the spirit of the animal, with their own autonomous life, their presence and their absence. They come and go, and you try to hold on to them a while in your mind's eye, or you try to get them to come out and stay still without losing that quick-moving, subtle, fleeting sense that you can't quite seize. What exactly did you see just then darting across your path or in front of your car or outside your window? There are incredible creatures "out there" living with us on this planet and just because they aren't immediately in our face doesn't mean they don't hold an important position.

JH: That's again where your work depicts just what I've been trying to say for years. The imagination is itself a great animal, or an ark of images that are all alive and move independently. They come and go. All shapes and sizes. Some images hang around like a loyal dog or a cow and others are so fluttery and shadowy, so impossible to catch.

MM: I have lost a lot of animals that just wouldn't stay in the painting. I tried and tried and then had to let it go.

JH: Animals wake up the imagination. You see a deer by the side of the road, or geese flying in formation, and you become hyperalert. I've found that animal dreams can do this too. They really wake people up. Animal dreams provoke their feelings, get them thinking, interested, and curious. As we get more into imagining, we become more animal-like. Not bestial but more instinctually alive, and with more savvy, a keener nose and a sharper ear. As Jung said, the old wise man is an ape, really. Perhaps I have a therapeutic intention with this book. I want to do something for the animals, but I also want to affect people: I want them to be closer to that ape—though, it may not be so therapeutic for the ape! You know, people come to therapy really for blessing. Not so much to fix what's broken as to get what's broken blessed. In many cultures, animals do the blessing since they are the divinities. That's why parts of animals are used in medicines and healing rites. Blessing by the animal still goes on in our civilized lives too. Let's say you have a quick and clever side to your personality. You sometimes lie, you tend to shoplift, fires excite you, you're hard to track and hard to trap; you have such a sharp nose that people are shy of doing business with you for fear of being outfoxed. Then you dream of a fox! Now that fox isn't merely an image of your "Shadow problem," your propensity to stealth. That fox also gives an archetypal backing to your behavioral traits, placing them more deeply in the nature of things. The fox comes into your dream as a kind of teacher, a doctor animal, who knows lots more than you do about these traits of yours. And that's a blessing. Instead of a symptom or a character disorder, you now have a fox to live with, and you need to keep an eye on each other.

MM: But I wouldn't want to forget about the real fox. I would like to see the same respect given to the real animal wherever it appears. I think it is important to see the animal as you do in dreams, but dream animals must not be segregated from the animals living out back under your porch or in the brush. One must be careful when adopting an "inner" animal that the connection to the animal world is not reduced to a feel-good-about-*me* condition. There is something else.

JH: Right. The therapies that talk about animal spirits and guides forget about that sadness.

Just look into the eyes of a dog. There is a soul in the animal, a soul of ancient sadness. There is a sadness in the soul of the natural world. All you have to do is stand in the woods or in a field and you feel it.

MM: ... and see it.

JH: Let's get back to the animals. They aren't the ones we can watch on TV nature shows. The "vanishing" in your paintings and the fleeting indeterminate quality of the animals and their ambiguous meanings in dreams have nothing at all to do with nostalgic sentimentalities about species extinction as pronounced on TV.

MM: A little nostalgia doesn't hurt, though. However, it is important for me that these paintings are not reduced to a one-dimensional nostalgia.

JH: Nostalgia is archetypal. It touches the longing for Eden, for the ark, for the arcadia land of pastoral nature where the lion and the lamb lie down together. Nostalgia is also very American. I suppose, a little nostalgia belongs to our feelings regarding animals. Maybe they are nostalgic too, and look at us, wishing we were all back in Eden, the ark, and arcadia—before the pesticides and slaughterhouses.

MM: Actual animals are also not at all nostalgic. They are keeping up with the times. Deer, raccoons, skunks, coyotes are moving in closer and closer, even wild pigs and bears. Cities are full of wildlife.

JH: But their moves of necessity and survival are not restoring arcadia. In fact, we put up warning posters about rabies and Lyme disease...We really don't want them too close. There remains a deep moat between them and us, despite the safari vacations, the snorkeling, and the nostalgia. We may long for their presence in some subliminal way; our behavior, however, keeps them "out there."

MM: That's right. That's why the animals in my paintings aren't completely "there," completely visible.

JH: The invisible is as important as the visible. And I see your paintings as being also about what I call the invisibles. The invisibles that have been forgotten and passed by. Perhaps we are learning what happens to our environment when we pass by the invisibles. If only we could look at the present-day situation from a completely different place. Perhaps the invisibles are doing exactly what is called for in the here and now, in this year of animal emergency. Perhaps there is intention in their vanishing. Perhaps there is a holocaust going on, or an animal sacrifice. Where have all the frogs gone, and why? The monarch butterflies? Perhaps they are withdrawing as the ancient gods withdrew from an inhospitable, irreverent world. Are the reasons only scientific, environmental? Are they sharing a planetary misery, carrying more than their share of it?

MM: Well, the odds are certainly against them. I think they'd want us, above all else, to reach beyond the human as far as we can possibly go. Not just watch them on TV for entertainment, but respect them by allowing them their rightful "place."

JH: That's why our inside animals are not like those on TV, where they are put into human stories. You don't see a leopard just as leopard. It is put into a story of predators, of extinction, or "the wonders of mating." Or you are taught a lesson about motherhood, about how risky animal life is and how everything has to hide in camouflage; or it's about big bucks competing for females. All *human* stories. Moreover, those wonderful shows—and the photography is really amazing—keep the animal out there, in nature, more and more visible, even at night, when our cameras invade their privacy. We are astounded by those close-ups such as you can never see in life.

MM: I question our ability to remember that these animals really do exist, living on the earth, and not just on TV. It's odd how the shows that are supposed to bring us closer to animals by raising consciousness about their extinction are strangely making the actual animals unnecessary. There they are, right in our own living rooms, virtual icons with enhanced lighting, magnification, and detail. While they are overexposed and proliferating on TV, they are rapidly and silently disappearing from the planet.

JH: I don't think we will be able to rid ourselves of the inside animal. The animal spirit will not be eclipsed by TV. And it may come into our dreams in unforeseeable ways.

MM: Unforeseeable, like invisible?

JH: I meant unpredictable—animals as archetypal eternal images, as inhabitants of imagination, may die but not go away. All this fascination with dinosaurs and extinct or legendary species shows how animal images continue to breed in imagination. So what they do in the psyche is unforeseeable.

MM: You mean by keeping them only partly visible, we are allowing them their freedom to be outside human control. Unpredictable.

JH: I think it's easier to depict the vanishing animal than it is to write about this elusiveness. In your images, the animals emerge or recede, they seem there and not there. They belong to both nature and imagination at the same time. I can't get that same presence or absence when I write about a pig or a polar bear.

MM: I'm not so sure. You hint at what the animal means, but you keep from saying it. You describe the nature of the giraffe or a moose at the same time you somehow let the animals stay half-hidden ...

JH: ... as metaphors, as they are in dreams. It's very hard to hold back the desire to interpret, to capture the animal into a meaning.

MM: Tell me about it, I struggle with this all the time. Recently, painting a snake came into a conversation. I said I was not interested in painting one. Snakes just have too much going on, and I'm not interested in all that symbolism. Then, boom, three encounters with actual snakes, keeping perfectly still so I could have a good look. It was then that I realized that I wasn't truly seeing *the* snake.

JH: We "civilized" human beings can't leave it at that. We can't resist putting that snake into some kind of story and giving it some kind of meaning. When I go to a zoo, I have to fight myself to keep from reading the little informational label and map on the cage so as to just see what is there and not put it into a scientific fact or story.

MM: But zoos are another story altogether. The purpose of the zoo is to provide that kind of information. Animals in zoos have been sacrificed for our access to that information. I think we are going to have to start realizing that zoos are the animal habitats of the future, depressing as this is. That zebra, munching on pellets in the zoos around the world, brings with it the loss of the plains and its herd. It becomes a kind of tragic representative of the changing link of animal to habitat.

JH: Maybe we have to rethink zoos. Look at them as small children do—more like a story book, a habitat of imagination rather than a replica of Africa or Antarctica—correct but fake. Suppose the zoo is more a place to imagine, to connect, and even to pray, than to learn.

MM: ... or a different kind of learning, which is what I hope this book can do. Here the animals are embedded in a habitat too, and that can move people to see the animals in a different way.

JH: Are you saying that studying animals, knowing about them, even feeling for them isn't enough? We have to *imagine* them. Get into them as imaginal beings, into them as images. That's what Adam did: he looked at these images parading by and read their names out of their natures. He was inside the animal. He knew the animals of his imagination. He and they were all in the same dream.

MM: What I'm saying is that I believe a little anthropomorphizing is necessary. For me to be inside means entering the animal's body and trying to see the world from there. It simply does not make sense to separate ourselves from the animal world when there are far too many concrete similarities.

JH: Or, words came first, since some theories say that we got our words from the sounds of animals. I like to think that the right words say something to the animals too.

MM: That's nice, a message to the animals. Hmm...

JH: In part I am trying to tell them something: a message about how they register in the human imagination, in our lore and fantasy, in our symbol systems, even what our zoology says about them. Like a report to them about how they are perceived. That's why I use so many different kinds of sources. Zoology is secondary, because there is basically only one source for all the kinds of stories—the zebra image itself. Tribal peoples would speak of a spirit zebra that gives rise to whatever we say about zebras, wherever we encounter that image—in a poem, in a zoo, or in the Serengeti. Our civilized mind makes a terrible mistake by contrasting "real" animals and animal "images," as if the one standing in the zoo and the one you meet in a dream are two different beasts altogether.

MM: That's what I meant when I said my paintings are about the real animal in an unreal world...an unreal world meaning various worlds...worlds that aren't literally depicted but nevertheless present a "place."

JH: The edges of your painted animals have to fade away and blur just as the hard line between fact and lore must be softened, sometimes eliminated. Your paintings and this book are like those old medieval bestiaries, which were, after the Bible, the most-read books for about a thousand years. Those animal books did not take into account today's distinctions between nature and imagination. They were pre-Cartesian, prescientific. And our book is too, reaching back to an archaic mentality, and also reaching forward to a radical phenomenology: a leopard is a leopard wherever it appears, utterly phenomenal.

MM: Scientific thought doesn't necessarily mean Cartesian thought. It depends on how you use science—"do science." The problem is we get obsessed with the literal facts that can block the imagination.

JH: Scientific method was designed for that very purpose—to rein in fantasy, and to correct the "fictions" of imagination with observed facts. But I think there are no objective facts without subjective fiction. Observation alone takes up only one half, the now-you-see-them half. Imagination involves that other half, the now-you-don't. In the nineteenth century wild animals were studied, hunted, collected as natural phenomena, facts.

MM: They were mostly painted that way too, and cast into bronzes; very detailed and naturalistic. You know, it's rare to see an animal in a painting during the great hundred years of modern art, from 1860 to 1960, say from Monet and Cézanne through Rothko. You see little dogs, carriage horses, and hunting scenes—and there are always major exceptions, like Picasso and Franz Marc—but it's interesting how much animals have been left out.

JH: And now as they are disappearing, they have found their way back into the imagination. The secret of the imagination is the disappearance of the actual. Their actual death is bringing them back to life, and depicting that "death," that absence, may be the best way to do "enough" for them. Gathering facts, symbols, fables, photographs, fossils, toys, slogans, carvings, the animal art books and bestiaries—all of it together can't do enough, can't fill that curious sense of obligation we feel toward them. We still feel something is left out.

MM: Something is left out: human humility.

JH: I envy you for painting. No matter how hard it is, at least you don't need to bring in all this material, all these references, to try to do justice to the animals.

MM: I try to escape from references. I want somehow to clear out all the junk about the animal. I want the mind to be quite quiet and not caught up by all that information. Once the animal has found its place in the painting, it seems to take care of itself, and one doesn't need those references.

JH: Your backgrounds are very important, too. They both let the animal stand out from it and disappear into it. Again, it's so much like dream country: usually only bits of a dream stand out against a vague screen. Your vague backgrounds...

MM: Edward Casey, the philosopher, wrote: "Landscape painting not only locates things; it also *relocates* them. It gives to things—concrete or abstract as they may be—*somewhere else to be.* Somewhere else than the natural world (if they are physical things) and somewhere else than the ethereal world (if they are objects of cerebration or contemplation). Somewhere else, in other hands, than the simple location, in which they are 'originally' or 'appropriately' or 'for the most part' located. Another place means another life—a second life. Thus things (including experiences of things) are not merely represented or remembered in paintings; they 'sur-vive' there in the sense of living on, literally living *over* their first, proper life."

JH: A "somewhere else" for them to live on and over.

MM: But then I ask myself, is that enough—a "somewhere else"? What about an actual ecological benefit? Then I answer: The ecological benefit can happen only when our usual perceptions are challenged and we begin to "see" things differently, imagine things differently.

JH: That's right—if it changes our usual perceptions, frees them even a little from our interpretations, if it brings us to feel into the animals with more kinship. When you know that the tigers are going, are leaving the planet forever, and the elephants and the frogs, you begin to mourn and to look around you with a different eye. I see your paintings as ritual objects, as if you are mourning the animals' leaving by eliminating their full-bodied presence.

MM: That's half of it, yes. The other half is that in order to fully appreciate something, does it have to be fully exposed?

JH: Dreams do this all the time. That's why I speak of dream animals. I'm not doing a dream book of animals, any more than you are doing naturalist paintings of animals. We are both struggling with the ghosts of the animal. Gaston Bachelard said the imagination requires absence and deformation. So I am always struggling with writing as much as I can about the dream and the animal and yet, at the same time, keeping it unclear, enigmatic, mysterious. I try to get them on the page and then encourage them to go away.

MM: Ha! I coax them into the painting and then encourage them to stay.

Source Notes

"The Animal Kingdom in the Human Dream" was originally published in *Eranos Yearbook* 51 (1982).

"Imagination is Bull" was originally given as a lecture at the Dallas Institute of Humanities and Culture in March 1981 and revised for a talk at the conference *Between the Horns of the Bull*, organized by the C. G. Jung Institute of San Francisco in March 1981. It has not been previously printed, and my revisions have aimed to keep the original oral form.

"A Snake is not a Symbol," "Horses and Heroes," "The Rat," "Lions and Tigers, or Why there are two Great Cats," and "Now You See Them, Now You Don't: A Conversation Between the Author and the Artist" were originally published in J. Hillman and M. McLean, *Dream Animals* (San Francisco: Chronicle Books, 1997).

"Going Bugs" was presented in November 1980 at the conference *Anima, Animal, Animation*, hosted by the Western New York Society for Analytical Psychology in Buffalo, N.Y.

"The Elephant in *The Garden of Eden*" was delivered as a talk at Boise State University in October 1986 and first published in *Spring* 50 (1990).

"You Dirty Dog!" was originally published in M. Ludington, *The Nature of Dogs* (New York: Simon & Schuster, 2007). The more colloquial, fuller, and fulsome version printed here was presented in June 2007 at the conference *Nature and Human Nature* at Pacifica Graduate Institute as "Nature in the Doghouse."

"Human Being as Human Animal: A Conversation with John Stockwell" was originally published in *Between the Species: A Journal of Ethics* 1/2 (1985).

"Let the Creatures Be: A Conversation with Thomas Moore" was originally published in *Parabola* 8:2 (Summer 1983).

"Animal Presence: A Conversation with Jonathan White" was originally published in *Talking on the Water: Conversations about Nature and Creativity* (San Francisco: Sierra Club Books, 1994).

THE UNIFORM EDITION OF THE WRITINGS OF JAMES HILLMAN